SHARKS

OF THE

WORLD

Rodney Steel

BLANDFORD

Paperback edition first published in the UK 1992
by Blandford, a Cassell imprint

Cassell plc,
Wellington House
125 Strand
London
WC2R OBB

Reprinted 1994, 1995 & 1998

Previously published in hardback by Blandford in 1985
Reprinted 1986, 1988 & 1989

Distributed in the United States by
Sterling Publishing Co., Inc.,
387 Park Avenue South, New York, NY 10016–8810

A Cataloguing-in-Publication Data entry for this title is available
from the British Library

ISBN 0–7137–2341–6

(M) 595·31 S

Typeset in Hong Kong by Graphicraft Typesetters Ltd

Printed and bound by Colorcraft Ltd, Hong Kong

Contents

Picture Credits   6

Preface   7

1   Sharks Great and Small   9

2   The Human Toll   26

3   Design for a Purpose   42

4   Relics, Rarities and Curiosities   74

5   The Great Man-Eater and Its Kin   85

6   Lesser Killers and Their Kin   102

7   Gentle Giants   130

8   Sharks of the Ocean Floor   140

9   Experiments in Evolution   151

10   Ancestors from Ancient Seas   157

11   A Role to Play   171

Appendix: Check-list of Sharks Living and Extinct   185

Glossary   187

Guide to Further Reading   189

Index   190

Picture Credits

Preface

Familiar to everyone, yet widely misunderstood and misrepresented, sharks were for many years regarded as primitive mindless killers whose physiological simplicity has enabled them to survive with little change for 300 million years or more.

However, with the advent of more sophisticated free-diving equipment that enables Man to enter the hitherto essentially inaccessible underwater world and, for a while, become a part of it, observers can now watch sharks deep in their natural environment instead of merely spectating from the deck of a ship or peering at sluggish aquarium specimens.

Accompanying this revolution in submarine exploration has been the development of photographic equipment capable of recording the underwater scene in all its wonderful variety and colour, as well as a wealth of new laboratory equipment incorporating modern electronic technology and all the astonishing versatility of computers.

Simultaneous arousal of public and scientific interest in sharks has led to renewed investigation of these enigmatic creatures, using all the new facilities and equipment which have become available. Hauling sharks out of the sea on fishing lines and simply identifying their carcases, which was about all that nineteenth and early twentieth century naturalists could hope to do, was replaced by proper studies of shark behaviour and analysis of their physiology.

The results have been a revelation. No longer are sharks regarded as little better than the vermin of the oceans. Large predatory species are, it is true, no less dangerous to swimmers or surfers for having become better understood. But the motivation for their attacks is now more comprehensible and, with better understanding, it is possible to offer advice to those who use the seas for commerce or for pleasure so that the risk of shark attack is materially diminished.

The picture that now emerges is of sharks as anything but primitive, with surprisingly large brains, sensory perception of totally unexpected sensitivity, and complex behaviour patterns geared to the demands of feeding and reproduction. There is nothing archaic about sharks and they are not just lethal automatons. They include some of the most efficiently adapted of all fish, specialised to meet the demands of a hunter's life in the seas, with different species capable of exploiting environments as diverse as inland lakes and the ocean deeps. Some sharks feed on minute plankton, others pursue prey as large as sea lions. There are even sharks that give birth to fully developed young which have been nourished inside the mother's body by a form of placenta.

This book will seek to explore this newly discovered world of the shark. As yet our knowledge is still very incomplete, but in a matter of only a few decades, the papers and reports on sharks have proliferated and with the volume of research now being undertaken it should not be long before even the more obscure corners of the sharks' world are opened up to human enquiry.

Rodney Steel
Battle, Sussex

Chapter 1
Sharks Great and Small

Introduction

Honed to perfection as a killing mechanism by 350 million years of evolution, the big killer shark is magnificently adapted to its role as an assassin of the ocean depths. The sleek, streamlined body, the batteries of needle-sharp teeth, the glaring eyes that miss nothing as they seek a glimpse of possible prey, the quivering snout with nostrils questing for scent of food – every centimetre of a typical shark is designed and proportioned for just one purpose: to kill.

Not all sharks are monsters capable of biting a man in half, however (Fig. 1.1). Such creatures are relatively rare. A good-sized shark might measure perhaps 4.5 metres (15 feet), and would live mostly on fish, not excluding other sharks (even smaller members of its own species). A fish of this size could comfortably take a man's arm or leg into its maw and hew off a limb with no more concern than a child might bite into a liquorice stick – or rip out a mouthful of flesh, leaving a gaping wound haemorrhaging into the ocean.

Fig. 1.1 Sharks huge, ferocious and minute: the great white (*Carcharodon carcharias*), a typical predatory shark some 6 metres (20 feet) long; the enormous but harmless whale shark (*Rhincodon typus*) measuring about 12 metres (39 feet) and the tiny *Squaliolus laticaudus*, which scarcely attains 15 centimetres.

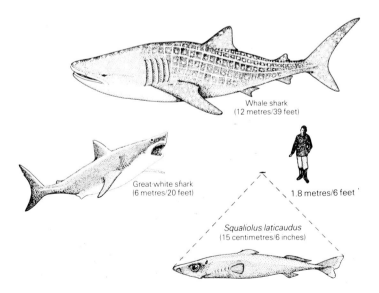

Whale shark
(12 metres/39 feet)

Great white shark
(6 metres/20 feet)

1.8 metres/6 feet

Squaliolus laticaudus
(15 centimetres/6 inches)

9

Many sharks never attain any kind of size at all, even when fully adult. Their lengths have to be expressed in centimetres rather than metres, like tiny *Squaliolus laticaudus* from the Philippines which measures only 15 centimetres (6 inches) when fully grown, and they represent no hazard whatsoever to swimmers or boatmen. Among these small sharks are such frequently encountered forms as the common dogfish (*Scyliorhinus*), which often finds its way to the fishmonger's slab as rock salmon and, as such, is a popular item on the menu of British fish-and-chip shops. On the other hand, some of the largest sharks are completely harmless. The massive and appropriately named whale shark (*Rhincodon*) of tropical seas may attain a length of 16 metres (50 feet) and a weight of several tonnes, but its gaping jaws contain only bands of small curved teeth that form a kind of rasp. It feeds on tiny floating crustaceans (krill) and other planktonic life, straining the sea water through long, wide gill clefts which are each provided with a set of gill-rakers to sieve this diminutive source of nourishment from the out-going current of water. The giant whales feed in a corresponding fashion although, being mammals, they do not of course have gill rakers, but achieve the same result with sheets of whalebone set across the huge mouth.

Almost as large, running to 13 metres (40 feet) or more, and equally docile, is the basking shark (*Cetorhinus*), which feeds on krill in a manner similar to that of the whale shark. *Cetorhinus* is a fish of temperate seas, however, and was at one time extensively hunted from the shores of New England, Scotland, Ireland and Norway for the oil in its liver. Like the whale shark, its teeth are very small and set in numerous rows, so that the basking shark is a totally inoffensive creature. The only danger it offers to Man is if it should collide with a small boat, either by accident or when being hunted. The sheer size of a basking shark is likely to result in substantial damage to a flimsily built craft and can easily sink a rowing boat.

On the other hand, there are sharks almost as large as whale sharks and basking sharks that are ferocious predators. The enormous great white shark (*Carcharodon carcharias*) can easily run to over 6 metres (20 feet) in length and, with jaws bearing rows of triangular teeth as much as 8 centimetres (3 inches) long, this sleek killer is evidently no placid plankton-eater. Its diet is mainly fish but, to sustain the enormous bulk of a full-grown great white, they must obviously be fish of large size. A 180-centimetre (6-foot) tall man swimming in the sea would be a snack of appropriate proportions for such a monster and the great white has a fully deserved reputation as a man-eater.

The great whites that roam the seas today, ranging into the temperate seas of high latitudes, are apparently a diminished remnant of veritable monsters that existed in former days: *Carcharodon* teeth in relatively fresh condition dredged from the ocean floor of the Pacific measure 12.5 centimetres (5 inches) in length and fossil teeth obtained from Tertiary rocks are of similar size. The mouth of such a creature would have possessed a gape exceeding 2 metres (6 feet), and these extinct relatives of the great white must have run to well over 13 metres (40 feet) in length.

On the evidence of the 12.5 centimetre (5 inch) teeth, nearly twice the size of those in the existing *Carcharodon carcharias*, some authorities have suggested a length of 30 metres (100 feet) for the extinct *Carcharodon megalodon*. However a less extravagant estimate seems more probable and, in all likelihood, this ancient giant possessed disproportionately large jaws.

The big predatory sharks are at the summit of oceanic food chains which begin with microscopic plankton and ascend, via small fish that feed on this nutritious 'soup', through larger fish preying on their less substantial brethren, and the more modestly proportioned sharks. Behaviour patterns of sharks are geared to two fundamental requirements: feeding and breeding. All but the largest also have to guard against being eaten themselves by giants like the great white, while no shark is safe from Man, who seeks them for either sport or commercial gain.

Predatory animals are invariably in a marked numerical minority compared with the prey on which they feed and sharks are no exception. They may congregate in what seem to be substantial numbers around boats or in the vicinity of shoaling food fishes but, compared with the teeming millions of mackerel or herrings, for example, they still constitute only a small percentage of the ocean's overall population.

Partly because their numbers are limited in this way, sharks have evolved a complex breeding pattern that is in marked contrast to the casual spawning of myriad eggs which characterises fishes in general. Many sharks of temperate seas are evidently migratory, following warm waters to higher latitudes in summer and then retreating again as winter draws on, and most of these species probably have breeding grounds where males and females congregate to mate. In the case of big open-ocean sharks, such an arrangement is almost obligatory, otherwise many would probably never find a mate with which to pair.

Fertilisation is internal, male sharks being provided with a pair of so-called claspers that project from the pelvic fins and are inserted into the female's cloaca to channel sperm into her oviduct. Mating sharks have

Mating dogfish (*Scyliorhinus caniculus*) with the male coiled around the female.

rarely been observed and knowledge of the procedure followed by large species is mostly speculative. Dogfish have been witnessed copulating in aquaria and, in these relatively small, slender, lithe fish, the males achieve their objective by coiling their bodies around the apparently passive females. Such a procedure is scarcely practicable for a massively pro- portioned, 6 metre (20 foot) mackerel shark or great white. Not only are the male claspers of many species provided with a formidable array of hooks and gaffs to secure the female, but considerable coercion is apparently employed: in some large species the backs of the females bear scars evidently resulting from healed cuts or slashes inflicted by the teeth of amorous males. In at least some species (e.g. *Prionace*, the great blue shark), females have substantially thicker skin than males, its depth exceeding the length of the male's teeth and thus precluding serious injury.

Despite their apparently vicious behaviour, the mating season is, in fact, probably a more hazardous period for male sharks than for females. While on the breeding grounds, it seems likely that males do not feed and become extremely thin, with the oil content of their livers falling almost to nothing. Since male sharks are usually about 25 per cent smaller than the females they are trying to seduce, and since their aggressiveness towards a prospective mate is inhibited by behavioural patterns to relatively in- nocuous love-bites, it is evident that a small, weakened male is quite likely to be killed by an unwilling female, while fishermen catching for the leather industry try to avoid females with their scarred hides and go only for males.

Furthermore, the males also sustain mating injuries, bleeding claspers surrounded by an oedematous area of tissue being a clear indication of recent copulation.

Among the smaller sharks, the males use their teeth either to physically restrain the females or to initiate mating behaviour, often by seizing hold of a pectoral fin. In a few instances, the teeth of males differ from those of females belonging to the same species, having evidently become modified specifically as an aid to mating (examples are *Deania*, *Halaelurus* and *Apristurus*).

Fig. 1.2. The silky shark (*Carcharhinus falciformis*), up to about 3.3 metres (nearly 11 feet) in length.

A black-tip shark (*Carcharhinus limbatus*), a member of the abundant and highly successful carcharhinid family. These structurally very advanced sharks give birth to live young that have been nourished inside the mother's body through a placenta-like connection.

In many species, pregnant females seek out carefully chosen nursery areas to lay their eggs or (in viviparous and ovo-viviparous species) to give birth to their fully formed young, probably abstaining from feeding during the time they are there. These nurseries are selected to provide an optimum environment in terms of security, water temperature and food for the hatchlings or newly born juveniles. Known examples of such areas include the outer rim of the continental shelf in the North Atlantic, Caribbean and Gulf of Mexico, where young silky sharks (*Carcharhinus falciformis*, Fig. 1.2.) begin their lives some 100 metres (325 feet) or so down, the shallow brackish water bays and estuaries of the northern Gulf of Mexico, where newborn bull sharks (*Carcharhinus leucas*) grow up, and oceanic banks like Serrana Bank in the western Caribbean (another silky shark nursery).

There is considerable evidence that most shark populations are segregated by both size and sex, the need to breed each year (or biennially in some species) being about the only occasion when this social system is seriously disrupted. The reason for a size-orientated social organisation is probably to secure the safety of the individual. Sharks are so voracious that they will readily eat other smaller sharks, even members of their own species, so it behoves smaller fry to keep out of their elders' way.

An example of segregation by size and sex is to be found in the marbled cat shark (*Galeus arae*, Fig. 1.3) of the Caribbean, which occurs at depths of 300–750 metres (1,000–2,500 feet) on the upper continental slope. While mature females are principally present in the middle to deeper regions of this range, sub-adult males favour the shallows and immature females are restricted to the middle depths; adult males occur throughout the depth range and are thus always available to mate with suitable females.

Fig. 1.3. The marbled cat shark (*Galeus arae*), about 50 centimetres ($1\frac{1}{2}$ feet) in length.

There are exceptions to these generalisations, however. Tiger sharks (*Galeocerdo*), for instance, demonstrate no apparent preference for specific nursery areas, nor do they segregate socially by size or sex.

The other major preoccupation of sharks, in addition to breeding, is feeding. It seems likely that, rather than a conventional spasmodic sense of acute hunger in the mammalian sense, they have a continual low-intensity feeding drive which is sometimes accelerated by the presence of other hunting sharks until the notorious 'feeding frenzy' is generated. A solitary shark, cruising a harbour entrance or prospecting along a shore line, will probably investigate, in a casual way, practically anything floating nearby. The long, twitching snout prospects this way and that for the scent of food, and flotsam and jetsam are given an investigatory nudge – often a preliminary move before taking a bite if the sensory organs of the snout confirm edibility, as human victims of shark attacks have confirmed, many of them reporting that they were first nudged before the shark came back to bite in earnest. However, an unaroused shark will, in all likelihood, only snatch at prospective prey in a desultory manner, perhaps making a quick lunge, that may or may not be successful, at a passing fish.

Smell is probably the primary hunting sense of sharks, but the thrashing sound of a hooked fish struggling on a line may also attract their attention and possibly constitutes an excitatory influence. The arrival of other sharks serves to introduce an element of competition. A formerly rather lackadaisical shark now begins to seek food in greater earnest, spurred on by the subconscious fear that a rival may steal anything it misses. Now any slow-moving or inanimate objects are not simply nudged but taken into the mouth for deliberate testing. Sooner or later, two or

Fig. 1.4. The lemon shark (*Negaprion brevirostris*), which attains a length of 3.3 metres (about 11 feet).

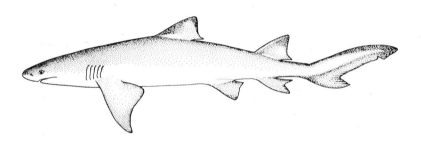

more sharks will go for the same thing and a fracas will result. The commotion draws in other sharks from further afield and, in a frantic melee of whirling, writhing sharks, a feeding frenzy develops. Shark will snap at shark and any individual injured so that it bleeds into the water is instantly torn to pieces by its brethren. Lemon sharks (*Negaprion*, Fig. 1.4) hooked from amid a school of these creatures in Lake Worth, eastern Florida, have been devoured in 2 or 3 minutes, leaving only the severed head to be hauled in on the end of the line. Feeding frenzies are frequently reported by seamen at night, when they are heard rather than seen, the surface waters under the stars apparently being a regular hunting ground for greedy sharks.

There is some evidence that at least a few species hunt in packs. Smaller forms, such as dogfish, are able to overpower much larger prey than themselves if they act in concert, in a similar way to a pack of wolves pulling down an elk, although with nothing like the intelligent cooperation that is the hallmark of pack-hunting mammalian carnivores.

Spiny dogfish (*Squalus acanthias*) have frequently been reported in large loosely organised schools, sweeping through an area and feeding as they go, with a swift congregation of fish wherever a source of food is discovered. The small green dogfish (*Etmopterus virens*), which only attains a length of about 25 centimetres, (10 inches) and is not really a dogfish at all, probably employs similar but even more savage hunting behaviour in the northern Gulf of Mexico. It usually swims at depths of 350–400 metres (about 1,100–1,300 feet) and is evidently a deep-sea fish, with a distinctive pattern of photophores (luminescent organs) along its body.

Trawls at any given spot usually catch either no green dogfish (Fig. 1.5) at all or an overwhelming abundance of them, suggesting that they do

Fig. 1.5. A pack of green dogfish (*Etmopterus virens*) attacking a squid.

indeed prowl in huge schools. Despite their diminutive proportions, they apparently feed almost exclusively on squid and octopus, their stomachs often being full of cephalopod beaks and eyes so large that the dogfish must have been barely able to swallow them. It has been suggested that a hunting school of these fierce little sharks will swarm over a squid or octopus far larger than themselves, tearing it apart with their razor-sharp lower teeth and perhaps maintaining the integrity of their deadly school (in an unthinking, instinctive manner) by reference to the elaborate lighting system arrayed along their bodies.

Curiously enough, large sharks are difficult to keep alive in captivity because, despite their voracity in the open ocean, they tend to refuse any form of food when imprisoned in a tank. Even introducing live fish or crabs often fails to stimulate their appetites and, quite frequently, the shark becomes progressively more torpid until eventually it dies.

Tagging of sharks has been undertaken in the hope of determining the mobility and movement pattern of individuals and of populations, as well as obtaining information on growth rates. Tags of various different types have been tried, including plastic and metal designs originally intended for use as cattle-ear tags. These have been fixed to the first dorsal fin of sharks, either caught on hand-lines by scientific expeditions in the eastern Pacific using small barbless hooks or else (in South Africa) brought alive to the research institute by members of the public (who received a reward contingent on the shark still being alive in an aquarium tank the day after delivery).

Recoveries in the eastern Pacific were mainly by sport fishermen, commercial tuna fishermen and Mexican government fishing exploration vessels but, in South Africa, reliance was again placed on the general public, suitably encouraged by a small reward for returning any tags found. Unfortunately, the wiles of the man in the street (or in this case, on the beach) seeking to make a fast buck tended to nullify some of the South African findings: initially most of the recoveries were so near the point of release as to be valueless and a larger reward was introduced for tags found more than 19 kilometres (12 miles) from the release point. Falsification immediately became obvious, with spurious recapture locations being claimed so that virtually none of the returned specimens now allegedly came from within this distance of the research institute's headquarters and loose tags, torn from fins by shark nets protecting bathing beaches, were attached to the fins of any available dead shark (normally no reward was paid for a tag by itself).

Nevertheless, sifting the various records indicated that offshore and oceanic sharks prowl quite extensive hunting areas but, in favourable seasons, will remain for long periods of time at a single location if the food supply there is good. Some species appear to be non-migratory (e.g. *Rhizoprionodon acutus* and *Mustelus canis* off Durban), others have clearly established migratory patterns, with dusky sharks (*Carcharhinus obscurus*) estimated to cover as much as 59 kilometres (32 nautical miles) a day during a 7-day period of southerly migration in autumn. In this connection, it is interesting to note that there is a record of a shark covering 128 kilometres (80 miles) in a single day. In June 1855, the *Rose of Sharon* (888 tonnes), en route from Sydney to Calcutta, anchored in Torres Strait. The crew caught a 5 metre (16 foot) shark, which the lascars cut up for food, throwing overboard the head and other inedible parts. The ship sailed that morning, anchoring again at 6 p.m., 128 kilometres (80 miles) further on. At 9 o'clock that evening, another shark was hooked, which, on being hauled in and opened, was found to contain the remains of the shark caught before the vessel weighed anchor in the morning. Migrations involve different age groups of a given species at different times and, as might be expected, are a more conspicuous feature of temperate seas, with their marked summer/winter temperature gradients, than of tropical waters.

More sophisticated methods of tracking sharks are now being employed. In Californian waters, angel sharks (*Squatina*) have been caught, fitted with sonic transmitters and then put back in the water so that their movements can be plotted by scientists in boats. Even more fascinating was the use of a satellite to track a basking shark off the west coast of Scotland. In June 1982, a team led by Dr Monty Priede of Aberdeen University located a basking shark in the Firth of Clyde and thrust a harpoon through its dorsal fin. Attached to the harpoon by means of a line incorporating a weak link designed to snap after 100 days was a radio-transmitter operating at 400 MHz. Whenever the shark was near enough to the surface for the radio signal to penetrate through the water, the transmission was picked up by French instruments on the American NOAA-7 satellite. Service Argos, the Toulouse-based organisation that was operating the satellite's radio-location equipment, then telexed the shark's position to Aberdeen. Unfortunately the weak link in the harpoon line broke prematurely after only 17 days but, during this period, the system functioned effectively and demonstrated that the shark had remained within a relatively small area. Despite the fact that sea water is opaque to radio waves, so that a transmitter-equipped fish below the surface cannot be tracked, the system tried out by Dr Priede could prove invaluable in research on shark movements and migrations.

The oldest known sharks are of Devonian age and date back some 350 million years. Already at this early time they had acquired sleekly contoured bodies – not quite of optimum hydrodynamic profile perhaps, but quite streamlined enough to make them among the fastest swimmers of the time. Their teeth were multi-pointed spikes, obviously well capable of impaling a struggling victim, and the prominent eye sockets suggest keen vision for discerning their prey in the deeps of the Devonian ocean. Although these ancient sharks had possibly not yet acquired the acutely developed sense of smell so characteristic of today's sharks, and their paired fins were little more than broad-based stabilisers, they were nevertheless cast in the mould of prospective oceanic conquerors and, in some cases, grew to a substantial size – one or two specimens indicate fish over 2 metres ($6\frac{1}{2}$ feet) in length.

Throughout the rocks that have been laid down since Devonian times by sediment accumulating on the sea floor, fossil sharks' teeth are

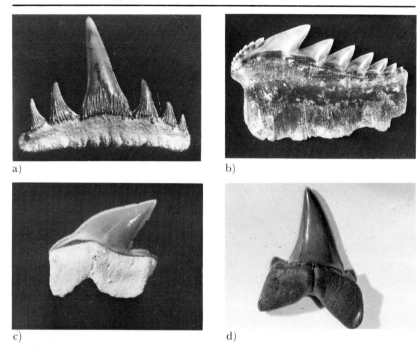

Fossil shark teeth: a) *Synechodus* sp., an extinct bullhead shark from the Palaeocene of southern England (width 14 millimetres/$\frac{1}{2}$ inch); b) *Notorynchus kempi*, an extinct seven-gilled shark from the Middle or Upper Eocene of southern England (width 30.5 millimetres/$1\frac{1}{4}$ inches); c) *Pseudocorax affinis*, an early isurid from the Upper Cretaceous of Belgium (width 7 millimetres/$\frac{1}{4}$ inch); d) *Odontaspis macrota*, an extinct sand shark from the Middle Eocene of southern England (height 27 millimetres/$1\frac{1}{10}$ inch)

abundant. They tell a story of progressive evolution as sharks tended to become ever larger and more powerful, developing teeth capable not only of skewering their prey but of cutting and sawing away whole mouthfuls of living flesh.

By the time the Age of Dinosaurs was at its height, some 150 million years ago, there were some quite formidable hybodont sharks abroad that measured nearly 3 metres (9 feet) in length and had paired fins of greater efficiency joined to the body at a narrow articulation so that they could be readily manipulated to enhance agility in the water. At the same time, a

Fig. 1.6. (Opposite) Sharks and their relatives through geological time. The ctenacanths seem to be close to the origin of living sharks (neoselachians), with some tiny teeth described as *Anachronistes* from the Lower Carboniferous of England and Wales possibly indicating the presence of modern-type sharks over 300 million years ago. The position of the enigmatic extinct edestids and their poorly known fossil kin is uncertain and they are not shown; they ranged from the Devonian to the Triassic but may not have been true sharks – relationship to the chimaeras has been suggested. Modern lamniforms possibly form three groups.

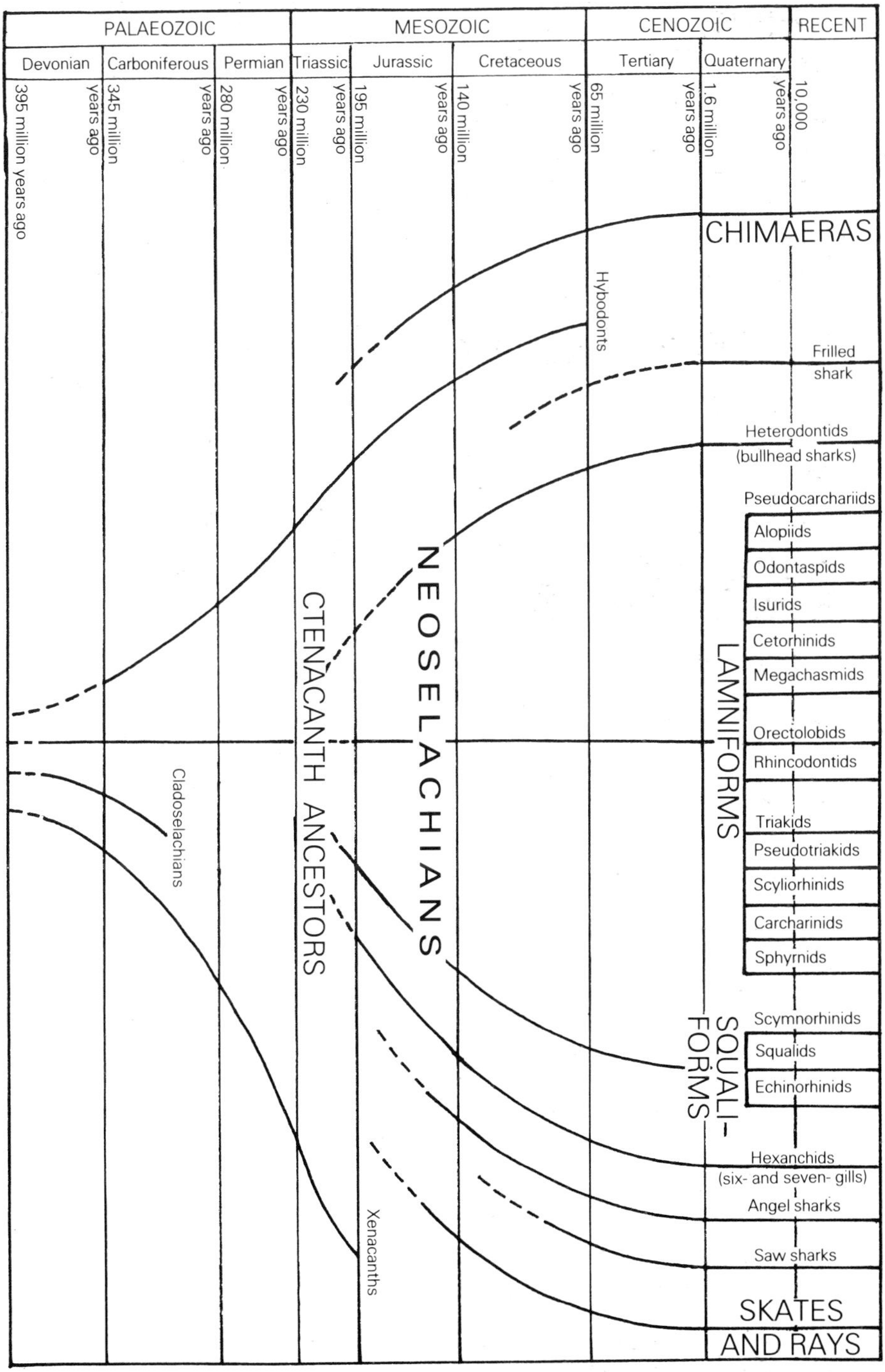

PALAEOZOIC				MESOZOIC			CENOZOIC		RECENT
Devonian	Carboniferous	Permian	Triassic	Jurassic	Cretaceous		Tertiary	Quaternary	
395 million years ago	345 million years ago	280 million years ago	230 million years ago	195 million years ago	140 million years ago	65 million years ago	1.6 million years ago	10,000 years ago	

CHIMAERAS

Hybodonts

Frilled shark

Heterodontids (bullhead sharks)

Pseudocarchariids

CTENACANTH ANCESTORS

NEOSELACHIANS

LAMNIFORMS

Alopiids
Odontaspids
Isurids
Cetorhinids
Megachasmids

Orectolobids
Rhincodontids

Triakids
Pseudotriakids
Scyliorhinids
Carcharinids
Sphyrnids

SQUALI-FORMS

Scymnorhinids
Squalids
Echinorhinids

Hexanchids (six- and seven- gills)
Angel sharks

Saw sharks

Cladoselachians

Xenacanths

SKATES AND RAYS

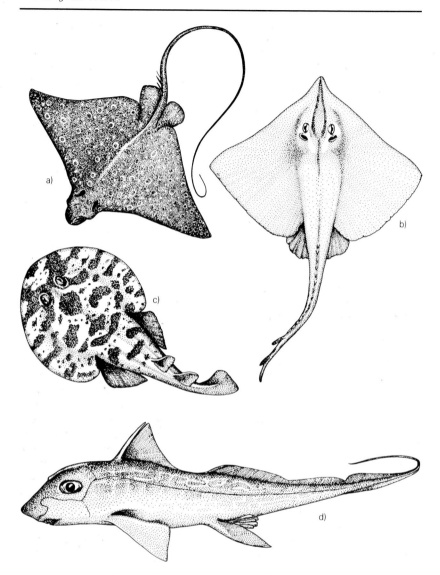

Fig. 1.7. Other elasmobranchs (cartilaginous fishes) related to sharks but not selachians: a) spotted eagle ray (*Aetobatus narinari*), b) skate (*Raja batis*), c) torpedo ray (*Narcine brasiliensis*), d) chimaera (*Chimaera monstrosa*).

number of short-lived (retrospectively speaking) experiments in shark evolution had already come to an end. Several families sought to live primarily on hard-shelled food, such as molluscs or brachiopods, and their broad, low-crowned teeth occur abundantly in rocks of late Palaeozoic age. Because, like all sharks, their skeletons were cartilaginous, they are rarely represented by any other fossil material and remain very poorly known, but by the dawn of the Mesozoic era (the Age of Reptiles), these aberrant lines had evidently vanished from the scene.

A few living species are seemingly not much further advanced than the old extinct hybodont stock, but really modern sharks had already begun to appear in some numbers long before the last dinosaurs died out. The two principal orders of living sharks, the lamniforms (predominantly although not exclusively active hunters, frequently attaining a large size) and the squaliforms (generally smaller bottom-dwellers, but with a few species that reach substantial dimensions) were firmly established as long ago as the latter part of the Cretaceous period, 100 million years ago. Their characteristic double-rooted, blade-like teeth are common fossils in Tertiary deposits and, by Miocene times, 20 million years ago, sharks had reached a peak of size, with predators as much as 15 metres (50 feet) in length cruising the high seas.

Several successful variants (Fig. 1.7) have diverged from the basic shark stock during the last 150 million years, the first of these offshoots to appear being the skates. The living banjo fish (*Rhinobatis*) made its debut in the Upper Jurassic, about 150 million years ago; this somewhat flattened bottom-dweller, which still retains dorsal and caudal fins and has only moderately enlarged pectorals, is transitional in structure to such grotesquely compressed types as *Raja*, which appeared in the Cretaceous and demonstrated a much higher degree of specialisation – a short flat body, broadly expanded pectoral fins extending forward along the sides of the snout, a slender tail and only a diminutive vestige of the median fins. Yet further along this road, diverging ever more widely from the original shark stock, are the rays (*Trygon* and its kin) with pectoral fins meeting in front of the snout and now so wide that the fish's body is broader than it is long. These were also to be found in Cretaceous seas, along with the first of the great eagle rays (*Myliobatis*, *Rhinoptera*) in which the pectoral fins may span 2 metres ($6\frac{1}{2}$ feet) from tip to tip but do not meet ahead of the cavernous mouth with its pavement of specialised crushing teeth. Slightly later arrivals on the scene, in the Eocene period, 50 million years ago, were the torpedo rays, in which some of the body musculature is modified into a powerful electric organ, while the huge devil fish are unknown until late in the Cenozoic.

Now a rather impoverished group of half a dozen genera and thirty or so species, the little chimaeras (or rat-fish) and the elephant fishes are also apparently derivatives of the early shark stock. The living examples of the group (*Chimaera* itself, *Hydrolagus*, *Neoharriotta*, *Rhinochimaera*, *Harriotta*, *Callorhynchus*) bear little resemblance to a typical shark, with their rat-like tails, long probing snouts, a hook-like copulatory organ on the forehead, skin flaps covering the gills, fan-shaped pectoral fins, a large spine in front of the dorsal fin, and crushing toothplates for pulverising the shells of the molluscs on which they feed – the upper jaw being solidly fused to the skull for additional strength. Nonetheless these active little swimmers are probably descended from some of the poorly known, mollusc-eating, shark-like fishes that prospered late in the Palaeozoic, about 300 million years ago. Chimaeras had already evolved early in the Mesozoic, but they have never, it seems, been a particularly numerous group, although modestly successful in their own somewhat unambitious way. The origin of their putative forebears is lost in the mists of time but it must be assumed that they separated from the central stem of shark evolution at a very early date, so that sharks and chimaeras have gone their separate ways for perhaps 350 million years.

Even today, the ocean deeps may still hide huge, unknown sharks. In 1976, a United States oceanographic research vessel working 40 kilometres (24 miles) off Oahu in the Hawaiian Islands hauled in a parachute anchor and found entangled in it the corpse of a 4.5 metre ($14\frac{1}{2}$ foot) shark like nothing that had ever been seen before. It proved to be not just a new species, but a representative of a totally new family – a massive plankton-eater with extraordinary protrusible jaws that lives in the abyss of the tropical ocean. There had never been any hint of such a creature's existence: no reports of remains washed up on remote beaches, no obscure sightings from ships at sea, and not even any accounts from fishermen of an unidentified giant shark being caught up in their trawl nets. It became known as the megamouth shark.

Emerging from the unknown depths of the sea to kill swiftly and silently with unparalleled ferocity, then vanishing back into an ocean which primitive peoples believed extended to the edge of the world, it is scarcely surprising that sharks became a subject of myth, legend, folklore and even veneration.

The archipelagos of the Pacific were once a centre of oceanic tribalism, with sea-going warriors feuding and fighting from their war canoes across wide areas of ocean. To them, sharks acquired the status of gods with supernatural powers – the kings of the ocean across which a fragile canoe ventured at its peril, with destruction in violent tropical storms an ever-present hazard and a lingering death from exposure and thirst the inevitable lot of the navigator who missed his tiny island home as he sailed the world's greatest expanse of sea. The natives of New Guinea regarded sharks as dangerous wizards and had a taboo against catching them, while many Polynesians revere the fierce blue sharks, which they never kill.

In the Hawaiian Islands, the king of the sharks was known as Kamo Hoa Lii and was supposed to live off Honolulu harbour; the queen of sharks, Oahu, allegedly dwelt at the bottom of Pearl Harbor. Legend has it that Kamo Hoa Lii saw a girl called Kalei swimming in the sea and fell in love with her. Kamo Hoa Lii, as befits a shark king, had magical powers and turned himself into a man so that he could marry this young woman. Their boy child was called Nanaue and bore on his back a mark like a shark's mouth. Kamo Hoa Lii gave strict instructions that the boy was never under any circumstances to be given meat, but one day this commandment was disobeyed. As soon as the meat passed his lips, Nanaue discovered the power to change himself into a shark. Craving more meat, he cruised the beaches in shark form and killed his fill of the islanders until at last he was caught. Nanaue's shark-body was taken to a hill at Kainaliu, which thereafter became known as *Pumano* (Shark Hill).

Using bamboo knives, the islanders hacked the corpse to pieces but, when the gods witnessed this sacrilege to one of their own sons, they vengefully took away the sharpness of the knives so that, even today, the bamboo from this area of Hawaii is believed to be weak and useless as a cutting tool.

The supposed magical properties of sharks are also reflected in the story of the *kapaaheo*, or shark stone, now in Honolulu's Bishop Museum. At one time, it seems, Hawaiian girls vanished with monotonous regularity from their favourite swimming beach in one of the island's beautiful bays, and these disappearances coincided with sightings of a mysterious stranger in the area. When local fishermen armed with spears went into the water with the girls, they were able to fend off an attacking shark, seriously wounding it. Not long after, the unknown stranger was found on the beach dying of stab wounds and, when he expired, he turned into the *kapaaheo*.

During construction of the Pearl Harbor naval base on Oahu, in the early years of the twentieth century, an ancient shark pen was discovered that consisted of a ring of rocks enclosing about 1.6 hectares (4 acres) of water. In days gone by, local gladiators fought with sharks enticed into the rocky enclosure by a bait of fish or human flesh, access to the ocean being via an opening on the seaward side. Armed only with a wooden dagger tipped by a single shark's tooth, the wretched warrior would have stood little chance against a tough-skinned adversary whose mouth bristled with similar teeth. As late as 1820, the explorer Otto von Kotzebue saw a large shark kept in an artificial enclosure of coral stones on the banks of the Pearl River and was told that children and sometimes adults were thrown into the pool.

Far to the southwest, below the equator in the Solomon Islands, sharks were venerated as the spirits of deceased ancestors. Any shark recognised as a regular inhabitant of a given area was regarded as a 'good shark' and provided with food, but if a strange shark arrived on the scene the islanders would confront it with a wooden effigy of their 'good shark' to scare it away. Human sacrifice to propitiate the shark gods was at one time common in the Pacific and the Solomon Islanders made underwater caverns for sharks to live in, in front of which were stone altars where the unfortunate human victims suffered their unpleasant demise – presumably if not already dead, they would drown anyway before a shark could be tempted out for its free snack. None of the big, active, open-ocean sharks would be amenable to living in caves, so it is probable that these sluggish specimens were nurse sharks (*Ginglymostoma*), which could be relied upon to remain *in situ* if meals were regularly forthcoming.

The half-god, half-man deity named Maui is a mythical creature that was widely venerated, not only in Polynesia but also in Micronesia and Melanesia. Allegedly, when Maui was fishing, he was insulted by the shark Mokoroa, so Maui killed Mokoroa and threw him up into the sky, where he is still to be seen lying upon the Milky Way. The island of Tahiti is said to be another of Maui's sharks, which escaped to its present location.

On the western shores of the Pacific, the Japanese included a shark god

23

in their pantheon – the god of storms – and sharks have always been used as a symbol of terror in Japanese legend. The Marshall Islanders fought religious wars over alleged slights to their shark gods, generally precipitated when a neighbouring tribe killed a shark, and the Samoans habitually used to hang a shark effigy in bread-fruit trees and coconut palms to protect the fruit. Attempting to ensure the success of next year's crops and fishing by burying a shark in a shrine was another practice once common in the Pacific, a local artist being enlisted to paint a tiger shark's striped image on the back of the grave, while two guards were stationed at either end of the tomb for a week.

The harmless, lethargic whale shark captured the imagination of the Vietnamese, for some unknown reason. At one time common in the seas off Indo-China, this huge plankton-eater was known in the area as *ca-ong* (which may be roughly translated as 'Sir fish') and shrines were built to worship the great beasts.

Pearl-divers in Ceylon used to employ snake-charmers to exert an imagined influence over the local sharks during the pearling season and, among the Pacific Islanders, there was once a regularly performed ceremony of shark-kissing: suitably high on the mild local narcotic known as *kava* (made from a shrub of the pepper family, *Piper methysticum*), natives would attempt to 'kiss' the local sharks. It was believed that once kissed, a shark never moved again and was thus rendered harmless. If the shark singled out for this attention was a drowsy nurse shark sluggishly dozing on the bottom, the demonstration would probably have been convincing enough, but any attempt to kiss a tiger shark might be expected to yield unfortunate results.

Although Westerners have not maintained such a picturesque shark folklore as the peoples of less sophisticated countries, seamen in the days of sail nonetheless nourished some curious beliefs about sharks. The capture of a shark was seen as an omen, particularly if it was a female carrying a full term foetus, and sailing ships habitually had the tail of a shark or porpoise nailed to the bowsprit for luck.

It was widely believed that, if somebody was dying on board ship, the sharks somehow knew this and would follow the vessel in anticipation of a meal when the body was put overboard. The Chinese who settled in California always had a great desire for their bodies eventually to lie among the bones of their ancestors in far-away China. Each family would therefore set aside funds for the transport, in due course, of their mortal remains back across the Pacific and this practice led to a steady trade in the shipment of coffined corpses westwards to China. The nineteenth-century sailors who manned the vessels carrying these bodies always swore that the sharks knew what was on board and followed in their wake for days. Sharks do undeniably have a sharp sense of smell but, apart from the fact that they greatly prefer fresh meat, it is more probable that they were simply attracted by rubbish thrown overboard from the galley, or by fish living among the weeds that habitually foul a ship's bottom.

One or two individual sharks became quite well known to local residents and sailors. Port Royal Jack was a massive shark that lurked at the entrance to Kingston Harbour, Jamaica, while Shanghai Bill cruised the waters not of Shanghai but of Bridgetown, Barbados. Both were believed to be man-eaters, but Shanghai Bill allegedly met his end when he tried to swallow a big sheepdog that had fallen or jumped into the water, got his teeth tangled in the dog's shaggy coat, and choked to death.

The West Indies were also the scene of the 'shark papers' incident in 1799. The United States brig *Nancy* (128 tonnes), was refused permission by the British (then at war with the Americans) to proceed to the West Indies, but her owners sought to circumvent this restriction by first sending the vessel under the command of Thomas Biggs to the Dutch colony of Curaçao, where false papers indicating Dutch ownership were obtained. When subsequently *en route* for the West Indies, the *Nancy* was intercepted off the south coast of Haiti by the British warship *Sparrow*, under the command of Lieutenant Willis. Unimpressed by the *Nancy*'s Dutch papers, Willis put aboard a prize crew and took the ship into Port Royal, Jamaica. During the course of further investigations, a Lieutenant Michael Fitton disclosed to Willis that, while captaining HMS *Abergavenny*'s tender *Ferret* on 30 August 1799, his crew caught a shark which was found to contain a set of ship's papers pertaining to an American vessel called the *Nancy*! Fitton's official deposition subsequently declared that he 'ordered some of the seamen to separate the Jaws and Clean them ... whilst others opened its Maw and therein discovered ... a parcel of paper tied up with string ...'. Evidently the *Nancy*'s skipper had thrown his genuine ship's papers overboard when interception by the British seemed inevitable, but their subsequent bizarre discovery revealed the fraudulent nature of the American brig's Dutch 'registration' and the 'shark papers' as they became known were a key item of evidence when, in November 1799, a court ruled that the *Nancy* and her crew were a legitimate British prize. The jaws of this shark, apparently a tiger shark, were eventually lodged in the Royal United Services Museum in London under the accession number 6020.

As a footnote to this curious catalogue of myth, legend and folklore, it may be noted that even the origin of the name 'shark' is itself obscure. It appears to have been introduced into the English language by members of Sir John Hawkins' expedition to the Caribbean which brought a 'shark' back to London for exhibition in 1569, a time when the name *tiburon* was commonly applied to these fish (and particularly to the bonnet shark, *Sphyrna tiburo*), this word probably being derived from the East or West Indies via Spanish or Portuguese. But where did Hawkins and his men find the word 'shark'? Perhaps it came from the Maya of central America, who employed a hieroglyphic form of writing. They had a verb *xoc* (pronounced 'shock') that was represented by a glyph depicting a fish with a prominent dorsal fin. When we speak of a shark, it seems probable that we are in fact using a Mayan word from the pyramid cities of Chichen Itza and Uxmal.

Chapter 2
The Human Toll

Sharks rarely make a clean kill. Even a hungry great white, a tonne or more of savage fury hurtling through the water, normally only savages its victim on an initial strike.

Australian skin-diver Rodney Fox was taking part in the South Australian State Spearfishing Championship at Aldinga Beach, just south of Adelaide on 12 August 1963. Approaching the end of his dive, Fox had no intimation of the danger looming up on him from the murky depths until the great white was nearly upon him. Almost before he realised his peril, the shark's massive jaws closed on his chest and back, forcing his left shoulder partway down the creature's gullet. Hurled through the water by the speed of the strike, Fox felt no real pain, only the crushing pressure of the jaws clamped on the left side of his thorax, apparently squeezing the organs of his body into his right flank. Short of a near miracle, Fox had only seconds to live before a merciful death snuffed out his life and his lacerated corpse was dismembered to disappear down the shark's cavernous maw.

Almost unbelievably, spearfisherman Rodney Fox recovered from these terrible lacerations inflicted by a great white.

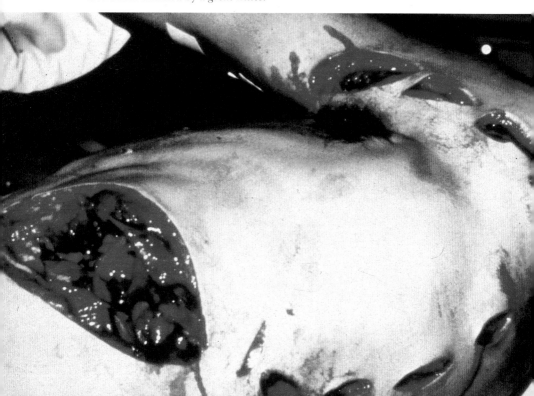

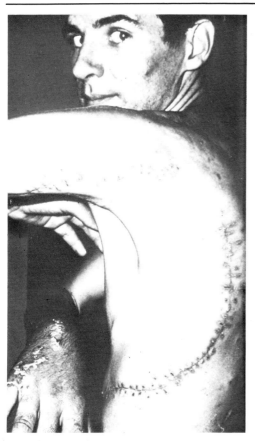

After the surgeons had done their work, Rodney Fox's fearful injuries healed astonishingly well but he will carry the scars for the rest of his life.

Shark attack victims (left to right) Brian Rodger, Rodney Fox and Henri Bource with a great white savagely mutilated by another of its kind when hooked.

Fox frantically drove his right fist at the only vulnerable area in the great fish's abrasively skinned face – the cold, pitiless eyeball. His fingers desperately clawed at the socket, but Fox's right arm slipped momentarily into the shark's mouth and, as he wrenched it free, the cruel teeth tore his hand and arm right down to the bone.

Now the shark had tasted blood. It came in again at the fearfully mauled Fox and seized the fish float, which was still attached to his diving belt. Dragged deep down by the diving shark, Fox sought frantically for the fastening of the belt. Then the shark's razor-edged teeth sheared away the connection and Fox was able to struggle to the surface. Hauled aboard a nearby boat, his condition was desperate: his rib cage, lungs and the upper part of his stomach were exposed, the flesh had been stripped from his arm, a lung was punctured and his ribs were crushed. He was rushed to hospital, where it took a 4 hour operation and 462 stitches to save his life. He still dives but, for the rest of his life, the scars of a killer shark's teeth will encircle his body.

Fox's friend and spearfishing rival, Brian Rodger, was equally fortunate to escape with his life after being mauled by a great white. Attacked during a 1961 spearfishing competition at the same locality, he had a leg fearfully lacerated by a shark's deadly teeth. Henri Bsource, another diver, lost a leg in Australian waters as a result of a shark attack – this time at Lady Julia Percy Island, Victoria, in 1964; 4 years later a shark took off his artificial leg in another attack.

Even more extraordinary was the escape of Iona Asai, a pearl-diver who was attacked while working the Great Barrier Reef from the lugger *San* in 1937. When Asai, swimming in about 9 metres (30 feet) of water, turned to confront his assailant, his horrified eyes saw a massive tiger shark heading straight for him only 2 metres (6 feet) away. He had no time to avoid the onrushing killer, which seized his head in its jaws. Like Fox, Asai went for the creature's eyes and squeezed the luminous orbs until the crushing grip on his head was released. Pulled into a boat, Asai was rushed to hospital where nearly 200 stitches were needed to suture his hideous wounds. He survived, however, and the identity of his would-be assassin was confirmed 3 weeks later when surgeons had to open an abscess on his neck; it was found to contain the tooth of a tiger shark.

For others, unluckier, inexperienced under water, or less cool-headed in the face of almost unimaginable terror, the outcome has not been so happy. Norman Clark was only 19 years old when he dived off a pier in Port Philip Bay, Melbourne, one day in 1930, during a yacht race. Before the appalled eyes of the watching crowd, Clark was seized by a massive shark 100 metres (110 yards) offshore and dragged under water. The great fish reappeared holding Clark by the leg while the youth beat frantically, but with evidently failing strength, at the creature's head. Clark was then momentarily released, but only to enable the shark to make a fresh assault, seizing its victim round the chest with such force as to hurl him out of the water before vanishing out to sea with what was left of the wretched Clark.

This horrific incident was only one in a long and melancholy catalogue

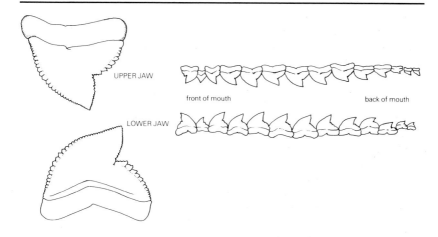

Fig. 2.1. The teeth of the tiger shark (*Galeocerdo cuvier*).

of fatal shark attacks in Australian waters that date back to the early records of British settlement. As long ago as 1806, the *Sydney Gazette* published a warning to parents that a shark was lurking in the vicinity of the harbour's hospital wharf and, in 1837, a boy aged 12 years died of tetanus after being seized by a shark in the Macleay River. Moreton Bay, Queensland, was known to be frequented by numerous sharks in the middle of the nineteenth century, one of which took off a native's foot but, generally speaking, these fish were apparently rather small individuals.

After the turn of the century, records of shark attacks around the Australian coast became more carefully documented. A particularly gruesome case occurred in Sydney on 6 January 1912, when a 'whaler' (*Carcharhinus obscurus*) seized a man and bit off the side of his thigh, together with his penis and scrotum. The shark was caught 48 hours later and, about 5 centimetres (2 inches) from the cloacal vent, were found the victim's penis and scrotum with attached tissue, still largely undigested.

Attacks on boats in Australian waters were also recorded, including one on a skiff off Bellambi Reef, New South Wales, on 16 June 1923, when four men out fishing were tipped into the water by a shark which smashed a hole in the bottom of the boat. One man tried to swim ashore and was immediately taken by a shark and two of the others became exhausted and sank, leaving but a single survivor to be rescued by a passing vessel. Similar attacks occurred on a canoe near Glenelg Jetty, South Australia, in 1929 and on a 3.5 metre (12 foot) dinghy at Rosebud, Victoria, the following year, although without fatal consequences to the occupants. Whether the sharks were consciously trying to tip these unfortunate people into the water is doubtful, as such behaviour would indicate quite a high level of intelligence. More probably, the boats were simply bumped to find out if they were edible in the instinctive manner that sharks usually employ and tipping a prospective meal into the water was an unexpected bonus.

South Pacific Islanders have also been attacked in their canoes on occasion and, in one particularly horrific alleged incident, about forty natives of the Ellice Islands group were crossing at night between islands several kilometres apart when a squall swamped one of the boats. Some sharks which had been following the diminutive fleet, occasionally snapping at the paddles (probably because they splashed the surface like fish), rushed in and seized the unfortunate natives in the water and, as a feeding frenzy built up, all but one of the remaining canoes were upset and their occupants devoured. Only two natives escaped to tell of their companions' terrible end.

Recreational use of Australian beaches by an increasingly urban population resulted in regular reports of shark attacks during the 1920s and 1930s. In the Sydney Harbour area, a boy was fatally mauled on 10 January 1919, at 7.30 a.m., when a shark seized him as he waded out for an early morning swim. Still alive when rescued by a passing boat, his right thigh bone was exposed and the femoral artery severed, so that he died shortly after being brought ashore. Five years later, almost to the day, on 19 January 1924, a 16-year-old youth was savaged in only 1 metre ($3\frac{1}{4}$ feet) of water in the Parramatta River; dragged from the water, he died within 3 minutes, the flesh of his right thigh being ripped to the bone from hip to knee. The same Parramatta River witnessed a further tragedy on 26 December 1929, when another 16-year-old was attacked again and again by a persistent shark that continued to maul its victim, even as rescuers lifted the boy into a boat with his left arm severed above the elbow and multiple lacerations of his chest. The youth died before he could be taken to hospital.

Fashionable Bondi Beach has always attracted surfers, but it has cost some of them their lives. On 12 January 1929, a boy seized in only 1.2 metres (4 feet) of water died in hospital after being rescued, his injuries including a massive lacerated wound extending from the top of his right hip bone to the middle of his thigh, the crest of the ilium having been torn off and fragmented. Less than a month later, on 8 February 1929, a 39-year-old man died before reaching Bondi's St Vincent Hospital after a shark had seized him, taking a huge bite, meauring 38 by 18 centimetres (15 by 7 inches), from his right thigh and severing the femoral artery.

Around the coast at Adelaide there were also tragedies. A swimming instructress, who was in addition a life-saving expert was attacked by a shark while swimming at 4 o'clock in the afternoon on 18 February 1926. Two men in a boat heard her screams and dragged her, still conscious, from the water but, with her right thigh almost bitten away and horrific lacerations of the body, she lived only a few minutes.

In those days, when antibiotics and other modern drugs were not available, a shark victim's prospects were poor, even if he or she could be taken to hospital before dying of shock and haemorrhage. A 22-year-old man, attacked at Coogee, Sydney, at 11 a.m. on 3 March 1922, had his right hand severed, his left hand mutilated (his little finger was gone and the ends of the third and fourth fingers were missing) and received a circular laceration, extending from the anterior of the anus to the promontory of the sacrum, which penetrated the deep spinal muscles of his back, as well as deep penetrating wounds of his left thigh. Despite expert surgery, gas gangrene set in before midnight and the offensive odour of putrefaction enveloped the patient's bed as he rapidly succumbed to overwhelming bacterial infection and septicaemia, dying at 5 p.m. on the day after the attack. In the case of a 20-year-old youth savaged at Maroubra Bay, Sydney, on 18 February 1929, on arrival at the hospital at 4.30 p.m., an hour after the attack, his injuries were found to include extensive lacerations of the thighs, abrasions of the right leg and foot and severe damage to his left hand. Despite the administration of gas-gangrene antiserum and irrigation of the lacerations with eusol (Edinburgh University solution, a chlorinated antiseptic), he was feverish the following day and, by 20 February, was in great pain and irrational, while the wounds were gaping, dirty and sloughing. Although there was no evidence of gas gangrene, he deteriorated progressively, the pulse became irregular, his temperature rose to 39.4°C (103°F), and he died within a week.

On the other hand, there were some notable recoveries, almost on a par with those achieved by a later generation of doctors in the famous case of Rodney Fox. A 30-year-old woman attacked at Bronte, Sydney, on 13 February 1924 had her right leg severed about mid-way up and her left foot so severely savaged that the bones were exposed. After surgical amputation of the right leg above the knee and the left leg below the knee, she made a complete recovery within a month. A 16-year-old youth seized at Coogee on 27 March 1925 sustained penetrating wounds of the left thigh that reached the bone and lacerations of the left leg which had exposed the tibia and fractured the fibula; all the wounds were full of sand where he had, amazingly, dragged himself ashore. Shocked but conscious, and in great pain on admission to hospital, he was operated on for the amputation of his leg at mid-thigh and was discharged $5\frac{1}{2}$ weeks later.

Nowadays powerful antibiotics are invaluable in controlling infection, particularly where deep, penetrating wounds such as those inflicted by the spike-like teeth of sand sharks (odontaspids) are concerned. Grey sharks (carcharhinids) have continuously-aligned cutting teeth in jaws of great crushing power and are capable of effecting complete limb amputations, slicing away flesh with such efficiency that massive haemorrhage from the cleanly severed skin and muscle is frequently fatal: treatment of grey shark victims usually requires enormous amounts of blood and plasma if the victim is to survive, while local use of antibiotic powder on the open wound is probably largely ineffective in countering infection due to the volume of exudate.

Leg injuries that involve severance of both femoral arteries seem invariably to be fatal within minutes due to catastrophic blood loss, and even the cutting of one femoral artery high up in the thigh is usually a hopeless proposition. Once a shark attack victim has been brought alive to the beach, however, the greatest danger is not haemorrhage (which would have already proved fatal if major blood vessels had been severed) but shock. Experience in South Africa suggests that the injured person should not be moved to hospital by ambulance for at least 30 minutes while morphine, saline and plasma are administered to counter shock. Bundling a severely mauled person into a car and rushing them to hospital has probably killed more people due to irreversible deep shock than it has saved. Shark-infested bathing beaches in South Africa are all now equipped with first aid packs containing saline, plasma and morphine for initial on-the-spot treatment.

The toll of shark victims nonetheless inevitably continues, as the splendid Australian beaches and subtropical climate combine to attract vacationers and sport fishermen in increasing numbers. A tragic case in July 1983 involved the three people aboard a prawn trawler that was wrecked during the night off the north Queensland coast near the Barrier Reef. Skipper Ray Boundy, aged 33 years, clung for 36 hours to floating wreckage, but his two companions were both taken by sharks: 24-year-old Dennis Murphy had his leg taken off and, in a courageous attempt to lure the attacker from his two companions, summoned his ebbing strength to swim away. It was to no avail. Dennis Murphy had only minutes to live and 21-year-old Linda Horton was also seized. Only Boundy survived.

Australia has always been a focus of shark attacks, with over 400 deaths since the beginning of the twentieth century, but South African beaches probably have the most notorious record of fatalities and maulings due to sharks, some sixty incidents having been reported along the coast between the Cape of Good Hope and Natal in just the 50 years from 1925 to 1975.

The beautiful Natal coast, with its magnificent sandy beaches, is a favourite vacation area and for the first four decades of the twentieth century was effectively free of sharks. Then, in the early 1940s, a series of attacks took place at Amanzimtoti, some 32 kilometres (20 miles) south of Durban, followed in 1944–51 by a number of incidents at Durban itself and then several attacks at Margate, 160 kilometres (100 miles) to the south. Amanzimtoti experienced further shark activity in the 1970s: a professional life-saver was seized by the leg 150 metres (165 yards) offshore in 1974 and a 16-year-old surf-boarder was savaged the following year when a shark caught his leg and endeavoured to pull him into the sea. Six people were killed by sharks on Natal's beaches between 1944 and 1952 and there were nineteen reported shark attacks.

Further north, in Mozambique, dangerous sharks not only prowl the coastline (there was a fatality at the popular resort of Xai Xai in 1974), but also range up the Zambesi River, sometimes as much as 200 kilometres (120 or so miles) from the sea.

These Zambesi sharks (*Carcharhinus leucas*) also occur in the mouth of the Limpopo, where three attacks occurred within 6 months early in 1961; a child was mauled 150 metres (165 yards) up the river in January of that year, a swimmer was killed the following May and, a few days later, in the same area, a man sustained serious injuries when a shark struck at him in shallow water. Mogadishu lido, Somalia, was the scene of a number of shark fatalities in the late 1970s and the 1980s, generally attributed to *Carcharhinus leucas*.

It has been suggested that the greatest danger from sharks occurs in warm tropical seas and Sir Victor Copplestone, the eminent Australian surgeon and shark-attack expert, suggested, in 1933, that a sea temperature of 21°C (70°F) represented something of a limiting factor for shark attacks. In the tropics, where the water never falls below this temperature, shark attacks occur all the year round. Areas at risk extend from Baja California, Daytona Beach (Florida), Daker (West Africa), the Red Sea and Formosa in the north to the Gulf of Guayaquil (Ecuador), Rio de Janeiro, Natal and Shark Bay (Western Australia) in the south. During summer months, sea temperatures rise in higher latitudes and the hazardous areas for shark attacks are extended. In the north, sharks may strike anywhere up to San Francisco, Buzzard's Bay (Massachusetts), northern Portugal, the Mediterranean and Sakhalin while, in the south, the danger zone embraces Antofagasta (Chile), Bahia Blanca (Argentina), the Cape of Good Hope, Cape Leeuwin (Western Australia), Melbourne and New Zealand's North Island.

There are objections to Copplestone's deductions, however. A sea temperature of 21°C is just about the degree of warmth that will tempt bathers, divers and surfers into the water. Sharks certainly penetrate to far higher latitudes than those demarcated by Copplestone's 21°C temperature limit and it is possible that the sharks are there all the time but the bathers are not – hence an apparent absence of shark attacks in water with a temperature below 21°C. In any case, there are records of sharks attacking people in the distinctly chilly seas of high latitudes, such as the fisherman at Wick, northernmost Scotland, in June 1960, who was bitten on the arm by a small shark netted along with his catch.

Although the beaches of the British Isles are not considered to be endangered by sharks, the offshore waters are nonetheless infested with them, at least during the summer months. There are highly profitable shark fisheries in the West Country based at Looe (headquarters of the Shark Angling Club of Great Britain), Falmouth, Fowey, Mevagissey, Plymouth and Torquay while, on the Channel coast, Emsworth, Gosport, Lymington and the Isle of Wight are all shark-fishing centres.

In the deep turbulent waters of St Catherine's Race, off St Catherine's Point in the Isle of Wight, there is an abundance of big threshers and porbeagles. They apparently come up-Channel following the shoals of mackerel that are their normal diet but winter fishing for mackerel has considerably reduced the stocks of these fish and big hungry sharks are now cruising closer to crowded holiday beaches in search of food. Under these circumstances, it is not perhaps surprising that sub-aqua club member Jimmy Johnson, aged 32 years, was attacked at Beesands, south Devonshire, on 1 June 1971 when only 50 metres (55 yards) from the beach, but drove off three charges by striking the 3.6 metre (12 foot) shark on the nose with a lobster hook, eventually struggling ashore unharmed. It was believed at the time that a mako shark was responsible, but some authorities consider it more likely to have been a porbeagle.

On the other side of the Atlantic, the beaches of eastern North America have been the scene of numerous shark tragedies and near tragedies. A series of attacks took place in Florida during an horrific 5 week period in

1958. No less than four incidents occurred in June and July of that year along a 96 kilometre (60 mile) stretch of western coastline between Sarasota and Sanibel Island.

Frank A. Mahala, a 17-year-old, was seized by the left leg on 24 June at 5.10 p.m. when wading in only 0.75 metres ($2\frac{1}{2}$ feet) of water some 5 metres (15 feet) from the shore at Turtle Beach, Siesta Quay. Dragged ashore by friends and rushed to hospital, Mahala had in fact been bitten several times by what may have been a tiger shark. He lost all sensation in his leg after the initial attack when the nerves were severed. (It seems to be a familiar occurrence that victims of shark attacks are numbed by the first bite.) Mahala eventually made a full recovery, as did 59-year-old Eric Cockerill, who was grabbed by the foot 2 days later while wading in 1 metre ($3\frac{1}{4}$ feet) of water on a sandbar 10 metres (30 feet) offshore at Sanibel Island at 5.30 p.m.. It seems probable that Cockerill had inadvertently trodden on a nurse shark, a relatively sluggish and usually inoffensive species, for, after momentarily retaining its hold on Cockerill's foot, the creature let go and apparently lost interest.

Nurse sharks, by and large, simply want to be left alone to mind their own business, and when, on 2 July, 22-year-old skin-diver John Hamlin found one resting 2 metres (6 feet) down on rocks 3 metres (10 feet) from the shore at Siesta Quay, he unwisely grabbed it by the tail. Less than happy at having its rest disturbed, this 2 metre (6 foot) nurse promptly planted its teeth in Hamlin's left leg, just below the knee. When its tormentor hastily let go of the shark's tail, it swam quickly away and Hamlin struggled ashore.

All these three victims made complete recoveries from their ordeals, but 8-year-old Douglas Lawton, who was seized by the leg in 1 metre ($3\frac{1}{4}$ feet) of water while 3 metres (10 feet) out near Sarasota on 27 July was less fortunate. His 12-year-old swimming companion heard the younger boy scream as he was pulled under and went to his aid. After a struggle the shark, apparently a tiger, let go and the victim was dragged from the water by his father and other rescuers, but his leg had to be amputated above the knee.

Further north along the eastern seaboard, the year 1960 witnessed the initiation of a sudden spate of shark attacks. At Sea-Girt, New Jersey, John Brodeur lost his right leg when he was seized while swimming across a shallow bay with his girl friend – so little water was there that he had in fact stopped swimming and was standing on the sea bed when the shark struck. Also in 1960, a swimmer who had ventured some 3 kilometres (2 miles) out off Ocean City, New Jersey, lost a leg in a shark attack and, on 24 August, at Bridgeport, Connecticut, a man was seized by the arm in 1.25 metres (4 feet) of water 75 metres (80 yards) offshore. The following year, the United States Fish and Wildlife Service undertook a massive 2-month shark hunt off New Jersey and Long Island between 13 August and 13 October which produced no fewer than 310 sharks, six of which were great whites ranging up to about 140 kilograms (300 pounds) in weight.

Evidently these east coast waters contain more sharks than was generally realised, although the notorious sequence of five shark attacks on the New Jersey coast in 1916 was still within living memory. On 2 July in that year, 24-year-old Charles Vansant was attacked in 1.5 metres (5 feet) of water at Beach Haven and subsequently died while, only 5 days later, Charles Bruder was killed at Spring Lake, some 30 kilometres (20 miles) to the north. Another 5 days passed while the shark apparently responsible continued to cruise northwards. Then, on 12 July, it struck again, killing a 12-year-old boy, Lester Stilwell, at Matawan Creek 50 kilometres (30 miles) up the coast in water fully 30 kilometres (20 miles) from the sea, at the same time biting would-be rescuer Stanley Fisher fatally in the thigh. Before the sun went down, another 12-year-old, Joseph Dunn, was seized further down the creek and lost a leg but, 2 days later, the massive hunt these attacks triggered off was brought to a successful conclusion at South Amboy, New Jersey, where the shark was finally caught and killed. When opened up, its stomach was found to contain parts of a shin bone as well as other alleged human remains.

Across the American continent, the cold California current curving down from the north might be expected to make the waters of the west coast too chilly for sharks but this is not the case. On 7 December 1952, two youths were swimming about 27 metres (30 yards) off shore at Pacific Grove, California, at 2 o'clock in the afternoon. Suddenly, 17-year-old Barry Wilson screamed as he was seized by a 3.6 metre (12 foot) great white, the force of the attack hurling him partly clear of the water before he was drawn under. As the victim re-appeared at the surface, wildly beseeching help, the shark apparently sheared off and Wilson's companion, 15-year-old Brookner Bradley, ploughed to his aid through the blood-stained water while an onlooker from the beach, John C. Basford, rushed into the sea to help, followed by four members of a skin-diving group.

They managed to get Wilson into an inflated inner tube and began struggling through rough seas to a breakwater but before they reached it, the shark struck again at the by then inert Wilson. By the time the unfortunate boy was finally brought to the safety of the beach, some 20 minutes had elapsed since the initial attack and Wilson was dead. The lower part of his right buttock had been torn away and the flesh had been ripped off the leg from thigh to knee, while his left leg was also hideously macerated.

For California, this horrifying attack was only the first of a sequence. Two shark attacks that resulted in only minor injuries were reported off Venice Beach, a surf-boarder was harassed off Santa Monica and a skin-diver in Monterey bay was fortunate to escape from a quite vicious attack. Then, on 28 April 1957, 25-year-old Peter Savino was lost while swimming in Morro Bay, near San Luis Obispo, although his death is not definitely attributable to a shark attack. However, an eye-witness glimpsed him rising to the crest of a wave about 300 metres (300 yards or so) from shore and holding up an arm dripping with blood before disappearing from sight. This visual evidence undoubtedly suggests that the unfortunate Savino had been seized by a shark.

A couple of years later, on 7 May 1959, a man was killed near San Francisco's Golden Gate and, on 14 June of that year, Robert Pamperin was seized while free-diving 45 metres (50 yards) offshore at La Jolla – a shark (seemingly a tiger) was seen heading out into the ocean with Pamperin's body clamped in its jaws. It has since been suggested that this incident was a carefully contrived hoax: Pamperin's body was never found and he was subsequently reputed to have been seen alive and well in Mexico, but the witnesses' accounts are well documented.

In the 1970s the San Francisco area became an increasingly popular hunting ground for great whites as protective legislation allowed the sea lion colonies along the Californian coast to increase dramatically in numbers, providing these voracious sharks with a ready source of their favourite prey. Within a decade, these waters had become one of the most dangerously shark-infested areas in the world.

In Europe, the Mediterranean – that mecca of seekers after holiday sun, sand and sea – has also acquired a record of shark attacks. The western end of this almost enclosed sea is apparently more or less safe but, from Monte Carlo eastwards, dangerously large sharks can be expected.

A number of attacks have been recorded since the mid-1920s at localities as far apart as the Bay of Monaco, Genoa, the Yugoslavian coast (Varazze), the Adriatic (Rijek), Israel, Egypt and Greece. Some of these incidents were fatalities and, from teeth found in the bodies of victims, it seems that porbeagles have been largely responsible. It was probably a shark of this type that mortally injured Maurizio Sarra off the coast of San Feliceo Circeo on 22 September 1962, while he was diving to harpoon groupers, and either a porbeagle or a great white probably killed scuba diver Luciano Costanzo off Piombino, in Italy's Gulf of Baratti, in February 1989.

In many cases, shark attacks on humans are half-hearted affairs in which a cruising shark apparently comes upon a swimmer by accident and takes a casual bite at a flailing arm or leg in passing, just as it might snap at a nearby fish. When the victim begins to thresh about in panic, the shark reacts by tightening its hold with the result that a mouthful of flesh or even a limb is torn off. Very rarely, if ever, does a shark devour a person completely: usually there is just a quick grab, a bite, and the victim is then thrown away like a plaything that has ceased to be entertaining. In other cases, injuries sustained by shark attack victims are slash wounds rather than obvious attempts to remove flesh, and may result from aggressive behaviour, perhaps associated with territorialism, rather than the satisfaction of hunger or curiosity. Occasionally, however, there is no doubt that sharks make positive attacks on a specific victim, usually someone swimming alone or as a member of a small party – sharks rarely single out an individual from a large group.

Even this usually fairly safe generalisation proved false during World War 2, when the crews of downed aircraft or sunken ships were sometimes left floundering in shark-infested waters for days on end.

The danger that shark attacks hold for shipwrecked sailors has always been an uncomfortable fact of seafaring life in tropical seas. On 23

October 1926 the British patrol boat *Valerian* foundered 29 kilometres (18 miles) southwest of Bermuda and sharks set about the crew of 104 struggling in the water; only twenty survived. The following year, the Italian cruise liner *Principessa Mafalda* sank with appalling rapidity off the Brazilian coast near Abrolhos Island on the night of 25/26 October following a boiler explosion, possibly caused by a broken propeller shaft, leaving most of her passengers and crew to swim for it: 314 of the 1,259 aboard were lost and many of the bodies recovered had allegedly been mutilated by sharks. In 1934, a British destroyer, leading a line-ahead formation out of Singapore during the night at a speed of 25 knots, accidentally ploughed into a big sea-going Chinese junk and cut it in half; only one member of the junk's eleven-man crew was rescued, all the others being seized by sharks that converged on the scene in a frenzied pack.

When World War 2 broke out, fighting was initially centred on Europe, spreading to the Middle East by the autumn of 1940. In December 1941, Japan struck at British and American possessions in the Pacific, however, and thereafter both the Pacific and Indian Oceans became the scene of wide-ranging maritime conflicts, with combat planes traversing hundreds of kilometres of open ocean to attack enemy ships and bases. Such open ocean in these latitudes is alive with sharks, including some of the biggest to be found anywhere in today's seas. The possible consequences for sailors whose vessels were sunk or airmen who came down in the sea were too horrible to contemplate. For many, this prospective nightmare turned to a fearful reality.

On 11 November 1943, the troopship *Cape San Juan* was torpedoed by a Japanese submarine in the South Pacific, but only 448 of the 1,429 aboard were subsequently picked up by the merchantman *Edwin T. Merridith*, with frenzied sharks climbing half out of the water onto life rafts to snatch terrified survivors even while the rescue operation was in progress. Swimmers stood little chance.

When another troopship, the 6,934 tonne *Nova Scotia*, was torpedoed by a German U-boat, on 28 November 1942, some 48 kilometres (30 miles) off the Natal coast most of the 900 or so aboard (including 765 Italian prisoners-of-war destined for colonial work camps) successfully abandoned the sinking vessel, only to perish horribly as they floated supported by life jackets: feasting sharks came in to take advantage of the helpless men and many of the bodies subsequently recovered had had their legs chewed off. Only 192 men were rescued, after spending some 60 hours in the water.

Right at the end of the war, when B-29 Superfortresses from the Marianas flew 4,800 kilometre (3,000 mile) round-trips to bomb Japan's cities and ultimately blasted Hiroshima and Nagasaki with atomic weapons, the United States cruiser *Indianapolis* was assigned to carry, from San Francisco to the air force base on Tinian Island, the inner cannon of the first of these nuclear devices, along with its precious uranium projectile.

The outward journey across the Pacific was successfully accomplished and the weapon carried by the *Indianapolis* subsequently incinerated

Hiroshima on 6 August 1945, but a week before that, at 12.14 a.m. on 30 July, the Philippines-bound *Indianapolis* was intercepted by the Japanese submarine I.58 some 965 kilometres (600 miles) southwest of Guam. A broadside of torpedoes struck the cruiser, already a war-weary veteran, and she rolled quickly onto her starboard side and sank. Despite the rapidity with which the *Indianapolis* went under, many of her 1,199-strong crew succeeded in getting off the foundering ship. But it was to be 4 days before rescue vessels reached the scene and, eventually, only 316 survivors were plucked from the water. The death role was 883, the worst naval disaster at sea in American history, and a large proportion of those who died were taken by sharks that converged on the area of the sinking, the blood spilling into the sea attracting wave after wave of these voracious killers. Many of the bodies recovered were horribly mutilated and even some of the people rescued had been savagely bitten.

The inevitable hazards of sea-borne travel still take their toll in peacetime. In March 1975, a ferry with 190 passengers aboard capsized near Sandwhip Island in the Ganges-Brahmaputra Delta of Bangladesh and at least some of the fifty passengers lost were in all likelihood taken by sharks.

It has been said that about 1,000 people a year end up being eaten by sharks, 70 to 80 per cent. of them off the coasts of Africa, South America and Asia, where such incidents are rarely recorded. Of the forty or fifty attacks a year that do get officially reported, some 40 per cent. are fatal. By way of comparison, those other great aquatic killers, the crocodiles, used to take an estimated 3,000 people a year, two-thirds of them victims of the huge salt-water crocodile, which can exceed 6 metres (20 feet) in length, while most of the rest were probably devoured by the only marginally less massive Nile crocodile.

Fig. 2.2. The oceanic white-tip (*Carcharhinus longimanus*), attaining a length of 3 metres (9¾ feet) and regarded by pioneer underwater explorer, Jacques Cousteau, as an especially dangerous species. An aggressive shark, rarely encountered inshore but abundant in the open sea, oceanic white-tips are quick to gather at the scene of a mid-ocean shipwreck.

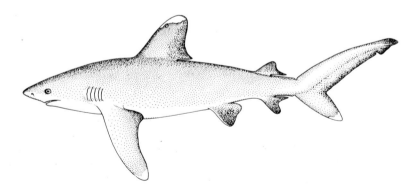

Fending off a shark whose intentions could well be unfriendly by using a shark billy.

Despite continuous efforts, greatly intensified during World War 2, there is still no effective means of protecting people in the water from shark attacks. Some of the activities which allegedly frighten sharks away, such as making a loud noise by shouting or hand-clapping, have been successfully used by underwater photographers to attract sharks, and aggressively swimming towards a shark that is slowly circling with apparent malicious intent is seemingly just as likely to provoke an attack as to circumvent one. The French underwater explorer Jacques-Yves Cousteau equipped his divers with billies for prodding away sharks. These consisted of a 1-metre ($3\frac{1}{4}$ foot) shaft of wood or aluminium, one end of which was provided with a circle of small nails to prevent the weapon from sliding too readily off a shark's hide but insufficiently sharp to cause any injury that would anger the fish. Cousteau's men also pioneered the use of cages into which they could quickly climb if threatened by sharks and evolved a technique for operating back-to-back in pairs when a shark attack seemed likely. The rubber suits used by SCUBA-divers are not a significant deterrent to sharks as experiments with a dummy have demonstrated: the dummy, suitably impregnated with pieces of fresh fish to give it an organic aroma, was dropped into the Red Sea, where sharks are abundant and, within minutes, a white-tip shark (*Carcharhinus longimanus*) had ripped off the dummy's leg.

Several chemical repellents have been tried, with negligible success. An anaesthetic known as MS-222, used by marine biologists and fishermen to immobilise fish, has little or no apparent effect on sharks. Incorporating copper acetate (believed to be objectionable to sharks) in a tablet along with a purple dye has been even less successful: sharks have actually been seen tracking along a trail left by this colouring substance as it is carried by underwater currents, presumably in the hope of finding something eatable at the end of it.

Using a nigrosine dye in conjunction with a chemical repellent does in fact seem to work in a tank. Sharks apparently learn to associate the dark-coloured water with the presence of the unpleasant chemical and avoid the spreading stain, but, if temporarily deprived of sight by being fitted with opaque eye covers, the fish will swim through the dye.

Air bubbling from a diver's aqualung equipment is said to deter a shark and perforated piping, through which air is pumped to generate a curtain of bubbles, has been laid off tropical bathing beaches. It works with some sharks, but tiger sharks seem indifferent to this bubbling effervescence, as do sand sharks. In Australia, an electric screen has been tried consisting of two wires, one suspended from buoys near the surface and the other held on the bottom by weights. During tests, several sharks were certainly turned away or temporarily paralysed, but the system was not considered to be infallible and installation costs were exorbitant. Conventional wire mesh barriers are simpler, cheaper and more effective, although regular inspection for corrosion is necessary – a barrier of this type installed at Aden but left unchecked for too long deteriorated to such an extent that a large shark eventually broke through and seized a woman bather by the leg.

Nonetheless there are substances that unequivocally do repel sharks. One genus of soles, the small flatfish *Pardachirus*, is apparently virtually immune to shark attacks. There are four species of this enigmatic creature, the best known being *Pardachirus marmoratus*, the Moses sole of the Red Sea and the western Indian Ocean. *Pardachirus pavoninus* (the peacock sole) ranges from the eastern Indian Ocean through the East Indies to the western Pacific, while *Pardachirus poropterus* (Indonesia and the Philippines) and *Pardachirus headleyi* (northern and eastern Australia) are less well known.

Beneath practically every one of the rays supporting the dorsal and anal fins of *Pardachirus* there is a pair of poison glands opening to the outside via tiny pores, with similar poison glands distributed randomly on the outer surface of the pelvic fins. These glands, when squeezed, exude a milky secretion which is highly toxic and capable of killing other fish and invertebrates – the active substance will even kill the Moses sole that produced it in the first place if it gets into the fish's circulation, e.g. in solution from the surrounding water through the gills.

The Moses sole probably uses the secretion from poison glands on the upper surface of its body as a deterrent to predators and, possibly, exudate from pores on the lower surface immobilises prospective prey on the sea floor as the sole cruises in search of food. As a deterrent it is certainly effective, very small quantities being sufficient to repel sharks for as long as 18 hours. Not surprisingly, the Moses sole is studiously avoided by sharks, but unfortunately the purified active toxin of its poison, a substance called pardaxin, is composed of a complicated 162-amino-acid sequence that can only be synthesised by a genetic engineering technique and, furthermore, has to be stored in a freeze-dried form which is 70 per cent. less effective than the fresh solution. However, some of pardaxin's effects are reminiscent of the qualities possessed by industrial surfactants: it reduces the surface tension of water by 60 per cent., foams in aqueous solution and disrupts the phospholipid membranes of cells. Investigation of a number of simple, inexpensive detergents showed that one of them was substantially more lethal to small pupfish than Moses sole extract and another was at least as deadly. Further tests of these two substances on lemon sharks, rendered cataleptic by being held inverted until they fell into a relaxed, trance-like state (tonic immobility), confirmed the first results. When released into the mouths of these lemon sharks, the two surfactants that had proved highly lethal to pupfish brought the sharks to instant struggling mobility, righting themselves in the laboratory tanks and returning to full conscious awareness. So far so good, but surfactants still remain unproven in the open ocean against wild sharks and the problem of packaging them for rapid deployment has yet to be solved.

The presence of a dead shark, or putrid shark meat, will also clear an area of sharks, as the Seychelles shark fishermen found to their cost when they started throwing the unwanted heads, tails and fins of gutted sharks back onto the shark grounds. Within days, an area formerly swarming with sharks had been completely abandoned by them. Contrary to popular belief, most sharks will not readily take carrion of any sort unless at the point of starvation and the belief that human corpses found mutilated by sharks were only savaged after death is ill-founded. Sharks like their meat fresh.

Chapter 3
Design for a Purpose

The common food fishes of the household menu, such as herrings, plaice or sardines, have a bony skeleton that is all too familiar to diners. This bony skeleton, of course, is present in all animals higher up in the evolutionary scale – amphibians, reptiles, birds and mammals.

Sharks and their relatives (the skates, the rays and the little ratfish or chimaeras) are different. The principal supporting structure of their bodies is not bone but cartilage, basically a flexible, semi-transparent, elastic material full of cell spaces that is formed from a complex protein which encloses a network of connective tissue fibres. Because of this feature, the shark group (known collectively as the Chondrichthyes, or 'cartilage fishes') are separated by zoologists from all other living fish (which are assigned to the Osteichthyes, or 'bone fishes').

Skeleton

In the bony fishes and the higher vertebrates, the skeleton (Fig. 3.1) is, in part, formed directly from embryonic connective tissue, but some bones (notably the long bones in the limbs of tetrapods) are preformed in cartilage and then gradually become ossified as growth of the immature animal proceeds: calcium salts are laid down within the structure of the cartilage so that it becomes relatively hard and brittle, with an opaque appearance somewhat similar to that of bone and, at the same time, blood vessels carry in cells (osteoblasts) to deposit true bone as the original cartilage is systematically broken down.

Because cartilage was thus seen as a precursor of bone in the higher vertebrates, the cartilaginous sharks were regarded as a primitive fish group, a concept supported by their great geological antiquity, tracing back 350 million years to the Devonian period, and also by one or two undeniably conservative features of their anatomy: the absence of a gill cover (or operculum), such as occurs in bony fishes, and the rather unspecialised tail fin formed by a simple upward diversion of the spinal column to support the upper lobe. However, the oldest of all known fish, the jawless ostracoderms that occurred as early as the Cambrian, over 500 million years ago, had massive bony head shields, so it would seem that the effective absence of bone in sharks may be not so much a primitive feature as a degenerate specialisation. The remote ancestors of sharks probably had bone, but the group as a whole gradually lost it, since its retention offered no particular evolutionary advantage. In fact, there is still some bone of a sort to be found in a shark's skeleton. Calcification of

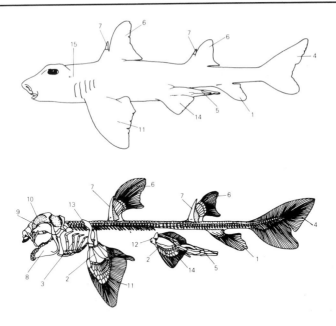

Fig. 3.1. (Top)A male bullhead shark (*Heterodontus*) with (bottom) its skeleton. 1. anal fin. 2. basal elements. 3. gill arches. 4. caudal fin. 5. claspers. 6. dorsal fins. 7. fin spines. 8. lower jaw. 9. upper jaw. 10. eye socket. 11. pectoral fin. 12. pelvic girdle. 13. pectoral girdle. 14. pelvic fin. 15. spiracle.

the cartilage in the bodies (centra) of the vertebrae is a well known feature of the spinal column in sharks and more or less corresponds to the deposition of calcium salts that occurs prior to the displacement of cartilage by bone in the limb bones of immature tetrapods; further significant deposits of mineralised tissue occur in the roots of the teeth, in the bases of the denticles that stud the skin and in the jaw and paired fins.

X-ray analysis of shark vertebrae in conjunction with transmission electron microscopy using a calcium-seeking fluorescent drug (tetracycline) has demonstrated the presence of calcified tissue in a thin layer covering the neural arches that form the upper part of the vertebrae and provide a channel for the spinal cord, as well as in the haemal arches below the backbone which protect the passage of blood vessels. What is more, the underlying cartilage in these areas proved to be full of large cells like those which occur where cartilage is being replaced by bone. In at least some sharks, this mineralised tissue is apatite (basically calcium fluorophosphate or calcium chlorophosphate in hexagonal crystalline form) which is laid down in irregular layers around the periphery of cell masses to form calcified plaques. These cell groupings have a discernible central point of origin from which they proliferate and seem to be constantly undergoing re-modelling. They occur in the braincase, jaws, gill arches, fin supports and vertebrae.

Skull

Nonetheless, the essentially cartilaginous skeleton of the Chondrichthyes is a convenient diagnostic feature of the group and serves to separate them from the bony fishes. In the absence of any external bones, the shark skull (Fig. 3.2) is a relatively simple structure, consisting of a trough-like braincase with a floor, side walls and an incomplete roof. At the front, there is a projecting rostrum with, at either side, a large pair of expansions for the olfactory capsules of the brain (sharks have a very keen sense of smell). Next come recesses (orbits) for the eyes incorporating exits for the eye-stalk, the optic nerve and the three nerves that run to the muscles of the eyeball. Beneath the orbits is the basal articulation where the upper jaw cartilage (the palatoquadrate or, as it is sometimes called, the pterygoquadrate) has its anterior point of anchorage. Behind the eye is the broad post-orbital process providing another point of connection for the upper jaw, followed by the paired otic capsules (containing the inner ear, with a medial opening on the upper surface of the braincase for the endolymphatic duct) and an articulation for the hyomandibular bone, which braces the joint between the upper and lower jaws against the braincase's lateral wall. At the back of the braincase is the foramen

Fig. 3.2. The skull of the frilled shark (*Chlamydoselachus*). (Top) The braincase with the upper jaw elements (palatoquadrates) removed. (Bottom) The complete skull with upper and lower jaws articulated. (Left) Dorsal view. (Right) Ventral view. 1. rostrum. 2. nasal (olfactory) capsules. 3 eye sockets. 4. basal articulation. 5. palatoquadrate. 6. post-orbital process. 7. otic capsules. 8. opening of endolymphatic duct. 9. hyomandibular. 10. occipital condyle. 11. optic nerve opening.

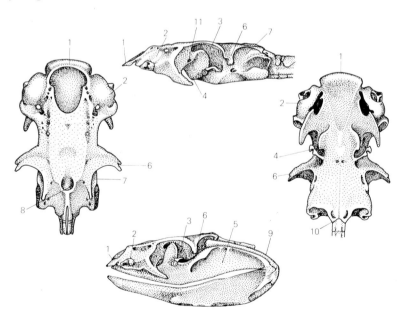

magnum, through which the spinal cord exits, and below it the occipital condyle for articulation with the first vertebra.

Gills

Immediately behind the skull is the gill area (Fig. 3.3). All living sharks lack an operculum which, in bony fishes, covers the gill slits and leaves only a single opening for the outgoing current of water. The oldest known fishes had as many as ten pairs of gill pouches, but modern bony fishes have a maximum of five, as do most sharks, although there are some apparently more primitive genera that possess six or even seven pairs of gills. Obviously some of the original gills have been lost and the fate of at least one of the primordial gill arches was evidently to become the jaws. Each functional gill arch comprises an upper component (the epibranchial) and a lower element (the ceratobranchial), both of which incline forwards from the point at which they meet. All vestiges of the most anterior gill arches originally present in the earliest fish, which had no jaws, have probably vanished altogether, but it is apparent that the upper jaw is a modification of an epibranchial, while the lower jaw was once a ceratobranchial. The hyomandibular bone, which braces the jaw joint against the braincase, is another modified epibranchial and, as further proof of this remarkable evolutionary adaptation, there is usually a small vestigial gill, called the spiracle, in the restricted space that remains between the hyomandibular bone and the upper jaw (Those sharks with six or seven pairs of gills, like *Hexanchus* and *Heptranchias*, have a fully

Fig. 3.3. The gill system. (Left) The section shows the mouth open on the right to admit a current of water while the gill slits are closed and the mouth closed on the left while the gill slits open. (Right) The skull and gill arches of the dogfish (*Mustelus*).

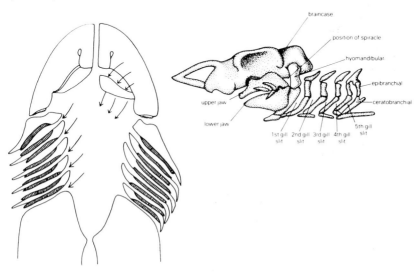

The seven-gill shark (*Notorynchus maculatus*) has two more pairs of gills than the five normally present in sharks. Opinions differ as to whether this is a primitive feature.

functional gill slit in this position.). Absent in some active, open-ocean sharks, the spiracle is still quite large and has been relocated behind the eye in many sluggish, bottom-dwelling forms.

At an early stage in their history, sharks apparently had wide gill openings leading out of the pharynx and through to the exterior but, in modern representatives of the group, the water flows through narrow slits. Running down close to the wall of the pharynx are the gill-arch elements (the epibranchial above, ceratobranchial below) and from them originates a septum that extends out to the external surface of the body and folds back to protect the next gill opening along with, on either side of it, the vascular, complexly folded gill tissue (offering the maximum surface area for gaseous exchange of oxygen and carbon dioxide) accompanied by a stiffening cartilaginous gill ray.

Spinal Column

The spinal column consists of simply constructed vertebrae, each comprising a centrum, through the middle of which runs the primitive notochord, and an upper element, the neural arch, that affords attachment points for the body muscles, as well as providing a channel for the spinal cord. Calcification of the disc- or spindle-shaped centra follows various distinctive patterns that can be revealed by transverse cross-sections or X-raying. In many sharks, heavily mineralised areas radiate out from the notochord at the centre like the spokes of a wheel (Fig. 3.4), sometimes broad and few in number, in other cases quite thin and

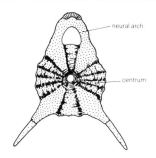

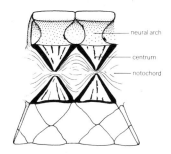

Fig. 3.4. (Left) Cross section of a vertebra from the porbeagle (*Lamna*), demonstrating the dark areas of calcification radiating from the centrum. Also shown is the neural arch. (Right) A longitudinal section through the spinal column of *Lamna*, displaying the constriction of the notochord as it passes through the vertebral centra. Also shown are the neural arches.

numerous; alternatively the whole centrum may be calcified to a varying extent (although usually more densely towards the middle), or mineralisation may be in the form of multiple, small concentric arcs.

Tails

The tails of sharks are of the apprently primitive heterocercal type (Fig. 3.5), formed by an upward bend of the spinal column which supports a superior lobe, aided by prolongations of the neural arches above and the haemal arches below. Some development of dermal rays further extends this stiffening structure dorsally and especially ventrally, where the lower lobe is without any spinal support but nonetheless sometimes almost equals the upper lobe in size. The tail provides the principal medium of propulsion in sharks; mackerel sharks employ short, strong tail strokes and hold the body essentially rigid, while other types use a more flexible technique that involves undulations along most of the trunk.

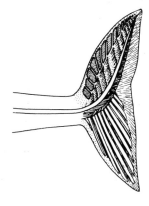

Fig. 3.5. The heterocercal tail of an extinct shark, *Cladoselache*, sectioned to show the spinal column diverted upwards to form the superior lobe while the lower lobe is supported by radial elements.

47

Fins

Sharks usually have two dorsal fins (some rather conservative types, such as *Chlamydoselachus*, *Hexanchus*, *Notorhynchus* and *Heptranchias*, have only one, as does the scyliorhinid *Pentanchus*) and, in lamniforms (but not in any living squaliforms), there is an anal fin on the mid-line of the belly just behind the vent. It has been suggested that all these median fins developed from a single continuous fin which in ancestral forms, ran along the back, round the tail and forwards under the body, but no known early fish exhibit such a structure. On the contrary, even the oldest of them seem to have discrete median fins, often supported anteriorly by spines, and it is perhaps more likely that this spiny origin was the true starting point for the median fins. In several families of living sharks (e.g. heterodontids, scymnorhinids, squalids), pointed spines with blade-like or rounded anterior edges still occur, apparently serving as cutwaters at the front of their dorsal fins. These structures were characteristic of early fossil sharks and there seems to have been a process of progressive reduction as the heavily ornamented spines of ancient sharks gave way to smooth unornamented ones and finally to the disappearance of spines altogether in modern lamniform sharks and a good many of the squaliform. The principal supporting framework in the dorsal fins now consists of a series of dermal rays.

Sharks swim primarily by means of muscular undulations passing backwards down the body to generate backward thrust at the tail, the muscles themselves being arranged in vertically orientated zig-zag blocks (myomeres) along the flanks. The paired (pectoral and pelvic) fins (Fig. 3.6) are essentially hydrodynamic aids to steering. In the oldest known sharks, they were little more than broad-based flaps supported by parallel bars of cartilage.

Eventually a more efficient construction was evolved. The root of each pectoral fin became effectively narrowed by a reduction in the number of basals (modern sharks typically have only three), while the fin area itself was extended considerably beyond the end of the radials (which developed into jointed structures endowed with greater flexibility). The pelvic fins remained fairly broad-based but, again, the fin area increased beyond the termination of the radials to leave a free posterior margin, with male individuals developing substantial copulating 'claspers' supported by stiff rods of cartilage. It was originally believed that these mating structures were indeed used to clasp the female, hence the name, but in fact the claspers are rotated forward and inserted either singly or together into the cloaca of the female while sperm from the male passes down rolls of skin which form a tube along the length of the clasper. (Female sharks customarily bear the scars of bites on their backs, suggesting spiteful mating behaviour on the part of males.)

With these improvements to the paired fins and the union of the respective left and right halves of the pectoral and pelvic girdles in the ventral mid-line to provide more substantial bases of support, sharks became far more manoeuvrable and hence considerably more efficient as

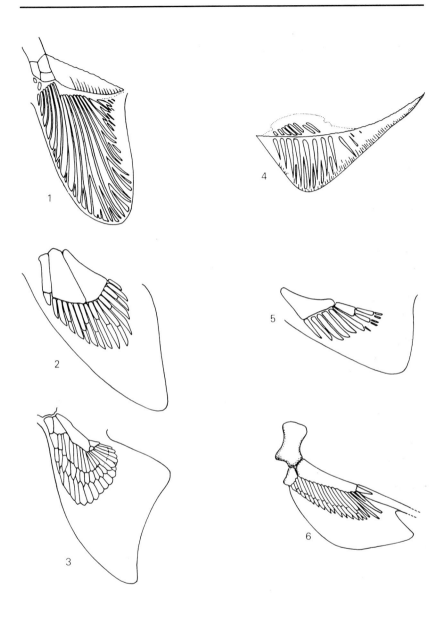

Fig. 3.6. The structure of the paired fins. (Left) The pectoral fins of: 1) the ancient Devonian shark *Cladoselache*, 2) the extinct hybodont *Hybodus* 3) the modern lamniform *Isurus*. (Right) Pelvic fins of 4) *Cladoselache*, 5) *Hybodus*, 6) the modern spiny dogfish *Squalus*. The radials of the modern forms have retreated from the edge of the fin to give greater suppleness and the articulation with the girdle elements becomes narrower for enhanced flexibility.

active high-seas predators, although some forms still prefer a more sluggish, bottom-dwelling life style.

Placoid Scales

The skin of sharks is covered by placoid scales – backwardly projecting tooth-like structures (Fig. 3.7) that make the hide intensely abrasive if it is rubbed the wrong way, i.e. from back to front. These scales vary in shape from one region of the body to another. They may, for example, be simple and rounded on the snout, shield-like on the belly, keeled along the flanks (to facilitate the shark's passage through the water), diamond-shaped

Fig. 3.7. Shark scales (dermal denticles): 1) cross section of a typical denticle showing its tooth-like structures; 2) dermal denticles of the whale shark (*Rhincodon*) in a) general view, b) lateral view and c) apical view; 3) dermal denticles of a grey shark (*Carcharhinus*) in a) general view and b) apical view.

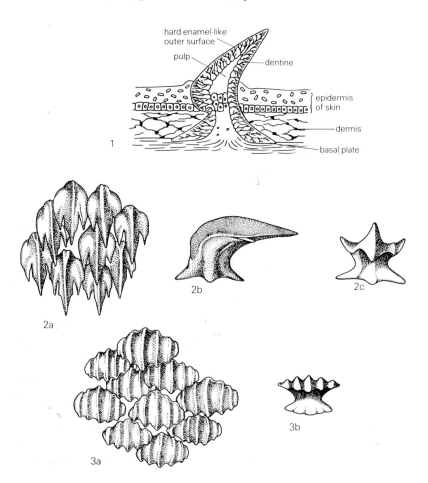

along the front edge of the fins, where a firm, sharp edge is required, and tiny quadrangular shaped structures where they line the pharynx (throat). The denticles of young sharks may be of a different pattern to the denticles of the same species when fully mature. Despite these modifications, dermal denticles all conform to the same basic structure. Implanted in the epidermis (the outer layer of the skin), there is a basal plate incorporating a pulp cavity supplied by nerves and blood vessels. Within this pulp cavity are cells that nourish the dentine from which the denticle is principally constructed – long processes from these cells pass through the dentine canals, ramifying throughout the projecting structure of the scale. A thin, hard covering of an enamel-like material sheaths the point of the denticle and its exposed surface, the resemblance of a placoid scale's construction to that of a tooth being unmistakable. The dentition, in fact, is really a series of highly specialised scales that, at one time in the history of sharks, must have lined the jaws and have now become adapted for biting, tearing or crushing. In very ancient fishes, a heavy external dermal armour was present, with a surface layer of bony denticles. The scales and teeth (modified scales) of sharks seem to be all that is left of these original denticles, the bony substratum having been lost early on in the evolutionary development of the group.

Dentition

Most sharks have the pointed, sharp-edged dentition that has been the hallmark of predators all down the ages, although some types developed rounded, low-crowned teeth for crushing the hard shells of molluscs and

The lower jaws of a porbeagle (*Lamna nasus*), viewed from the side, showing how new teeth rotate upwards into use from inside the jaws while worn-out teeth are shed from the outside of the jaw margin.

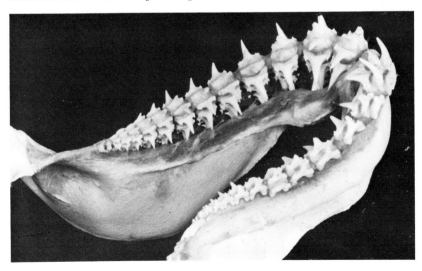

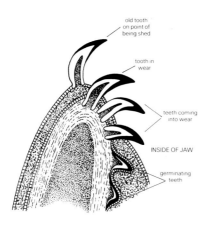

old tooth
on point of
being shed

tooth in
wear

teeth coming
into wear

INSIDE OF JAW

germinating
teeth

Fig. 3.8 Semi-diagrammatic cross section across the upper jaw of a shark to show the succession of dental replacement. New teeth form on the inside of the jaw, move up to the apex as they come into wear and are, in due course, shed to the outside.

crustaceans, while in a few plankton-eating species the dentition is vestigial. Generally speaking, only a single row of teeth, along the margin of the jaws, is functional at any one time, but half-a-dozen or more rows of replacement teeth are arrayed behind them, continually developing deep inside the mouth and gradually working their way to the front as teeth in the earlier series are lost due to wear or accidents. In many sharks, the teeth of the upper jaws differ from those of the lower, the complementing crown types producing a superbly efficient shearing or tearing mechanism when they interlock as the jaws close; the dentition also varies in structure from the front of the jaws to the back, teeth mid-way along the series frequently being much larger and of a different type to those at the front or back. Tooth replacement varies from species to species, but most sharks apparently lose only a few of their worn-out teeth at a time, one every 8 days or so being a typical replacement rate. However, dogfish (*Squalus*) and a related squaliform genus (*Isistius*) seem to replace a whole set at once, the replacement row moving into place immediately. In other sharks, the replacement rate in the upper jaws is different from that in the lower jaws.

Sharks do not, it seems, feed systematically at a carcase in the way that lions or tigers do. Their initial attack on a victim too large to be swallowed whole is usually aimed simply at taking out a mouthful of flesh, as seals found with huge bites torn out of their haunches or entire rear flippers bitten away amply testify. In the case of an attack on a man, this often results in a leg being taken clean off, especially if the bite goes through a knee joint, or the removal of a huge quantity of muscle from calf, thigh or buttock, leading to fatal haemorrhaging from ruptured arteries. In many cases, the flesh is effectively stripped from the tibia, fibula and sometimes the femur as well when the victim struggles to get free and the shark fights to make off with its pound of flesh.

Experiments have been conducted with a 'shark-bite meter' (gnathodynamometer, Fig. 3.9) consisting of a cylinder in which stainless steel

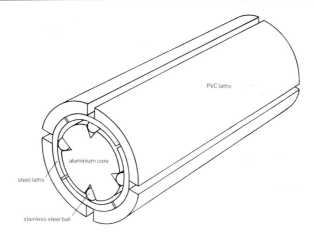

Fig. 3.9. The gnathodynamometer devised to find out the power of a shark's bite.

ball-bearings occupy depressions along an aluminium bar, being held in place by four steel laths with the whole instrument encased in polyvinyl chloride and wound with adhesive tape and fibreglass filaments. This device is fitted inside a 1.5 kilogram (3 pound) fillet of bonito, blue runner or barracuda and lowered into a shark tank in an aquarium.

As the sharks snap at the bait, their jaws close on the meter, compressing the outer casing down onto the ball-bearings so that they indent the aluminium core. By measuring the depth of these indentations, it is possible to compute the biting strength of the shark. It was found that the jaws of a big shark can dispose of 3 tonnes per square centimetre (about $6\frac{1}{2}$ tons per square inch) when they close, with as much as 60 kilograms (132 pounds) being exerted by a single tooth – quite sufficient to hew off a man's limb!

The living sharks of today's seas have two-rooted teeth in the majority of cases, the crowns usually being adapted for shearing or sawing flesh as the shark clamps its jaws on its victim and then throws its head from side to side – quite slowly and deliberately in the case of a tiger shark, very rapidly if it is a blue shark. Many ancient extinct sharks had single-rooted teeth of a less specialised type that necessarily meant tearing or cutting flesh from a victim in a less sophisticated manner. These long-departed forebears of modern sharks probably often engulfed their prey whole, aided by the suction effect of establishing a negative pressure in the orobranchial chamber (plankton-eating whale sharks are known to use this method today, as do carpet sharks on small fish).

The belief that sharks have to roll on their backs in order to bite because of their long pointed noses is ill-founded. The nose is supple and endowed with muscles enabling it to be raised out of the way (it can also be moved this way and that to sniff out prospective prey), while the jaws are only loosely attached to the skull and are protruded as the mouth opens to

The supple, inquisitive nose of a hooked porbeagle (*Lamna nasus*), showing the sensory pores of the electrically sensitive ampullae of Lorenzini.

A hammerhead (*Sphyrna zygaena*) with its extraordinarily expanded head.

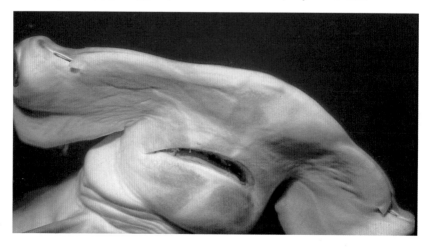

provide entirely adequate clearance for biting. When a shark snatches at a bait, it may roll as it turns away, which possibly contributed to this fiction, and sharks will also roll to look upwards with their laterally orientated eyes at the occupants of fishing boats – especially hammerheads, which have their eyes on broad lateral expansions of the head.

There is considerable evidence that at least some sharks deliver slashing blows with their teeth (presumably the upper ones) as a means of deterring or putting to flight a prospective antagonist. A number of divers attacked by sharks, such as grey reef sharks (*Carcharhinus falciformis*) which are believed to be territorial, have sustained injuries suggesting a slash rather than a bite, and it is possible that these attacks (often presaged by distorted swimming movements known as agonistic display) were intended to scare away an intruder rather than secure a meal. Furthermore, some bathers who have been attacked by sharks have been gashed rather than bitten, while scars and partially healed wounds are also found on the bodies of sharks, suggesting that they have themselves been the subject of a slashing (rather than a biting) attack by some adversary of their own kind.

Digestive System

Although some sharks have crushing teeth for dealing with hard-shelled prey, none can chew their food which must perforce be bolted whole. The digestive tract is relatively short, simple and S-shaped, the stomach being little more than a muscular expansion at the end of the oesophagus from which there is a double bend into the intestine, passing thence more or less straight to the rectum (Fig. 3.10). It lacks the convolution seen in more highly evolved vertebrates but this is made up for by a spiral valve (Fig. 3.11) which increases the surface area available for the absorption of nutrients. In the stomach, tubular glands secrete digestive enzymes (notably pepsin) which, in the presence of hydrochloric acid (also secreted by gastric glands), undertake the preliminary breakdown of food protein.

Fig. 3.10. The internal organs of a male shark.

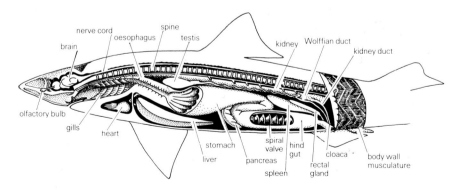

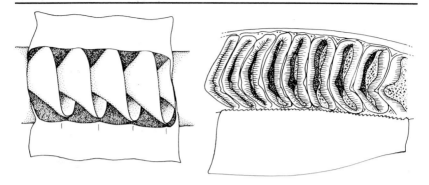

Fig. 3.11. The spiral valve of a shark's intestine, which substantially increases the internal surface area available for the absorption of nutrients. (Left) The relatively simple structure found in the dogfish. (Right) The densely fimbriated spiral valve of the megamouth shark (*Megachasma*).

More enzymes pour into the intestine from the pancreas and from the glandular epithelium of the gut itself as partially digested food is passed along from the stomach, with all the shark's nutritional requirements (salts, sugars, fats, amino acids, vitamins, etc.) being absorbed along the spiral valve.

The stomachs of freshly killed sharks often contain large items of essentially undigested food. A 4.5 metre (15 foot) tiger shark that was captured and sent to the aquarium at the Taronga Park Zoo, near Sydney, Australia, in August 1950, persistently rejected horse meat, vomiting it back within a few days, and when the animal died some 3 weeks later its stomach was found to contain the well preserved bodies of two 1.2 metre (4 foot) dolphins.

Apart from suggesting that sharks are able to store ingested prey in their stomachs for a limited period, these observations pose the question of how the creature could regurgitate only the unwanted horse meat.

Because of its cold-blooded metabolism, a shark's nutritional requirements are probably quite modest for its size and one substantial meal will doubtless suffice for a good many days (breeding males and pregnant females of some species apparently abstain from feeding altogether for long periods when they are· on the breeding grounds). For most of the time, sharks cruise in open water with minimum expenditure of energy and, as there is a negligible energy demand for maintaining body temperature, they do not need the large, regular intake of food that a calorie-hungry mammalian carnivore requires.

Reproductive and Urinary Systems

The reproductive organs of sharks are combined with the urinary system. A very generalised type of kidney is present, with a large renal corpuscle (Fig. 3.12) where waste products of the body's metabolism (mostly in the

Fig. 3.12 The kidneys of sharks have very large renal corpuscles (left) compared with the kidneys of marine bony fish (right) in which the renal corpuscles are small.

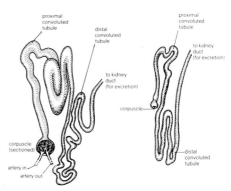

form of urea) are filtered from the circulation. All fishes need to maintain an osmotic balance between the fluids in their bodies and the water outside. Organic membranes are normally semi-permeable, allowing small molecules to move readily from one side to the other but preventing the passage of large molecules. This osmotic pressure means that water molecules can easily pass through, but large molecules in solution cannot. Hence freshwater bony fish, which live in a medium more dilute than their own body fluids, tend to absorb too much water and have large kidney corpuscles to filter off the excess. Marine fishes, on the other hand, are surrounded by saline water with a higher salt concentration than their body fluids and so tend to lose water, their renal corpuscles consequently being small.

Despite their large renal corpuscles and substantial water-filtration capacity, sharks avoid dehydration by re-absorbing most of their nitrogenous waste in the form of urea and trimethylamine oxide, thus increasing the total concentration of materials in solution without elevating the salt content. Water loss by osmosis is therefore prevented. This re-absorption occurs as the filtrate is drained from the kidney's renal corpuscle down a tubule surrounded by blood capillaries: the nitrogenous waste products are extracted as required and returned to the circulation so that the shark maintains a correct physiological balance between its body fluids and the surrounding seawater. As a further aid to osmoregulation, sharks also have a rectal gland whose function apparently is to secrete sodium chloride.

In males (Fig. 3.13), there are a pair of large testes in the anterior part of the peritoneal cavity from which sperm pass down the Wolffian ducts to the seminal vesicle for storage, eventually being expelled during copulation directly into the female cloaca by means of the tubular channels running along the pelvic claspers. A pair of large siphon sacs extend forward from the claspers beneath the skin of the belly. These fill with sea water through a fleshy funnel at the base of each clasper when the clasper is flexed prior to copulation and their contents apparently flood the sperm along the clasper groove during coitus. In addition, epithelial cells lining the inside of the sacs secrete a mucus-like polysaccharide-protein sub-

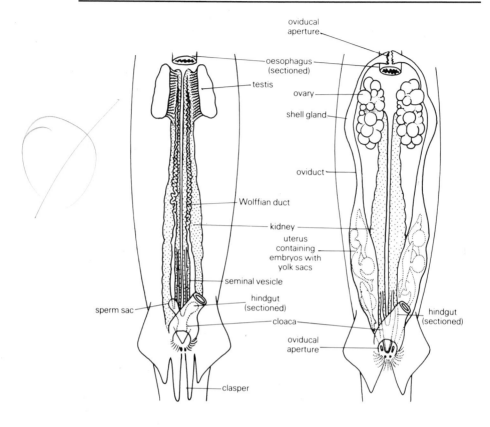

Fig. 3.13. The reproductive system of (left) a male shark and (right) a female shark.

stance that lubricates the clasper during mating and also possibly plays a part in transporting seminal fluid and sperm. In females, the ovaries (or ovary when only one – usually the righthand one – is functional, as in some species) release mature ova into the peritoneal cavity, whence they enter the paired oviducts via a median oviducal aperture (Fig. 3.13) and pass backwards down them to be fertilised *en route* by sperm from a male. Immature females have the cloacal openings of the oviducts closed by a hymenial membrane which is disrupted at the first mating.

Some sharks simply lay their eggs in a conventional manner (oviparity), mostly in the form of leathery cases with spiral attachment filaments at the four corners. Others retain fertilised eggs (usually enveloped only in thin membranous shells) within their bodies in ovisacs near the distal ends of the oviducts. In some species, these retained eggs soon rupture and the hatchlings then remain free within the mother to utilise the contents of their yolk sacs for the completion of their development, eventually being expelled fully formed from the cloaca (ovo-viviparity or aplacental viviparity). In other forms (grey sharks and hammerheads) a placenta-like outgrowth of the ovisac's wall contacts the embryo's yolk-sac and provides a channel incorporating an umbilical artery and vein and a vitelline canal for the transmission of nutrients direct from the female's blood stream. A variation of this system in some of these viviparous species apparently provides for the secretion of 'milk' from the uterine wall, whence it is directly absorbed by the embryos.

Within a single genus, one species may lay eggs while another gives birth to fully-formed young (examples are *Galeus melastoma* and *Galeus polli* respectively), while nurse sharks (*Ginglymostoma*) can apparently adopt either viviparity or ovo-viviparity, whichever is best suited to the prevailing conditions.

In the case of some ovo-viviparous or viviparous forms, it is alleged that the first two embryos to develop eat all the others within the mother's body: certainly pregnant females containing only one or two juveniles have been caught, which is difficult to account for in view of the number of eggs shed from the ovaries. Embryos of the sand tiger (*Odontaspis taurus*) certainly eat eggs as they are shed into the female's oviduct, and the innate savagery and potential self-reliance of the unborn young was amply demonstrated when ichthyologist Stewart Springer opened a freshly caught pregnant female sand tiger and received a bite from one of the juveniles in her oviducts.

The hatchlings of oviparous species emerge fully developed and well able to forage for themselves, although the mortality rate from predators (including other sharks, even of the same species) is inevitably high.

Although dogfish have been seen mating, with the male coiled around the female to insert his claspers in her cloaca and inject the sperm, there are no eye-witness reports of the big oceanic sharks copulating under natural conditions. In many cases, their mating habits and reproductive methods are essentially unknown, although it is obvious that a massively proportioned mackerel shark, for instance, could not perform the same sexual gymnastics as a small, slender dogfish. Many of these large forms possibly breed in the deepest waters of the ocean, where pregnant females and their emergent young are safe from the attention of predators, including cannibalistic relatives.

Circulatory System

The circulatory system of sharks is relatively simple, with a four-chambered heart lying doubled back on itself beneath the gill region so that de-oxygenated blood returning along the veins from the body is sucked into the most posterior of the four consecutively disposed chambers (the sinus venosus), then passes forward to the atrium which contracts and drives the blood down into the ventricle lying folded beneath it. Powerful muscles in the walls of the ventricle and the conus arteriosus next shunt the blood up through the gills, where carbon dioxide is exchanged for oxygen, and then the arterial system carries the newly charged blood back into the circulation.

Respiration

Sharks lack the opercular gill cover that bony fishes open and close to maintain a flow of water through their gills. But water somehow has to be kept moving in and out of the gill slits to bring in the oxygen essential for life-giving metabolic processes and carry away unwanted carbon dioxide. In the absence of an operculum, the only way a shark can normally do this is to keep moving. Some sharks do, in fact, contrive to rest on the bottom, doubtless positioning themselves so as to make use of natural water currents, and divers have found large reef sharks (*Carcharhinus perezii*) resting in submarine caves off the Mexican coast at Isla Mujeres that seem to draw sufficient water through their mouths, even when stationary, to maintain a rate of 20 to 28 respirations per minute (the water in this area is oxygen-rich due to fresh water seeping through the sea floor). Many of the big oceanic species are believed never to rest, however: all their lives they must swim to live and a shark caught in a net so that it cannot move is doomed to drown.

Buoyancy

Most sharks are also obliged to swim in order to avoid sinking. Bony fishes have evolved a swim bladder in the form of an elongate sac arising from the anterior part of the digestive tract that can be filled with air to provide buoyancy. Sharks do not have this feature. Like all vertebrates, however, their specific gravity is slightly higher than that of sea water, so they do not naturally float – a shark that has been killed will immediately sink.

One or two species have acquired an ability to inflate their stomachs with air and thus acquire buoyancy (sand sharks in aquariums have been observed rising to the surface to gulp air), while many have oil-rich livers which undoubtedly reduce quite materially the specific gravity of the fish. In the cases of some deep sea sharks as much as 90 per cent. of this liver oil is the hydrocarbon squalene, which has a specific gravity of only 0.86 and is 80 per cent. more effective per unit of weight at producing aquatic lift than cod liver oil (with a specific gravity of 0.926). Out of the water, the livers of these abyssal species represent 20-30 per cent. of the creature's total weight, but in their proper salt water environment the lift produced by the liver oil makes the shark neutrally buoyant so that it can cruise effortlessly just above the sea bed seeking its prey with a minumum of water disturbance from swimming movements. The manner in which sharks synthesize squalene is a matter for speculation, and unlike most liver oils it cannot be readily broken down by the liver to be used as a food reserve. Fine tuning of the liver oil content to give the desired neutral buoyancy must therefore be dependant on varying the relative quantities of other lipids that are present, but how sharks achieve this is unknown.

Some large pelagic sharks also have quite substantial quantities of squalene in their livers – in the basking shark, for example, it may constitute up to almost 50 per cent. of the liver oil, but not enough to make it float of its own accord.

Brain

As might be expected in so magnificently efficient a predator, the shark has aquatic sensory perception of almost unparalleled acuteness, although its brain (Fig. 3.14) is seemingly of such elementary construction that the animal has been regarded customarily as little more than an automaton, its life entirely controlled by conditioned reflexes. Conscious thought, reasoning, affection, even fear and pain, seem to have little or no place in the pitiless world of the shark, where kill or be killed is the sole criterion by which it lives out its remorseless existence, but experiments with captive sharks in laboratory or aquarium tanks indicate that these creatures do in fact have a substantial learning capacity. They can be taught to distin-

Fig. 3.14. The brain of *Scymnorhinus*: (left) dorsal view, (right) ventral view and (below) lateral view.

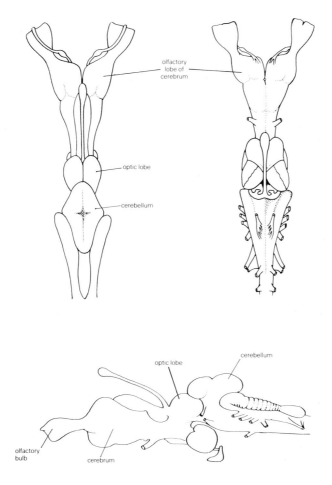

guish targets of different shapes by rewarding them with food when they touch the 'correct' one and will also learn to recognise a sound cue with similar conditioning. Once this knowledge has been acquired, it is retained for some considerable time and the experiments can be repeated successfully even after a substantial interval has elapsed.

Lemon sharks even proved capable of distinguishing a white target from a red one, although this may be attributable to differing degrees of brightness rather than colour as such. Interestingly, a white square and a white circle proved more difficult for the shark to differentiate than a white square and a white diamond.

These tests strongly indicate that sharks possess a capacity for learning and the modification of behaviour patterns as a result of conscious experiences which is far more sophisticated than they are generally given credit for. Other observations, such as the propensity for porbeagles to apparently 'play' with floating objects, similarly suggests that the reasoning powers and general awareness of these fish may have been seriously underestimated.

In fact, many sharks have a ratio of brain weight to body weight that is comparable to that of birds or even mammals. The squaloid sharks do not rate very high by this criterion, but makos, porbeagles, great whites, grey sharks, and hammerheads have notably large brains. A need for increased sensory inputs to enhance motor control in these active pelagic species was probably a major factor in promoting elaboration of their brains, but the acquisition of learning capacity has been a concomitant development.

The vertebrate brain is effectively divided into three segments: the fore-brain, the mid-brain and the hind-brain. In sharks the fore-brain comprises the well developed olfactory lobes, which receive impulses from the nostrils, with behind them a barely discernible cerebrum. In Man, the cerebrum forms two hugely expanded hemispheres which are the chief seat of human intellect, but in sharks it may possibly constitute a major centre of vision, receiving nerve impulses from the optic lobes of the mid-brain, as well as providing a relay station for olfactory nerve impulses on their way in from the nose. Sharks probably use their acute sense of smell far more than vision when seeking prey, at least until close to their intended victim. The two nostrils, one on each side of the snout, usually close to the mouth and sometimes connected with it by grooves, are imperfectly divided so that there is an incurrent and an excurrent flow of water. They lead to the paired olfactory sacs, which have a convoluted lining of elongate cells, each bearing a sensory hair that projects above the epithelium and, at the other end, terminates in long nerve fibres connecting with the olfactory nerve. The scent of blood in the water will attract sharks from miles around and incites the notorious 'feeding frenzy' in which large numbers of sharks apparently go berserk in the presence of fresh blood, attacking virtually anything that moves (including each other), snapping and biting in a fearful turmoil of frenetic slaughter. Human victims of shark attacks are usually subject to more strikes once blood has been drawn, but curiously it is rare for would-be rescuers to attract attention: the shark will continue to go for the haemorrhaging victim of its initial attack. It is for this reason that no one with an open cut, sore, boil or abscess should enter shark infested waters, nor is it safe for menstruating women to bathe where sharks occur.

The mid-brain has as its most conspicuous feature the paired optic lobes, one on each side, which receive visual impulses from the eyes, and also constitutes the major coordination centre of the brain to which sensory stimuli from the nose, the eyes and the organs of hearing and balance are relayed. This function was taken over by the cerebrum as evolution progressed, with consequent massive enlargement of the cerebral hemispheres (as in Man), while the mid-brain declined in relative importance.

The hind-brain of sharks, as in other vertebrates, includes the cerebellum, where movement is co-ordinated so that posture and balance can be maintained. The cerebellum is, in fact, a development of the primitive brain stem's acoustic area, to which impulses from the ear travel, and it is the ear and (in fishes) the lateral-line system that are the primary organs of balance.

Sensory Organs

Eyes

In a shark, the lens of the eye is suspended within the eyeball by a circular membrane and is normally held at a distance from the retina (where the image is focussed) designed to provide optimum long range vision. The human eye has an elastic lens which focuses by altering its shape under the influence of ciliary muscles, acting indirectly through the circular suspensory ligament surrounding the lens. Fish in general have a different system (Fig. 3.15) to provide them with close-up vision when necessary: they possess an almost spherical inelastic lens, but it hangs from a ligament at its upper margin and has a muscle-like protractor structure at the lower edge which can contract and swing the entire lens forward to focus on near objects. The lens of a shark eye seems to be capable of very little movement, however, and it is uncertain to what extent they are able to focus on close objects. A significant specialisation of sharks' eyes is the presence of a tapetum lucidum – a reflecting layer behind the retina – which enhances vision in conditions of dim illumination. Normally light entering the eye is focussed by the lens onto the retina, where there are light-sensitive cells (rods for perceiving faintly illuminated subjects, cones for colour and elucidating fine detail) that transmit an image to the brain. Most of this light is then absorbed by a pigmented choroid layer. In sharks, there is a reflective layer behind the retina, the tapetum lucidum, consisting of thousands of polygonal platelets silvered by guanine crystals, that reflects light which has already passed once through the retina back onto the photo-sensitive cells, thus effectively using the same illumination twice over to amplify the image. These tapetal plates are almost parallel to the retina at the back of the eye but become nearly perpendicular (as well

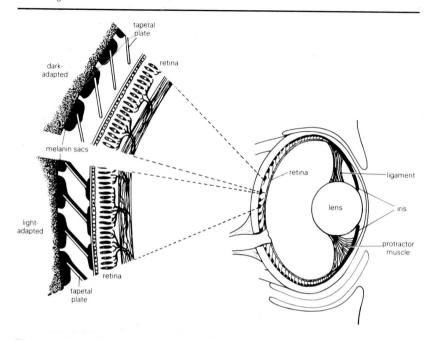

Fig. 3.15. The eye of a shark in section. Towards the front of the eye, the tapetal plates become nearly perpendicular as well as more numerous.

as more numerous) towards the front and, in surface-dwelling species, are guarded by sacs containing a dark pigment (melanin) that runs out to occlude the reflective surfaces when they are not required. Sharks that permanently live in deep water apparently lack this occlusal mechanism, which they do not need since they never normally rise into brightly lit surface water.

Experiments have been conducted with lemon sharks to try and determine the sensitivities of their vision. A tiny electrode was inserted just in front of the eye to intercept the optic nerve and record the impulses passing along it while light of different wavelengths was directed into the eye in flashes of 0.02 seconds duration. The electroretinograms obtained indicate marked sensitivity to blue and green light (with wave lengths of approximately 450 nanometres (4,500Å) and 530 nanometres (5,300Å) respectively), but only limited ability to discern red at 682 nanometres (6,820Å) and no reaction at all to deep red at 782 nanometres (7,820Å). Since sea water is largely opaque to red light, with only 58 per cent. transmission at 700 nanometres (7,000Å), but transparent to blue (98 per cent. transmission at 450 nanometres/4,500Å) and green (96 per cent. transmission at 525 nanometres/5,250Å), the effectiveness of a shark's visual adaptation to life in the sea is apparent.

Further tests on lemon sharks disclosed an ability to distinguish individual flashes of a flickering light down to 45 impulses per second – a lot less than a dragonfly (220 per second), but close to that of the

64

cockroach (40 to 50 per second) and wolf spider (50 per second). Vertebrates, in fact, tend to have lower flicker-fusion thresholds than the rest of the animal kingdom, that of the bush baby being only 10 per second, although pigeons rate a high value of 140 per second.

Sharks are evidently endowed with considerable ability to discern the brief, flickering movements of prospective prey in the dimly lit undersea world and it has been determined that this ability is dependent more on reflectance than colour, except at the red end of the spectrum where vision is lost. It was once widely claimed that natives were never attacked by sharks, only white-skinned swimmers being at risk. The numerous recorded attacks on black- or brown-skinned victims obviously refutes this belief but, nonetheless, the fact that sharks' eyes are particularly sensitive to reflectance suggests that a Caucasian may well be at greater risk in the water than a Negro.

The light-sensitive cells in the retina of a shark's eye are difficult to differentiate into typical rods and cones, which in many animals do not exhibit as much difference in appearance as their names suggest. Whether sharks had cone cells at all was in some doubt, but it seems that, although their retinas are predominantly composed of rods and display the rapid initial increase of sensitivity under dark conditions typical of other animals with retinas composed predominantly of rods (cats are the best known example), cones are nonetheless present. The visual acuity of a shark's eye is probably low, however, and may not exceed 5 per cent. that of a man's, while colour perception (also a function of cone cells) remains an unknown quantity. Great whites allegedly show a tendency to strike at warm coloured (yellow, orange, apricot etc.) floats, even in the presence of an appetising bait, and this species will attack dummies in an orange safety vest while leaving a similar dummy attired in a black wet suit severely alone. One interesting discovery is that the photoreceptor cells of a shark's retina are quite easily damaged by intense light: these fish do not, of course, normally subject their eyes to unfiltered light above the surface of the sea for more than a few moments and their retinas are obviously not able to withstand prolonged bright illumination.

Each individual photoreceptor cell contains a photopigment, which, in the case of the rods, is the Vitamin A-based substance called rhodopsin. This absorbs light at approximately the 500 nanometre ($5,000\text{Å}$) section of the spectrum, corresponding to the green light predominantly transmitted by the upper levels of oceanic water. Sharks that habitually live in very deep water, where only blue light remains, have a golden visual pigment with optimum absorbency shifted towards the blue end of the spectrum at 470–480 nanometres ($4,700$–$4,800\text{Å}$).

Adaptation of the shark eye to darkness occurs rapidly when illumination is removed. Dilation of the pupil to admit more light and withdrawal of melanin from the sacs shielding the tapetal plates results in a thousandfold sensitivity increase after just 12 minutes, but the process thereafter slows and yields only a further hundredfold increase in the next 45 minutes, with a tenfold increment in the ensuing 8 hours. This pattern of eye-sensitivity enhancement can be plotted on a graph and produces a

65

Carcharhinid sharks have a protective nictitating membrane that covers the vulnerable eyeball as the shark takes its prey.

smooth curve, unlike dark adaptation in the human eye which yields a graph with an abrupt shift after 9 minutes – interpreted as marking the change from predominantly cone-dominated (photopic) sight to rod-dominated (scotopic) vision – and the human eye also reaches its ultimate threshold faster than a shark's eye (in about 30 minutes).

Some sharks (e.g. carcharhinids, hammerheads) have a nictitating membrane that covers the eyeball as a protective measure when the creature is about to bite at its prey, while the presence of a round or slit-like pupil that adjusts its aperture (albeit rather slowly) according to the ambient light is a specialisation not present in bony fish: the iris sphincter apparently responds autonomously to variations in illumination, while the dilator is under nervous control.

Ears

Precisely what sharks can hear is unknown. They do not have ears with the sophisticated, spirally coiled cochlea of the mammalian inner ear that enables these most advanced of vertebrates to distinguish sounds transmitted through the air and, ultimately, to provide a capacity for verbal communication and the composition of music. Sharks do not even have the ear drum and middle-ear cavity of primitive amphibians and reptiles, with a bone to transmit sound waves to the series of sacs and canals that constitute the inner ear (Fig. 3.16). Like fishes in general, sharks require only to perceive sound waves transmitted through the relatively dense medium of water and have no reason to develop the sensitive amplification system found in terrestrial vertebrates in order to detect the tiny disturbances set up by sound waves travelling through the air. They have, instead, an elementary auditory system more obviously designed to monitor movement and balance than to detect specific sounds; on either side of the braincase, the paired otic regions contain two sac-like

Fig. 3.16. The inner ear of
Scyliorhinus. 1. utriculus. 2. sacculus.
3. macula. 4. anterior canal. 5.
posterior canal. 6. horizontal canal.
7. ampulla.

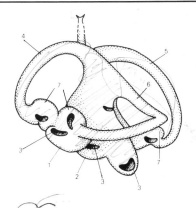

structures with three associated canals. This is the inner ear, still present as an organ of balance in higher vertebrates but of decreasing importance as the cochlea acquires greater size and sensitivity, until eventually the old inner ear becomes dismissively termed the vestibule. The two sacs comprise an upper utriculus and a lower sacculus, each with a sensitive spot (or macula, orientated horizontally in the utriculus, vertically in the sacculus) lined with epithelial cells and containing a calcified otolith – in sharks, a rather crumbly, amorphous mass of crystals. During development, this otolith forms out of a gelatinous membrane that invests the tips of sensory hairs arising from the macula's epithelial cells. Linear motion and accelerations due to gravity cause the otolith in its capsule to lag momentarily behind the movement, thus enabling the sensory hairs embedded in it to register the change in orientation or speed and transmit a message to the brain-stem and thence to the cerebellum.

The three canals of the inner ear form semi-circular structures, orientated at right angles to each other, that constitute outgrowths of the utriculus. Each canal has, at one end or other, an enlargement (ampulla) where it joins with the utriculus and, within the ampullae, are epithelial cells similar to those of the maculae, with sensory hairs embedded in a gelatinous mass (cupula). Their function is to register turning movements as liquid in the canals surges and displaces the cupulae. Since the canals are at right angles to each other, they are able to detect movement in any one of the three spatial planes.

Fish have few visual landmarks to help them judge their position and speed unless they are swimming near the bottom and the sensory function of the inner ear is thus vitally important to them. If sharks can hear at all in the accepted sense, then a sensitive macula located in the lagena, an outgrowth of the sacculus, may provide a rudimentary acoustic receptor.

Lateral-Line System

In all fish, however, there is an accessory sensory system known as the lateral-line system (Fig. 3.17). This incorporates clusters of epithelial cells (neuromasts) from which arise sensory hairs embedded in gelatine. These

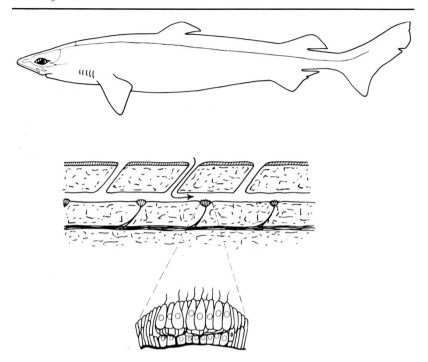

Fig. 3.17. (Above) Path of the lateral line system beneath the skin of a typical shark. (Below) A diagrammatic vertical section along a lateral line canal.

closely resemble the hairs of the inner ear's maculae and ampullae, but are located in a tube (usually closed, with pores connecting it to the surface of the body) that runs the length of each flank and branches to form a complex pattern around the head and jaws. Evidently the sensory cells respond to the movement of the water as the shark swims and turns, providing another sensory input to aid orientation and balance.

The Spiracular Organ

Inside the spiracle there is a further sensory structure, the spiracular organ, which is supplied by the anterior lateral line nerve and apparently supplements the sensory functions of the lateral line. Consisting of a blind tube or pouch about 5–7 mm ($\frac{1}{4}$ inch) long and not more than 0.2 mm wide, the spiracular organ is lined towards its upper end by patches of sensory hair cells and opens via a tiny pore into the spiracular cleft (or into a pocket of the spiracular cleft). There are no otolith-like structures present, so the spiracular organ is evidently not sensitive to gravity, but in at least some sharks (carcharhinids, spiny dogfish) it is associated with muscles of the upper jaw cartilage. Its precise role nonetheless remains a mystery, although it is evidently a receptor of some sort.

Pit Organs

In addition to the lateral-line system, sharks have pit organs (Fig. 3.18) scattered along their bodies in numbers and patterns that vary from species to species. These minute sensory centres comprise a bud-like aggregation of elongate supporting cells surrounding a small number of somewhat shorter pear-shaped sensory cells, each of which bears a hair-like projection at its upper end that is embedded in a gelatinous cupula capping the entire structure. In less advanced sharks, like *Heptranchias* and *Notorynchus*, (the seven-gill sharks), the pit organs are

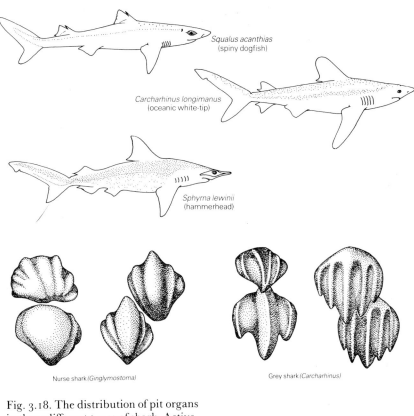

Squalus acanthias
(spiny dogfish)

Carcharhinus longimanus
(oceanic white-tip)

Sphyrna lewinii
(hammerhead)

Nurse shark *(Ginglymostoma)*

Grey shark *(Carcharhinus)*

Fig. 3.18. The distribution of pit organs in three different types of shark. Active species have more pit organs than sluggish bottom-dwelling forms. Pit organs are protected by modified dermal denticles which often have a very different appearance to the general pattern of scales typical of a given species. Pit organ scales (left) and normal scales (right) of representative sharks.

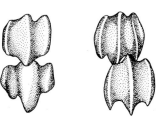

Lemon shark *(Negaprion)*

situated in slit-like grooves, but the more typical species have a pair (sometimes two or three pairs) of enlarged, modified dermal scales (Fig. 3.18) to protect each of their pit organs.

Below the throat of most sharks, there are two transverse series of pit organs (a mandibular row and an umbilical row), while down the body these structures, generally speaking, occur in two longitudinal regions: along the path of the lateral line itself and higher up towards the middle of the back. Some species (the spiny dogfish, for example) have relatively few pit organs, forming a sparse lateral row that reaches the upper lobe of the tail and a so-called parasagittal row extending back no further than the first dorsal fin. In *Carcharhinus*, the pits are much more numerous but are still essentially restricted to the same regions of the trunk, although the lower series extends almost to the tip of the tail and the upper row occurs all the way along the back. A very abundant distribution occurs in hammerheads, with pits extending all over the upper part of the body and tail, some of them even occurring low on the flanks below the lateral-line system.

The function of pit organs is still obscure. Some organisation of these structures into vertical or obliquely orientated rows is evident and they must obviously provide sharks with sensory inputs transmitted by the nerve fibres that penetrate the central structure of the pit organ. Perhaps they are sensitive to twisting movements of the shark's body as it seeks its prey or maybe they are just another means of picking up sound vibrations carried through the water from nearby prospective victims or potential enemies, as well as warning of sea-bed obstructions detectable from currents swirling around rocks or reefs. Since the innervation of pit organs seems to be derived from the same nerve that controls the papillae of the mouth and pharynx, they may even have a taste function, perhaps facilitated by brushing the adjacent spiny denticles against prospective prey to dislodge tiny fragments of skin or flesh. Bathers attacked by a shark frequently report that their assailant first brushed past them and these contacts with a shark's rough hide can tear away quite large areas of human skin and flesh. The notorious great white, however, has a reputation for charging straight into the attack without any preliminary investigation.

Perception

The combined sensitivity of the inner ear and the lateral-line system provides sharks with an acutely responsive means of maintaining their equilibrium and orientation as they twist and turn at high speed in search of prey. That they are somehow able to detect, and recognise from a considerable distance, the distressed thrashing of a hooked or injured fish seems to have been amply demonstrated, as any experienced shark fisherman will have discovered: sharks appear with great rapidity as soon as a big fish (or even another shark) is hooked.

Equipped with this formidable array of sensory detectors, it is scarcely surprising that sharks have made a good living in the seas for some 350

This scyliorhinid cat shark, *Holohalaelurus*, is accompanied by a remora, or sucker fish, which will sometimes secure itself to a shark by means of the sucker on its head; remoras feed on the parasites that infest a shark's skin and thus pay their way as hitchhikers.

million years and prospered at the expense of their fellows. So keen are their various means of perception that it seems they can even hear the low frequency sounds generated by muscles as the molecules within them cross-bridge to achieve contraction. Place your thumbs over your own ears to cover the ear canal, and then with your elbows raised bunch your fists. You can just detect a low rumbling noise, like distant thunder. The sound incorporates an abundance of low frequencies at around 20 Hz.

Such low frequency sounds are close to the limit of human hearing which has a maximum range of 20–20,000 Hz, but sharks are apparently very sensitive to sounds in the 20–40 Hz range. When an underwater loudspeaker is used to broadcast sound emissions, sharks take little or no interest in any sounds other than those in the 20–40 Hz range, although they are able to distinguish sounds of up to 1,000 Hz. On perceiving low frequency emissions, however, they home instantly on the source, swinging left and right as they come in to enable their sensory systems to pinpoint the objective, and frequently savage the loudspeaker. It seems that 20–40 Hz sounds correspond to the noise emissions of contracting muscle tissue, which will be generated in abundance by potential prey seeking to escape, struggling injured fish (or humans), or the threshing of a hooked shark. A steady note elicits little interest, only an irregularly pulsed sound drawing a shark's close attention, so that the uneven, low frequency engine note of a helicopter in all likelihood attracts sharks – which would be unfortunate for an imperilled swimmer hoping to be rescued by one of these aircraft from a threatening shark.

It is also evident that some of the sensory pores in the head region of sharks – the ampullae of Lorenzini (Fig. 3.19), named after Stefano Lorenzini who first described them in 1678 – are sensitive to weak DC and low frequency AC electrical fields, as well as having some measure of purely mechanical sensitivity, and can detect the bio-electrical activity

71

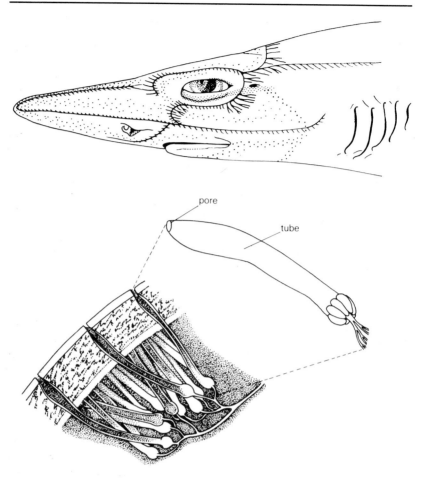

Fig. 3.19. (Top) The location of the ampullae of Lorenzini on the head of *Mustelus* with the subcutaneous lateral line pathways. (Bottom) A section through the skin of the snout to show the ampullae of Lorenzini.

that characterises all living creatures. Small prey fish generate weak DC electrical fields and, in experiments with sharks temporarily deprived of olfactory, mechanical and visual receptivity, it has been found that they can still find a flatfish concealed in the sand. On the other hand, they are unable to locate electrically-shielded prey fish, or pieces of dead fish, but can be deceived into attacking a buried electrode emitting an electric field. The occasions when great white sharks have bitten at metal boats or divers' protective metal cages may be explained by the strong electrical fields these metal objects possess. It is significant that active predatory forms have far more ampullae than the more sluggish bottom-dwelling types: *Galeus*, for example, has over 1,500 such sensors, but the somewhat unenergetic skate *Raja* has only 700-odd while the notably lethargic torpedo ray has a mere 220.

Scientists from Woods Hole Oceanographic Institution in Massachusetts set up an experiment in the shark-infested waters of Cape Cod to test the sensitivity of the great blue shark (*Prionace glauca*) to electric fields. An apparatus was constructed consisting of two pairs of salt-bridge electrodes 60 centimetres (2 feet) apart on a beam with, between them, an odour port through which small quantities of menhaden chum (chopped-up bait) was pumped. Suspended at night 5 metres ($16\frac{1}{4}$ feet) beneath the glass viewing well of a research vessel, 25 kilometres (15 miles) south of Martha's Vineyard with an 8 microampere direct current passing through one or other of the electrode pairs and a single underwater light to illuminate the scene, the equipment quickly drew the attention of a number of 2–3 metre ($6\frac{1}{4}$–$9\frac{3}{4}$ foot) great blues. Presumably attracted initially by the scent of chum permeating through the water, they nonetheless almost ignored the odour source when launching their attacks. On the night when sharks were most active, a total of forty strikes were made at the test apparatus, only two of which were on the odour port, while seven were on the unactivated electrode and no fewer than thirty-one on the live dipole. This marked preference must be regarded as highly significant.

It is also possible – even probable – that sharks can sense the electric fields induced by wind-driven and tidal ocean currents flowing through the Earth's magnetic field, thus enabling these creatures to follow ocean currents during migrations or to compensate for passive drift. Since a shark swimming through the Earth's magnetic field also induces its own local electric field, with a voltage gradient that varies with its compass heading, it may well be able to navigate with its own built-in electro-magnetic compass.

It looks very much as if the impressive array of sense organs employed by sharks have developed largely to complement each other and to help sharks to hunt in the shallow waters of the continental shelf, where the marine life on which they can prey teems in abundance but sediment stirred up from the bottom frequently reduces visibility to a metre or less. With eyes that are designed to pick up faint, flickering movements rather than to perceive detail, electrical receptors on the head, a lateral-line system and widely distributed pit organs, a prowling shark cruising in murky offshore waters must be literally bombarded with sensory impressions that transform the watery gloom into a world full of sound and movement.

Chapter 4
Relics, Rarities and Curiosities

Almost a living fossil, the frilled shark (*Chlamydoselachus*) is so primitive that it resembles some of the long extinct Devonian sharks which died out 350 million years ago more than it does the typical sharks of modern seas. In 1885, Samuel Garman of Harvard's Museum of Comparative Zoology even went so far as to maintain that it really was a living survivor of those ancient fossil killers.

In fact, the elongate, dark brown, pale bellied frilled shark (Fig. 4.1) is not a straggler left over from the remote past of the Palaeozoic, but it undoubtedly represents a very low level of shark evolution, having evidently failed to progress beyond an exceedingly conservative structural condition. Behind its flattened head, there are six pairs of gill openings, in addition to a small spiracle, which is one more than modern sharks typically possess, although it is by no means certain this is a primitive condition since the Mesozoic hybodont sharks of 150 million years ago only had five pairs of gill openings, as apparently did the even more ancient sharks of the Devonian. The frilled shark owes its common name to the remarkable fold of skin that originates at the edge of the first gill slit and extends right across the undersurface of the neck to function like an

Fig. 4.1. (Top) The frilled shark (*Chlamydoselachus*). (Bottom left) The jaws of *Chlamydoselachus* and (right) teeth from one of the transverse rows arranged across the margins of the mouth.

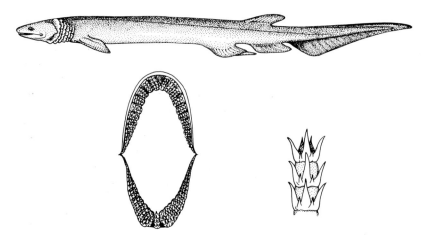

imperfect operculum (the cover that, in bony fishes, shields the gill openings). By means of a long hyomandibular bone that forms a sliding brace for the lower jaw, the mouth at the extremity of the broadly rounded snout can be gaped widely open, while the ligaments attaching the upper jaw to the cranium simultaneously allow the front of the skull to be raised, thus keeping the mouth cavity in line with the body so that prey can be readily swallowed. All the teeth are of the same basic type: typically three-cusped (tricuspid) hooks arranged in a series of transverse rows across the edge of the jaws. There are about fourteen of these rows on each side of the upper jaw and thirteen rows either side of the lower jaw, with an additional small series where the two halves of the mandible join. Each transverse row has several teeth functional at any one time; replacement teeth push up from behind and the broad base of each tooth is forked to interlock with a pair of excavations in the base of its successor. Embryological studies indicate that each tooth is formed by the fusion of simple denticles, analogous to dermal scales, and with some 300 of these tricuspid elements arranged around its mouth, a frilled shark is deploying nearly 1,000 hook-like fangs to prevent any prey seized from wriggling free.

As befits a deep-sea fish hunting its prey in the dark waters below the 180-metre (600-feet) mark, the frilled shark has large elongate eyes to catch every faint glimmer of light, while the sensitive nostrils are situated on the sides of the snout.

The notochord, which underlies the spinal cord and was the original stiffening element around which vertebrates developed their backbones, consists of a stout, continuous rod of cartilage extending from the skull right back to the tip of the tail. This is a very primitive arrangement. In more advanced sharks, the notochord becomes greatly reduced as hard vertebral centra develop around it and usurp its supportive function: there is only incipient restriction of the notochord in *Chlamydoselachus* to indicate the start of this trend.

The pectoral fins are broad and rounded, while the pelvic fins, the single dorsal fin (supported by essentially unfused radials) and the anal fin (with some of its radials accreted to form basal elements) are located well towards the rear of the sinuous body, close to the tail fin, which has an elongate, pointed upper lobe but only a small lower lobe. The serpentine frilled shark is not well adapted for speed, but would be adept at swimming among rocks; the juxtaposition of the pelvic fins, dorsal fin and anal fin near the powerful tail fin suggests that these propulsive organs are grouped together to form a posterior fulcrum from which this remarkable shark can strike at its prey. Along the lower surface of the belly, there are a pair of longitudinal body-wall thickenings (the tropic folds) with a midline groove between them, but the function of this feature is unknown.

The stomach is small and proportionately narrow, while the liver comprises two very long lobes that correspond to the elongate conformation of the body. Even in adult frilled sharks, the epibranchial arteries, which carry oxygenated blood from the gills to the dorsal aorta (and thence to all the organs to the body), remain opposite the gill arches that provide a supporting structure for the gill membranes. In other sharks, there is a re-orientation of these arteries during embryological development so that, in adults, they lie opposite each gill slit instead of each gill arch. Lateral-line grooves are open throughout almost their entire length in *Chlamydoselachus*, as they apparently were in the ancient Devonian sharks, with only modified dermal denticles to partially roof the canal and provide some degree of shielding. In modern sharks, the canals of the lateral-line system are almost entirely enclosed and only communicate with the surface through pores.

Obviously well adapted to its chosen way of life, the frilled shark has been under no selective pressure to change and seems to have remained effectively in a primitive state of suspended evolution. Its fossil history, curiously, is poorly known: some teeth have been reported from the Pliocene of Tuscany, Italy (*Chlamydoselachus lawleyi*), and a single isolated tooth of doubtful identity was found in the Miocene of Trinidad, while other species occur in the Miocene of North America and the Eocene and Miocene of Europe. Such an apparently archaic shark might be expected to have a long fossil pedigree, but this is not the case. Indeed, its existence in modern seas was unsuspected by Western scientists until almost the end of the nineteenth century.

In the years 1879–81, the naturalist Ludwig Döderlein brought back with him to Vienna his collection of Japanese fish. Included in this material were two specimens of a hitherto unreported shark-like fish of elongate shape – the creature now known as *Chlamydoselachus*, the frilled shark.

One of the two specimens turned out to be a pregnant female and, from it, an embryo was obtained which Döderlein gave to another scientist, C. Röse, while the preserved carcases of the two frilled sharks passed to the collection of the Vienna Natural History Museum.

The year after his return, Döderlein carefully wrote up a description of this new shark and entrusted his longhand draft to a certain Hofrath Steindachner for publication. Unfortunately Döderlein's manuscript was subsequently lost and never achieved publication. The first scientific description of the frilled shark to appear (and with it the promulgation of its Latin name, *Chlamydoselachus*) was written by Samuel Garman and appeared during 1884, followed by a further report in the *Proceedings of the American Association for the Advancement of Science* (published in 1885). These articles were based on a female specimen apparently purchased by Harvard's Museum of Comparative Zoology from a Professor H.A.Ward, its origin being Japan.

A further specimen was brought to the Museum of Comparative Zoology in 1887 by a Japanese graduate student, Saitaro Goto, and this too was described by Garman while, in the same year, Albert Günther reported the capture of three frilled sharks by the research vessel *Challenger* in the deep waters of Yeddo Bay, Tokyo. Working in Japan itself, T. Nishikawa published, in 1898, a description of a female frilled shark containing about a dozen eggs and this article came to the attention of a dedicated young student of fishes at Columbia University, New York.

Bashford Dean was born in New York in October 1867, the son of a lawyer, graduated in biology from the College of the City of New York in 1886, and later entered Columbia University as a graduate student, where he ultimately became a faculty member. An extraordinary personality by any standards, Dean combined an avid dedication to the study of fish, both living and extinct, with such improbable additional qualifications as an expert knowledge of European armour and an ability to draw with both hands simultaneously.

Dean's work on early fossil fishes led him to examine the supposedly primitive sharks for clues to the evolution of fishes as a whole and, in particular, to study the Port Jackson shark (*Heterodontus*) and the frilled shark. He especially wanted embryos of different ages to see whether development recapitulated the early stages of shark evolution, and it was to obtain embryos of the Port Jackson shark that Dean planned to visit Japan, for it was known that this form breeds extensively in Japanese waters.

The youthful and dedicated New Yorker spent 12 months in Japan between 1900 and 1901, working at the Misaki Marine Laboratory on the Miura peninsula, which juts into the central basin of the Sagami Sea. Dean discovered that about a dozen examples of the frilled shark, some of which were pregnant females containing eggs, were landed each year from the waters of the Sagami by fishermen. With his keen interest in embryology as a source of information on a species' past evolutionary history, Dean began to study the developing embryos of frilled sharks. Using his ambidextrous skill as a draughtsman, he built up a complete record of this enigmatic shark's lengthy gestation, which may last as long as 2 years. Only one ovary (usually the right-hand one) is normally functional and it seems that eggs ripen throughout the year – there is no specific breeding season as Nishikawa at first thought. Normally between three and twelve large, ellipsoid or rounded eggs with tough keratinoid capsules are present and from these the embryos emerge within the female's body, each still attached to its nourishing yolk sac, while the ruptured egg capsule is expelled. The embryos have external gills and probably use them to obtain oxygen from sea water entering the uterine cavity (some diffusion of oxygen through the walls of the uterus is also possible). A mature egg of *Chlamydoselachus* may measure as much as 100 millimetres (4 inches) across and is amongst the largest known cells of any living animal.

Dean returned to the Misaki Laboratory in 1905 and, in all, obtained some forty or so adult specimens of the frilled shark from the Sagami Sea, including twenty-six females, ten of which yielded eggs (fifty-six in all – some in a blastula stage of development with cells multiplying around a central cavity, some as gastrulas in which the dividing cells form two distinct layers corresponding approximately to the adult's skin and gut lining, and some as definite embryos ranging from 1.15-3.9 centimetres/$\frac{1}{2}$ -$1\frac{1}{2}$ inches in length according to age). The Japanese fishermen knew *Chlamydoselachus* as the *rabuka* (silk shark), *tokagizame* (lizard-head) or *kagurazame* (scaffold shark) and, by 1905, examples could be bought in the Yokohama fishmarkets for between $25 and $50 – a large sum to the

Japanese in those days – while Dean subsequently had eggs and embryos sent to him from Japan for study in the United States.

Meanwhile, this rare and extraordinary shark had been recognised elsewhere in the world. R. Collet in 1890 recorded the discovery of an eviscerated female specimen measuring 61 centimetres (24 inches) among a collection of specimens obtained by the Prince of Monaco at Funchal, Madeira, in 1889. The same zoologist published, in 1897, a description of a female frilled shark 1.91 metres ($6\frac{1}{4}$ feet) long hauled up from below the 180 metre (600 foot) mark in Varanger Fjord, Norway, and in the early years of the twentieth century there were catches of *Chlamydoselachus* off Cezimbra, Portugal (in 1900), off Corunna, Spain (in 1906), off Morocco (in 1909 and 1913) and off San Sebastian (in 1925), with subsequent recoveries from as far afield as California, Australia, New Zealand and off the Namibian coast.

Evidently the frilled shark is fairly widespread, but it is a rare fish that normally frequents the deeper, colder waters of the continental shelf. It takes squid as a bait, but what its normal food includes nobody really knows.

Fig. 4.2. (Top) The bullhead or horn shark (*Heterodontus*). (Bottom) The skull of *Heterodontus* showing the amphistylic jaw articulation in which the hyomandibular is of only moderate significance as a means of bracing the upper jaw (palato-quadrate) against the braincase, an additional articulation between these two elements occurring in the ethmoid region.

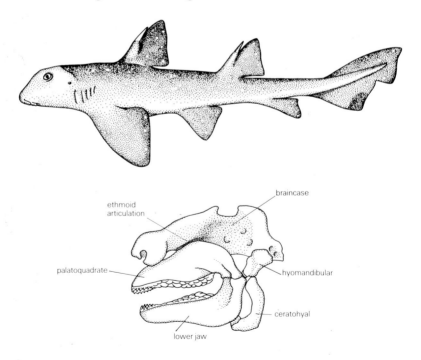

Jaws of the Port Jackson shark (*Heterodontus portusjacksoni*).

The original object of Bashford Dean's journey to Japan was to seek out the Port Jackson shark (*Heterodontus*, Fig. 4.2). Widely believed at the time to be a markedly primitive shark, this creature possesses a short, blunt-snouted head that has resulted in it being called the bullhead shark.

Viewed from below, the extraordinary mouth of a horned or bullhead shark (*Heterodontus*) with its crushing teeth for eating shellfish, crustaceans and sea urchins.

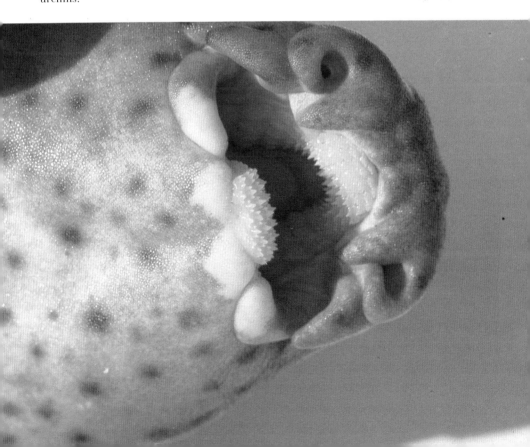

It is not particularly big, the largest specimens only running up to about 1.5 metres (5 feet) in length, and is not regarded as dangerous to man.

Heterodontus has small, sideways-looking eyes with a pair of longitudinal ridges on the head just above them, a small spiracle and the conventional five pairs of gill slits found in most sharks. The dentition comprises small anterior teeth and, at the back of the jaws, elongate ridged grinders – very much the sort of combined biting and crushing equipment that occurs in the fossil skulls of the extinct hybodont sharks which lived 100 million or so years ago during the Age of Dinosaurs. Like the old hybodonts, *Heterodontus* also has a thick pointed spine running up the front of both the dorsal fins, while the pectoral fins are proportionately large, an anal fin is present and the tail is rather short.

It used to be generally accepted that *Heterodontus* is indeed a close relative of the hybodont stock, but there are now grounds for believing that it is not really particularly primitive at all, having evolved as an offshoot of the rather sluggish carpet-shark group (the orectolobids). A few features suggest some structural advances, such as the presence of well-calcified vertebrae constricting the notochord and the loss of the primitive articulation between the palatoquadrate and the braincase behind the orbit, but the upper jaw suspension is nonetheless still essentially amphistylic – a supposedly archaic construction in which the palatoquadrates are braced against the braincase anteriorly and ventrally as well as being supported by the hyomandibular bone posteriorly (Fig. 4.2).

Heterodontus is usually found in the shallow waters of warm latitudes in the Pacific and Indian oceans, occasionally being encountered as deep as 150 metres (500 feet) but quickly heading for shallower water if alarmed. It lives mainly on molluscs (hence the grinding teeth at the back of the jaws) but also eats fish, crustaceans and sea-urchins – the stomachs of some captured specimens have proved to be full of finely powdered echinoid tests, while the teeth are sometimes severely stained from the consumption of purple sea-urchins. The spines of the fins and the prominent supra-orbital ridges apparently assist *Heterodontus* to force its way beneath rocks in search of prey, the dorsal spines often being worn down to only half their normal length as a result of this practice. Unfortunately, the fondness for molluscs that bullhead sharks display makes oyster beds very attractive to them and they can cause considerable damage to these commercial enterprises.

Aquarium specimens of *Heterodontus* have frequently been witnessed copulating, the male holding the female by a pectoral fin while his tail curves across her back in front of the second dorsal fin, only one clasper at a time being thrust into the female's cloaca. The dorsal fin spines may also have a function during copulation, providing a means of securing a purchase. The eggs are laid in the shallows throughout the year, although spring is the principal breeding season. The horny, dark brown egg cases are up to 15 centimetres (6 inches) long and bear two tough spiral flanges, each forming about half-a-dozen screw-like turns around the case which help to wedge the egg in among rocks. Normally two eggs at a time mature within each female and they are laid in communal nests containing up to about sixteen eggs. The actual process of laying may take as much as 2 hours per egg, with the spirally flanged case gradually screwing its way out of the cloacal opening. Allegedly, the female then takes each egg in her mouth to place it in a secure rocky cleft or niche.

The Port Jackson shark itself is *Heterodontus portusjacksoni*, also known as the oyster-crusher or pig shark. *Heterodontus japonicus*, the Japanese bull-head (the *sasiwari, nekozame, sazaewari* or *sazaiwari* to the Japanese) is smaller, ranging up to only about 1 metre ($3\frac{1}{4}$ feet) in length with distinctive dark bands surrounding its body; *Heterodontus zebra* of the western Pacific is about the same size while *Heterodontus quoyi* (from the west coast of South America) and *Heterodontus francisci* (California and western Mexico) do not apparently exceed 60 centimetres (2 feet). The status of *Heterodontus galeatus*, described from the waters around Queensland and New South Wales, is uncertain.

The fossil record of *Heterodontus* can be traced a long way back in time, with an imperfect skeleton some 150 million years old occurring in the Upper Jurassic of Bavaria and other fossil remains indicating the presence of this ancient form in the Cretaceous and early Cenozoic of Europe, southern Asia and Africa, as well as the Miocene of Australia.

Looking more like the popular concept of a shark than the elongate *Chlamydoselachus* or the rather clumsily proportioned bullheads are the hexanchoids, often called comb-toothed sharks because their teeth bear an unmistakable resemblance to combs. Examined more carefully, however, it becomes evident that this group is a small assemblage of rather rare, bottom-dwelling, deep-sea forms that exhibit a number of very conservative features suggesting relationship with the squaliform assemblage. The fact that they have more than the normal shark's quota of five gill slits (*Hexanchus* itself has six, *Heptranchias* and *Notorynchus* seven) is a noteworthy characteristic, while the vertebrae of comb sharks are very weakly calcified, the notochord being in consequence but little constricted, and the upper jaw is attached to the skull in the old-fashioned hybodont manner: the palatoquadrates hinge on the braincase through an articulation with the post-orbital process and an attachment point beneath the eye socket region, although the reduced hyomandibular bone has lost its former function as a brace for the jaws and there is instead a knob on the mandible that fits into a socket in the palatoquadrate.

Fig. 4.3. The dentition of *Hexanchus griseus* showing the characteristic comb-like lower teeth (left side).

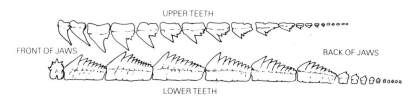

UPPER TEETH

FRONT OF JAWS   BACK OF JAWS

LOWER TEETH

The characteristic comb-like dentition (Fig. 4.3) is best developed in the lower jaw, where each of the elongate, blade-shaped teeth bear a dozen or so small cusps along their crowns, whereas, in the upper jaw, the teeth have slender, curved primary cusps. The pointed snout overhangs a large mouth, the streamlined body carries only a single dorsal fin, and an anal fin is present, while the long tail has a very small lower lobe. In the pectoral fins, the propterygial cartilage lacks radial elements; these supporting structures are borne solely on the two remaining basals.

Little is known of the hexanchids' habits. They live on the edge of the continental shelf, where the sea floor plunges down into oceanic depths, and apparently spend their time cruising just above the bottom feeding on fish or crustaceans.

The six-gill or griset (*Hexanchus*) is a sizeable shark, running to as much as 5 metres (15 feet), a reported 8 metre (26 foot) long specimen allegedly caught off Cornwall in the middle of the nineteenth century being regarded as an unreliable record. It is known to dive as deep as 1,850 metres (5,900 feet) and, if hooked, will often simply go steadily deeper and deeper, despite every effort to arrest its progress, until eventually the line runs out. Unless the fisherman is operating from a very large boat, with particularly strong tackle, there is then no option but to cut the line if a really big six-gill is on the other end, as this powerful shark can easily drag a small boat beneath the surface or jerk the fisherman into the sea. As befits a deep-water species, *Hexanchus* is a uniform dark brownish grey above, shading to a paler hue below with a light-coloured streak along the middle of each flank. Adults have three-cusped dermal denticles protecting the body, while the brown-hued juveniles exhibit a series of modified denticles along the top of the tail fin that are twice the normal size.

The largest and most widely distributed species of *Hexanchus* is *Hexanchus griseus*, the blunt-nose six-gill (Fig. 4.4), which occurs in the temperate waters of the Mediterranean and the Atlantic, Pacific and Indian Oceans. It rests on the bottom by day and feeds at night; high water temperatures towards the surface and inshore probably act as a barrier to it, although six-gills have been seen inshore in the warmer parts of their range (Cuba and the Mediterranean). To the north, the species is present through the North Sea to Iceland, having been caught at 1,025 metres (3,360 feet) in the Shetland-Faroe channel, while the most southerly limit of the six-gill's distribution appears to be Mauritius. The shovel-nose shark (*Hexanchus corinus*) of the Californian coast is probably only a variety of *Hexanchus griseus* and it is likely that this massive shark occurs in the deeper waters of the Gulf of Mexico and off South America.

A somewhat smaller species, *Hexanchus vitulus* (the big-eyed six-gill) runs to only perhaps 2.1 metres (7 feet) in length and seems to prefer warmer seas than its big relative, occurring off Florida, in the Philippines, around Madagascar and down the east African coast from Kenya to Natal.

Free-swimming mouse-grey-coloured *Hexanchus* young measuring 40–70 centimetres (16–18 inches) have been caught, and a pregnant female 4.5 metres ($14\frac{1}{2}$ feet) long was found to contain 108 embryos.

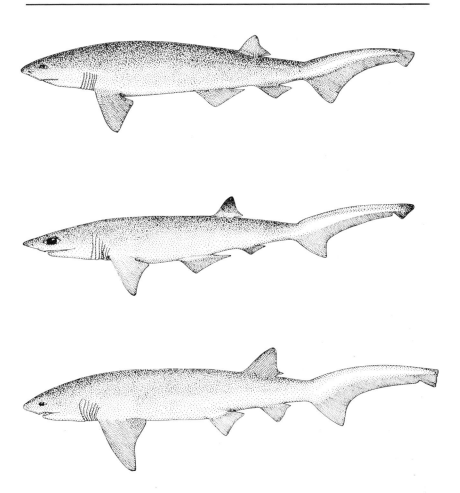

Fig. 4.4. (Top) The blunt-nose six-gill (*Hexanchus griseus*), up to 4.5 metres (15 feet) in length. (Centre) The seven-gill (*Heptranchias perlo*), up to perhaps 3 metres (10 feet) in length. (Bottom) The broad head seven-gill (*Notorynchus maculatus*), growing to 2.5 metres (8 feet).

At one time fished by the Cubans on hook-and-line for oil and taken in the North Sea to be sold for human consumption in Germany (the flesh is alleged to have a purgative action), the six-gill now has no commercial value, but is regarded as a nuisance by fishermen in the Mediterranean and on the Iberian peninsula because it drives away marketable fish and has a voracious appetite for hake. Off Cuba, *Hexanchus* takes dolphins (*Coryphaena*), small marlin and swordfish, crabs and shrimps; they also snatch bites out of hooked sharks and one specimen was found to contain a torpedo ray.

Closely related to *Hexanchus* is *Heptranchias*, the seven-gilled shark or perlon (Fig. 4.4). A smaller form than the six-gill, running to only 3 metres (10 feet) or so in length, with a narrow head and tapering snout, this browny grey shark occurs in the Mediterranean, the Atlantic and the Pacific. Like its relative, it is a bottom-dweller in deep water, but has occasionally been reported to enter shallow roadsteads or lagoons in tropical West Africa. It lives essentially on fish (especially hake, to the disgust of Spanish fishermen) and is not considered to be dangerous to Man. Males apparently become sexually mature at a length of 60–75 centimetres ($2-2\frac{1}{2}$ feet), females at 1 metre ($3\frac{1}{4}$ feet). Up to twenty embryos have been found in pregnant females, each with a large oval yolk sac that shows no sign of attachment to the oviduct wall, birth taking place when these juveniles are no more than 25 centimetres (10 inches) in length.

Although known to the Japanese as the *aburazame*, or oil shark, because of the oil obtainable from its liver, the seven-gill is of no commercial importance, as much because of its rarity as anything else since its flesh is apparently excellent to eat.

Whether *Notorynchus* is really a separate genus from *Heptranchias* is doubtful. Like the perlon, it has seven pairs of gill slits, but the head is wider, with a broadly rounded snout, and the inordinately long tail makes up perhaps a third of the creature's 2.4 metre (8 foot) overall length. One species, (*Notorynchus maculatus*, Fig 4.4) has been found off the Californian coast; this dark blue-grey shark with irregular black blotchy markings and pale ventral surfaces is slightly smaller than *Notorynchus pectorosus* from Australian waters.

Hexanchids occur as fossils as far back as the early Jurassic, about 190 million years in the past and, by the end of the Cretaceous, 65 million years ago, they were evidently widespread, for their comb-like teeth are found in deposits of that age in places as far apart as southern England and New Zealand.

Chapter 5
The Great Man-Eater and Its Kin

All of the big killer sharks that prowl the modern oceans are lamniforms, an order (Lamniformes) that also includes a substantial number of smaller forms, as well as a few very large but completely harmless plankton-eaters. Five pairs of gill clefts are universally present in all these sharks, but spiracles are either small or absent. In the most conservative genera, the snout is formed by three conjoined cartilaginous rods, which are sometimes reduced or even lost in more advanced forms, and the otic region of the braincase – where the hearing organs are accommodated – is comparatively short (Fig. 5.1). The upper jaw cartilages are not fused to the skull and extend forward as far as the nasal capsules (towards the tip of the snout), as well as being prolonged backwards in some species to project behind the level of the occiput.

The two halves of each jaw are usually only loosely joined anteriorly (i.e at the symphyses), but lamniforms that habitually tackle tough-skinned prey (like the tiger shark, which feeds on marine turtles) may have tightly-fused symphysial unions. Predatory lamniform sharks are able to protrude their upper jaws below the pointed snout, thus enabling them to tear a hunk of flesh from prey too large for swallowing whole.

There is considerable variation among lamniform sharks in the shape and form of their teeth (Fig. 5.2) but, within a given species, the dentition is of a similar type right around the upper or lower jaws, from the front to the sides, and is therefore an invaluable means of identification: teeth left embedded in the planks of a boat, or even in the body of a shark's victim, are sufficient to positively identify the attacker.

No other shark is surrounded by as much myth, legend and fantasy as the great white (*Carcharodon carcharias*). The ultimate expression of power and savagery in lamniform evolution, this notorious man-killer undoubtedly deserves its unsavoury reputation, even if its size is often

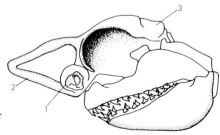

Fig. 5.1. The skull of a lamniform shark (*Isurus*). The upper jaw is separate from the braincase and projects forward as far as the nasal capsule (1), while extending posteriorly beyond the occiput. There are three rostral supports (2) and the otic region (3) is short.

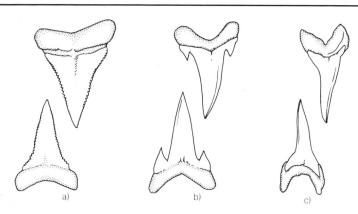

Fig. 5.2. Teeth of a) *Carcharodon*, b) *Lamna* and c) *Isurus*. Upper jaw teeth are above and lower jaw teeth below.

exaggerated. As is customary among sharks, the females are larger than the males but, even so, 4.5 metres (15 feet) would be a good average length for a female. Such a shark would nonetheless constitute a formidable antagonist if encountered by a swimmer or SCUBA diver. With its conical snout, stoutly proportioned body and gaping jaws lined by multiple rows of triangular teeth up to 8 centimetres (3 inches) long, this massive predator has no enemies save others of its own kind and Man himself. Even a run-of-the-mill specimen can weigh 1.3 tonnes (3,000 pounds) if it is in good condition, and unusually big examples of the species may run over 6 metres (20 feet) in length with a weight in excess of 3 tonnes (7,000 pounds).

Stories of giant great whites exceeding 9 metres (30 feet) are usually unverifiable. There was, for example, the alleged 30-footer taken off Soquel, California, with the carcase of a 45 kilogram (100 pound) sea-lion in its stomach, or the 11.1 metre (37 foot) great white supposed to have been trapped in a herring weir at White Head Island, New Brunswick, in June 1930, for which there is only hearsay evidence, not to mention Captain E.S. Elkington's story that, in 1894, a shark 1.2 metres (4 feet) longer than his 10.5 metre (35 foot) launch lay alongside his vessel for half-an-hour just outside Townsville, Queensland. The jaws of a great white taken off Port Fairey, Victoria, in 1842, were presented to the British Museum (Natural History) in London but claims that this fish was 10.85 metres ($36\frac{1}{2}$ feet) long seem to be a substantial exaggeration because the largest tooth in the dentition is only 5.7 centimetres ($2\frac{1}{4}$ inches) in length, which suggests a figure of around 5.15 metres ($17\frac{1}{2}$ feet) for the overall measurement. However, in May 1978, the English shark-fishing expert, Trevor Housby, was fortuitously on hand when fishermen in San Miguel harbour, in the Azores, harpooned a veritable giant. Lanced through the gills and brought ashore, this monster great white proved to be 9 metres ($29\frac{1}{4}$ feet) long, with pectoral fins spanning 4.17 metres (13 feet 8 inches) and teeth measuring 76 mm (3 inches).

The most feared silhouette in the underwater world: a great white shark
(*Carcharodon carcharias*) in Australian waters.

However, even a modest-sized 4.8 metre (16 foot) great white can exert
a biting pressure of 3 tonnes per square centimetre (20 tons per square
inch) and, with a single snap of its jaws, will hack out a chunk of flesh
measuring 28 by 33 centimetres (11 by 13 inches). A whale killed off South
Australia had sustained five shark bites, each measuring 48.5 by 60
centimetres (19 by 24 inches), suggesting an adversary about 7.8 metres
(26 feet) long.

For a predator of this power, a man is obviously no more than just a
tasty snack, although a claim by the sixteenth-century French naturalist
Guillaume Rondelet, that whole men in armour had been found inside
sharks off Nice and Marseilles, is even harder for a modern zoologist to
swallow than it would have been for a great white. This alleged example of
the sardine's revenge must, it seems, belong to the same category of myth
as Jonah's sojourn within a whale, but there is no doubt that a large
specimen of *Carcharodon* can engulf some very substantial prey. Larry
Mansur, a Californian commercial fisherman, caught a 5 metre (16 foot)
shark near Los Angeles in July 1976 that contained the bodies of two
whole sea-lions, one weighing 78.75 kilograms (175 pounds) and the other
56.25 kilograms (125 pounds), while, on 2 October 1954, the body of a
13-year-old boy was found in the stomach of a 0.9 tonne (2,000 pound)
great white caught at Nagasaki. Rondelet's other claim that 'two tunny
and a fully clothed sailor' were discovered inside a Mediterranean shark is
rather more reasonable, even if still subject to scepticism.

The melancholy catalogue of fatalities attributable to attacks by great whites has been rather more adequately documented since the beginning of the twentieth century. Often found in quite shallow water, this most feared of sharks is also the most single-minded in its onslaught. Other dangerous big sharks, like makos or tigers, will usually circle a prospective victim, weighing up the situation before finally deciding to make an attack, and very often their first pass is itself something of an exploratory manoeuvre: the fish will brush past the object of its enmity or simply nudge it with its nose to test its prospective edibility. Not until this preliminary reconnoitering has been completed will the real attack come, so that the swimmer or diver may have some chance of bluffing his or her way to safety – perhaps a bold show of determination will give a not particularly hungry shark a reason to reconsider the situation (if the mental processes of sharks can be assessed in such charitable terms) and the creature will turn away in search of easier prey.

But great whites are different. If they are really hungry, they mean business right from the start. There are no preliminary skirmishes. A famished great white goes straight in, mouth gaping, jaws thrust forward, driven on by a single, dominating, all-powerful impulse: it feels hungry, and that most basic of requirements must be satisfied.

Rodney Fox never saw the great white that savaged him off Aldinga Beach in 1963 until he felt the cruel teeth lacerating his flesh. He was conscious only of a sudden stillness in the water around him, '... a silence, a perceptible hush'. Perhaps his adversary had been stalking him unseen through the shallow water, which was only 15 metres (50 feet) deep at that spot, Fox's attention being concentrated on adding to his catch as he sought to defend his South Australian Spearfishing Championship.

In fact, Fox may have been lucky – incredibly lucky – not just because a boat was only yards away when he struggled, bleeding and mutilated, to the surface; not because the people who pulled him out of the water had the presence of mind to leave his wet suit on him to help hold the shredded flesh together; not because a policeman just happened to be on hand when the boat reached the shore, with a car instantly available to take Fox on the first stage of his journey to hospital in Adelaide (an ambulance met the car half way); and not because the surgeon on duty that afternoon had just returned from a specialised course in thoracic surgery in England. Fox was lucky because his adversary seems not to have been all that hungry. With Fox's body firmly grasped in its jaws, even a moderate-sized great white could have practically bitten him in two had it so desired.

Perhaps the rubber wet suit did not taste right, or perhaps because, in a desperate attempt to prevent a further onslaught, Fox grabbed hold of the shark itself and wrapped his legs around its body in what must have been a totally unexpected act of apparent aggression, the great white seems to have faltered. It may be significant that the shark then latched hold of Fox's fish float. It was fully recognised that dead and bleeding fish being trailed through the water by a diver were likely to attract sharks and boats (one of which rescued Fox) were on hand to take each competing diver's catch on board. Maybe this was what really instigated the attack on Fox and a mouthful of wet-suited human being proved not to be the palatable snack of fresh fish that was anticipated.

For whatever reasons, the shark which attacked Fox did not kill and devour him, as it certainly could have if it wished.

The lesson of this horrific experience is that, even if a great white does attack, it may be only a half-hearted snatch. A tonne of shark with teeth 8 centimetres (3 inches) long is still going to do a lot of damage, even if it is not all-out for a maximum effort, and the extensive lacerated wounds which will inevitably be sustained by the victim are likely to prove fatal if skilled medical attention is not quickly available. The fact remains, however, that the great white's reputation as a dedicated killer may be over-stated. It is far too big and powerful to trifle with, but many great white attacks, including fatal ones, are probably not really premeditated attempts to kill outright so much as the grabbing of a succulent mouthful in passing – a fully grown human being is probably too large for a great white to swallow whole. How else is it possible to explain the fact that only about a third of great white attacks on people prove fatal, the majority of the victims managing to reach safety, albeit in a badly mauled state? It is inconceivable that the great white is such an inefficient hunter that most of its prey manages to escape, even after the shark has secured a purchase with its jaws. The answer, probably, is that if the victim is small enough (e.g. a small sea-lion or a child) then it will be engulfed whole; otherwise a bite (or bites, in the case of an easily subdued subject) will suffice. And a great white can take a very large bite.

The experiences of Rodney Fox's two diving friends, Brian Rodger and Henri Bource, tend to bear out this re-assessment of the great white. When Rodger was seized by one of these sharks off Aldinga Beach in 1961, his entire lower torso ended up in the creature's mouth – and yet he lived. Granted he discharged his speargun into the shark's head, which even one of these voracious creatures must have regarded as a distinct discouragement. His shredded leg was laid open to the bone, but he nonetheless managed to wrap the rubber sling of his speargun round his thigh as a tourniquet while trying to struggle towards the shore. A rowboat picked him up, but he was 3 hours on the operating table at the Royal Adelaide Hospital before the surgeons were sure they could pull him through.

And Bource? Like Fox, he never saw the shark that hit him until it was too late, but he experienced the same eerie silence of a sea suddenly empty of the seals and fish that moments before he had been photographing. Seized by the left leg, he was dragged deep under while the shark shook him like a terrier with a rat until his limb had been severed. Freed to float to the surface, he was dragged aboard the dive boat where an emergency tourniquet was applied to his thigh, and an ambulance summoned to Port Fairey by the boat's radio rushed him to Warrnambool Hospital. Bource was another lucky survivor.

Fox, Rodger and Bource all continued to dive after recovering from their injuries. In 1965, a year after Bource's narrow escape, the three were aboard the tuna fishing boat *Glenmorry* off South Australia, fishing for great whites, along with ace shark fisherman Alf Dean and underwater photographer Ron Taylor.

While Taylor hung over the transom to record the action on camera as great whites came racing in to take the enticing baits put out for them, Henri Bource hooked a massive specimen and began reeling it in. Before the fish could be pulled close enough for gaffing, another great white attacked its helpless cousin and wrenched a huge mouthful of flesh from its back. It could not have looked easier, as the three veteran survivors watched their catch mangled before their eyes. If the shark which seized Rodney Fox had prosecuted its attack with comparable determination, the young Australian would never have survived the first onslaught.

Because of its murderous reputation, it is possible that the great white has been blamed for attacks actually carried out by other species. Not everyone is ineluctably convinced that the 2.5 metre ($8\frac{1}{2}$ foot) fish killed by taxidermist Michael Schliesser at South Amboy, New Jersey, in 1916, after the notorious sequence of five shark attacks within a 2-week period along the New Jersey coastline, was indeed a great white, although it was identified as such by no less an authority than Dr Frederick A. Lucas, the director of the American Museum of Natural History in New York. Nor is it certain that this was the creature responsible for all five attacks, three of which took place in a tidal creek. Great whites are not known to leave marine waters, but bull sharks (*Carcharhinus leucas*) certainly do, and they are present off the United States east coast during the summer months, though not in any abundance. Furthermore, the 'human remains' found in the shark caught by Schliesser were initially reported as 'the shinbone of a boy and and what appeared to be part of a human rib'. Later the shin bone was categorically stated to be Vansant's (the first fatality) and then, by some chroniclers, Bruder's (the second victim).

Richard Ellis, the American shark authority, has investigated in detail the whole sequence of events along the New Jersey coast during that sultry summer fortnight of July 1916 and, while accepting that the shark killed by Schliesser in Raritan Bay (a salt water enclave open to the sea) probably was a great white as claimed, it is by no means certain that it was responsible for all (or even any) of the five attacks. The depredations of a bull shark seem in some respects a more likely bet, especially for the three attacks that occurred in Matawan Creek.

On the other hand, there is little doubt that the incidence of great white sightings and attacks on the American west coast has increased very substantially from the mid-1970s onwards. San Francisco has become the focus of these occurrences, which rose from perhaps one every couple or so years in the 1950s to nearly fifty in the period 1973–83, including thirteen attacks on surfers.

Great whites probably really are more numerous today than ever before this century in the notorious San Francisco 'red triangle', bounded in the north by Tomales Point, in the south by Monterey Bay and in the west by the Farallon Islands. The reason seems to be that the seals and sea-lions upon which they prey, once decimated by uncontrolled human hunting, are now protected in the United States by a 1972 Act which prohibits the killing or harassment of marine mammals. Their numbers have multiplied beyond anybody's fondest hopes but, as the colonies increase, so sightings of their mortal enemy, the great white shark, have become more frequent. Now San Francisco is regarded as the great white capital of the world and its lovely beaches are no longer the happy family playgrounds they once were.

On 19 December 1981, surfer Lewis Boren disappeared off Monterey. His surf-board came ashore next day with a huge scallop hacked out of its edge, and his body was washed up 24 hours later with most of his left side above the hip missing. Tooth marks in the board, indubitably those of a great white, indicate a fish perhaps over 6 metres (20 feet) in length: mercifully, it seems that Boren must have died almost instantly and, like Fox and Bource, probably never saw his assailant before its jaws closed on his flesh. The Boren fatality served to underline once more how lucky Rodney Fox's escape 18 years earlier had been, for the American's wet suit certainly did not make him any less attractive as a prospective meal to the great white shark that killed him and his injuries demonstrated all too gruesomely what could have happened to Fox if the Australian's assailant had clamped its jaws with real determination instead of making what seems to have been a merely half-hearted assault.

The next year, on the 4th of July public holiday – the mid-summer high spot of the surfing and bathing season – popular Stinson Beach had to be closed because of a great white sighted off shore. The horror engendered by Boren's terrible death had fully alerted the citizens of San Francisco to the danger lurking off their magnificent coastline and nobody was now going to chance their safety when a shark was reported in the vicinity.

Surfers, always at particular risk from shark attacks because of their need to go far out to catch a big roller, now use shorter, more manoeuvrable boards. From below, silhouetted on the surface, a surfer floating on one of these boards with his (or her) legs trailing in the water looks almost uncannily like an elephant seal swimming – and elephant seals are one of the great white's favourite prey species, the shark usually attacking from underneath.

So large protected seal colonies mean more great whites, which mean greater risks for bathers and, in particular, surfers. No one would want to see the marine mammals deprived of their fully deserved protection, but the balance of nature around San Francisco's beautiful bay area has undoubtedly swung in favour of the great white – perhaps the only place in the world where this magnificent shark is not becoming increasingly rare. An additional potential hazard is the possibility that a shark which has once tasted human flesh – not by any means its normal prey – may find it so palatable and so easy to come by that the creature becomes a rogue man-eater, a marine analogue of the man-eating tiger.

Inevitably, the fearsome reputation of the great white has attracted sportsmen seeking to challenge this leviation of the deep to mortal combat with rod-and-line or, latterly, speargun, as well as luring cameramen (and women) to dive in search of the ultimate in submarine photography.

Doyen of great-white anglers was the celebrated writer of Western novels, Zane Grey. Originally trained to be a dentist, like his father, he hankered instead for the great outdoors. Fishing the Delaware vied with Western writing as a recreational activity and, when *The Virginian* was published in 1902 and instantly became a best-seller, the youthful Zane soon put dentistry behind him.

A burgeoning output of cowboy dramas, that included the classic *Riders of the Purple Sage*, quickly made Grey a very rich man with the time and money to devote to his consuming passion for fishing. Only now it was no longer the sylvan reaches of the Delaware and the sophisticated artistry of the freshwater angler. Grey sought the spume and spray of the open ocean and brute force encounters with the world's greatest game fish: tuna, swordfish, marlins, sailfish – and sharks. From the Atlantic to the Pacific, he pursued and fought the largest fish a rod-and-line fisherman could essay to land. Records were his single-minded aim and many were the acrimonious letters he penned in prosecuting his claims to paramountcy as a big game fisherman. This unyielding determination to be credited with the biggest and the heaviest trophies did not endear him to the more casually sporting United States deep-sea angling establishment and Grey eventually became something of a lone wolf, cruising the South Seas on his sleek yacht in perennial pursuit of ever-more impressive prizes.

Sharks really only constituted quite a small part of Grey's angling activities, and he became particularly enamoured of the mako as a target for his line – the way in which these fish jump when hooked is highly spectacular and was described by Grey in articles published by the magazine *Natural History*. Nevertheless he also reeled in his share of great whites, and was photographed aboard ship with the recumbent carcase of a 1,000 pounder that almost dwarfs the small frail figure of the elderly author sitting gloatingly beside it.

The most famous of modern-day great-white fishermen is the Long Island professional, Frank Mundus. Allegedly the model for the bitter, obsessive Captain Quint who came to such an unpleasant end in Peter Benchley's best-seller *Jaws* (providing the book's principal character with a meal), Mundus is in fact a totally dissimilar personality, with a penchant for parading the decks of his 13-metre (42 foot) charter boat *Cricket II* in fancy dress to amuse his customers when the fishing is slow, as well as a proclivity for a little mild practical joking.

As a shark fisherman, however, he is without peer on the American east coast and probably anywhere in the world. He quit school at the age of 16 years, became a crewman on charter boats fishing out of New Jersey ports and, eventually, acquired a vessel of his own, the *Cricket*. Moving up to Montauk, Long Island, Captain (as he was now styled) Frank Mundus became the owner of *Cricket II* and rapidly established himself as a shark fisherman par excellence. His name was made in the biggest possible way in June 1964 when he found a huge female great white following the chum (bait) slick behind *Cricket II* as he headed back to harbour with two porbeagles hanging from the ginpole and a defective engine that needed urgent mechanical attention.

But spluttering engine or no, this was a monster that Mundus had to have. Overboard went all the mackerel bait they had left, along with a baited hook. The shark ate the mackerel and simply spat out the hook. She would have been a rod-and-line absolute record, but obviously these tactics were not going to bring her to the gaff, so Mundus simply harpooned her. In all, five harpoons were thrust home, with red beer kegs attached to the lines, and for 5 hours, the 13 metre (42 foot) boat was towed around the ocean while frantic (and eventually successful) efforts were made to fix the recalcitrant engine.

Even when the monster tired, it took another 3 hours to tow the shark, still struggling feebly, to the shore, where a bulldozer dragged it up the beach and a 0.30 calibre rifle bullet administered the *coup de grâce*. Had Frank Mundus lost this mammoth prize, his estimates of its size would no doubt have been greeted with polite disbelief, but it was impossible to refute the fact of a 5.3 metre ($17\frac{1}{2}$ foot) carcase with a 4 metre (13 foot) girth lying on the beach. It could not be weighed, because there simply was nothing available that would accommodate such a giant, but Mundus estimated she would have tipped the scales at over 2,000 kilograms (4,500 pounds) and when Perry Gilbert, Cornell Professor and celebrated shark expert, visited Montauk a year later to view the trophy's head on the wall of one of the resort's restaurants he agreed that it 'could easily have weighed more than 4,000 pounds'.

One of the largest fish ever caught with hook-and-line was a great white pulled in by Alf Dean at Denial Bay, near Ceduna, South Australia, on 21 April 1959. Using a 58.5 kilogram (130 pound) test line, Dean landed a 5.05 metre (16 foot 10 inch) specimen weighing 1,210 kilograms (2,667 pounds). In 1986 Donnie Braddick and Frank Mundus took a 1,565 kg (3,450 lb) great white 4.9 metres (16 feet 8 inches) long off Montauk, Long Island, using 22.7 kg (50 lb) line, and during November 1987 Vic Hislop reeled in a 2-tonne great white on a handline off Melbourne. Spearfishing for sharks underwater is a conspicuously hazardous pastime, requiring cool nerves and, in the case of the great white, an explosive head on the end of the spear – even a very modestly proportioned specimen in the 3.6 metre (12 foot) class would be too much of a good thing to take on with an unarmed spear. Furthermore, a shark has such a tough hide that an ordinary manually propelled weapon is likely to simply glance off unless the assailant has the skill (or luck) to take out an eye or find the soft, vulnerable belly area around the cloaca. Stories of knife fights with sharks underwater should invariably be treated as highly suspect, because the water's resistance so impedes the striking force of a man's arm that his blade could scarcely be expected to do more than glance off a shark's armoured dermis.

Using an explosive-headed spear, however, a great white measuring 4.2 metres (14 feet) was killed in Australian waters during the 1960s and, for those intrepid skin-divers prepared to let a great white get really close to them, the Australians have developed 'shark billies', which work on a spring principle, and, when rammed against a shark, discharge a shotgun cartridge loaded with 20-gauge pellets at point-blank range.

Photographing great whites offers an even greater hazard than hunting for them with rod-and-line or a speargun. No one would be well advised to swim around anywhere near the vicinity of a great white unprotected and a technique that has been employed with some success is to construct a steel cage in which the photographers can shelter while filming through the bars. Chunks of horse meat or other delicacies are attached to the structure as a shark lure and, even if a great white takes a run at the cage, some of the shock should be absorbed by the freely suspended cage simply swinging away in the water. Nonetheless, great whites of only medium size, around 3 or 3.6 metres (10 or 12 feet) in length, have proved capable of doing quite severe damage to these cages, bending the tough steel structure with ease as their pointed snouts were driven between the bars to try and reach the intrepid photographers within. A fully mature great white, measuring perhaps 6 metres (20 feet), would probably be capable of destroying the cage, as novelist Peter Benchley felt was an only too likely outcome when, in 1974, he was occupying a diving cage off Dangerous Reef, on Australia's Great Barrier Reef. For an American television production, the author of *Jaws* was to be filmed from another cage by underwater-cameraman Stan Waterman, who had been one of the team that completed the film *Blue Water, White Death* (about the great white) in 1970.

On the 'Blue Water' expedition, Waterman on one occasion encountered a great white unexpectedly when diving in an area off Cairns where only smaller sharks were expected to occur. Alone in the water and unprotected by a cage, Waterman was too much of a professional to allow such trivial details to distract him. He focussed up and triggered his camera as the massive grey shape with its accompanying pilot fish cruised towards him, the expressionless black eyes gazing unblinkingly out at this human intruder in the submarine world. Then the huge shark turned almost disdainfully away and continued on to disappear into the blue-green mist of the distant depths. And Waterman had some unique footage in the can – the first film ever shot of a free-swimming great white taken by an unprotected diver.

But the 4.2 metre (14 foot) great white that went for Benchley was a creature of very different mood. This one wanted a meal – and quickly. Only the bars of the cage separated it from one – Benchley – and, from the furious agression of its attacks, there seemed every probability that this barrier would not remain inviolate for long.

Fortunately the steel held and Benchley lived to write another day, but it was an astonishing contrast to Waterman's earlier experiences on the 'Blue Water' expedition, when even great whites attracted to the photographers' diving cages by baits of horse or cow meat and whale-oil chum never really looked vicious enough to jeopardise the security of the protective bars, although they provided some exciting footage for the movie production.

Giant teeth some 12.5 centimetres (5 inches) or so in length recovered from the Pacific floor by the *Challenger* expedition of 1873–76 suggest that stories of great whites measuring 9 or 12 metres (30 or 40 feet) in length may not be entirely imaginative. This nineteenth-century research vessel was dredging the sea floor at a depth of 4,300 metres (14,300 feet) in the

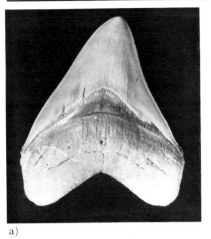

a)   b)

a) A fossil tooth of *Carcharodon megalodon*, 11 centimetres ($4\frac{1}{2}$ inches) high, from the Middle Eocene of Carolina, USA. b) A tooth from an immature specimen of the living species *Carcharodon carcharias* (the great white) measuring 3 centimetres ($1\frac{1}{4}$ inches).

south Pacific at a location known as Station 281 when two large *Carcharodon* teeth were brought up. Both were covered by a coating of manganese dioxide – one only slightly, the other more deeply – and, since it has been determined that this deposit accumulates at a rate of 0.15–1.4 millimetres ($\frac{5}{1000} - \frac{55}{1000}$ of an inch) per 1,000 years, it is possible to work out the length of time that these teeth had been resting on the bottom of the Pacific. The more thickly-coated one, with manganese dioxide 3,640 μ thick, had been there for 24,206 years while the more thinly coated specimen with manganese dioxide only 1,700 μ thick had lain on the sea floor for 11,333 years. Although technically of Pleistocene age, in geological terms these dates are almost modern: the ice of the final glaciation that brought the Pleistocene Ice Age to an (apparently temporary) end was already in retreat 15,000 years ago, and *Homo sapiens* was present in Europe 30,000 years ago, so modern Man was certainly contemporaneous with specimens of *Carcharodon* far exceeding in size any examples so far fished from today's oceans.

Enormous *Carcharodon* teeth also occur as fossils, extending the range of this genus back to at least the Paleocene period, 60 or so million years ago. Assigned to a separate species, (*Carcharodon megalodon*), they are of worldwide distribution, turning up in North America, Britain, Europe, the West Indies, central and South America, Australia, New Zealand and the East Indies. Tantalisingly, nothing else is known of this extinct monster, since its cartilaginous skeleton would only be preserved under exceptionally favourable conditions. However, in 1909, the American Museum of Natural History in New York attempted to reconstruct its jaws on the basis of teeth 10.1 centimetres (4 inches) in length and came up with a mouth 2.74 metres (9 feet) across that had a gape of 1.83 metres

(6 feet). To provide scale, a number of men were photographed sitting inside this extraordinary model and a snout-to-tail measurement of 24 metres (80 feet) was computed for the entire animal.

There is little doubt that this is an over-enthusiastic estimate. For one thing, it was assumed that all the teeth in the jaws were the same size. In fact, the lateral teeth of the living great white are a lot smaller than those in the centre of the jaws and, if this fact is taken into account, an estimate of perhaps 13.1 metres (43 feet) would be more realistic. This is not by any means the maximum theoretical size of *Carcharodon megalodon*, however. Fossil teeth from the appropriately named Sharktooth Hill, near Bakersfield, California, are nearly 15.2 centimetres (6 inches) long and must have belonged to a veritable giant measuring perhaps 16.5 metres (55 feet) with a weight of 20 tonnes (nearly 45,000 pounds). A living specimen of *Carcharodon megalodon* would have been an awe-inspiring sight and apparently there are great whites of approaching 9 metres (30 feet) still existing in today's oceans. Suggestions that the abyssal depths of the Pacific continue to harbour *Carcharodon megalodon* itself seem too far-fetched, however. A fish of such a size would require a substantial amount of food in the form of prey and the great oceanic deeps support only a limited fauna, totally inadequate for the nutritional needs of a 15 metre (50 foot) killer shark.

Despite the almost morbid fascination that the great white engenders, and the thousands of words that have been written about it, *Carcharodon carcharias* is still a creature of mystery. It is known to live principally on fish, from fast-swimming types to sluggish bottom-dwelling skates and rays, with seals and sea-lions also often falling victims of its greedy voracity along the shores of California, the maritime provinces of Canada, New England, South Africa and South Australia. It will also feed on turtles, small cetaceans and the carcases of large whales, and its propensity for seizing swimmers is notorious, but the great white's life history is still obscure. Almost nothing is known of how or where they breed, although during 1934 a pregnant female was allegedly caught in the Mediterranean at Agamy, near Alexandria, and when landed by three boatloads of Egyptian fishermen, after a struggle lasting several hours, it was found to measure 4.2 metres (14 feet) and to weigh $2\frac{1}{2}$ tonnes (5,600 pounds): upon opening it, nine juveniles, each 60 centimetres (2 feet) long and supposedly weighing 486 kilograms (108 pounds), were found inside. Identification of this shark as a great white apparently depends on photographic evidence only and the claimed weight of the juveniles is manifestly suspect, since apart from this one instance no great white less than 1.2 metres (4 feet) long has ever been reported and a 12.7 metre ($4\frac{1}{4}$ foot) specimen caught in 1974 off Bayshore, Long Island, weighed only 16.20 kilograms (36 pounds), a somewhat plumper 1.25 metre (4 foot 2 inch) juvenile accidentally caught in trap nets off Rhode Island tipping the scales at 22.95 kilograms (51 pounds). The mystery of the great white's breeding habits therefore remains essentially unsolved. Furthermore, it has proved impossible to keep specimens alive in aquaria for study. A 2.55 metre ($8\frac{1}{2}$ foot) male hooked off Florida and released in a tank at Marineland simply lay on the bottom for 35 hours until it died, while in August 1980 a 2.1 metre (7 foot), 132 kilogram (300 pound) female accidentally caught in a net off San Francisco was placed in the doughnut-shaped 'roundabout' tank at Golden Gate Park Aquarium but had to be taken out and returned to the sea after 3 days when it became disorientated and began crashing into the side of the tank: electrolysis caused by corrosion in the structure was affecting the shark's electrical receptor system.

Large predators are always relatively few in number compared to the animals on which they prey and *Carcharodon* is obviously not a common genus. In fact, it might even be justifiable to regard it as endangered but there are no statistics of populations on which to base any assessment of its numbers. Reduction of the great white's normal prey species through human depredations has resulted in steady depletion of whale, turtle and seal stocks, so that this mighty shark is already probably hard pressed to hold its own in poached and polluted modern seas (save only on the Californian coast apparently), while an almost obsessive hatred of the great white, nurtured by the media and the motion-picture industry has made the killing of this species appear to be the ultimate macho status symbol, as well as providing a supposedly beneficient service to the world in general and mankind in particular.

Perhaps few people would mourn the passing of the great white. We get along very well without giant carnivorous dinosaurs such as *Tyrannosaurus*, or the extinct sabre-toothed cats, and *Carcharodon* is after all something of an anachronism – a left-over from prehistoric time, unchanged for millions of years save apparently for a substantial reduction in size from the giants of Miocene (or even Pleistocene) days. Yet, in the very magnificence of its superb adaptation to the role of ocean killer, the great white embodies a grace and cruel beauty that the world would surely be the poorer without, as well as leaving still unresolved the tantalising conundrum of its life history: how it is born, how long it lives, where it dies.

Carcharodon is an isurid shark, belonging to a family (Isuridae, some-times known as the Lamnidae) that takes its name from the genus *Isurus* (mako sharks) and includes also the bulky, voracious porbeagles (*Lamna*) as well as several not very well known fossil genera that are now extinct.

Typically pelagic denizens of the open sea, isurids sport the characteris-tic type of colouration found in oceanic sharks, the upper part of their bodies being bluish grey, shading to white on the belly. Collectively, they are known as mackerel sharks – not because mackerel form a major part of their diet (although in temperate waters they do), but in allusion to the accessory stabilising keels that are prominently developed on either side of the tail (Fig. 5.3), superficially resembling the very similar structures seen in mackerel. The spiracle is reduced in isurids and may be absent altogether, its value to a free-swimming form that rarely prowls near the bottom being limited and, although two dorsal fins are present, the posterior one (located immediately above the anal fin) is of only moderate size. The pectoral fins are a graceful sickle-like shape and the tail fin is of

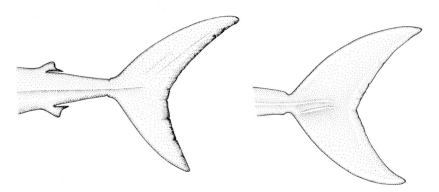

Fig. 5.3. The tails of the fast-swimming mackerel sharks have lateral stabilising keels. In *Isurus* (left) there is only one pair of keels but *Lamna* (right) has a double keel each side, with a small subsidiary stabiliser below the principle one.

approximately half-moon configuration but with the upper lobe always somewhat longer than the lower one – and, in some species, very much longer.

Reproduction is ovo-viviparous, the young being born alive, but it seems likely that, in at least some species, the largest of the unborn young devour their smaller brethren within the mother's body, so that por-beagles, for example, normally have only four young in a litter – two from each oviduct.

Because of their close similarity, the species of *Isurus* and *Lamna* are sometimes included in a single genus, but there are sufficient differences between the mako sharks and the porbeagles to justify separation, although they are undoubtedly closely related and should all be assigned to one and the same family.

Makos (*Isurus*) are quite slenderly proportioned and more elongate than the porbeagles, with the first dorsal fin located rather far back. Unlike the porbeagles, makos (or blue pointers) have smooth-edged teeth that lack auxiliary cusps, an ideal armoury for impaling the large, active fish upon which makos principally subsist, such as scombroids (mackerel, tunny etc.) and clupeids (herrings, tarpon). Makos also probably take squid and are known to attack such formidable adversaries as swordfish: a 328.5 kilogram (730 pound) specimen of *Isurus* taken near Bimini, in the Bahamas, had inside it an almost intact 54 kilogram (120 pound) swordfish complete with sword, while a 360 kilogram (800 pound) mako seen attacking a swordfish off Montauk, Long Island, and later caught was found to contain 67.5 kilograms (150 pounds) of the swordfish's flesh.

Although nowhere near as big or as powerful as a great white, mako sharks can still exceed 3.6 metres (12 feet) in length and are considered dangerous to Man. They are of negligible commercial importance, except as a subject for sport fishermen, who regard them as an exciting game fish: when hooked, a mako will jump perhaps 4.5 metres (15 feet) clear of the

The ferocious tooth batteries of a mako shark (*Isurus*), showing the flexible snout and protrusible jaws.

surface with terrifying energy, a leap that would require an initial take-off speed of 35 kilometres per hour (22 miles per hour), the maximum speed that these fish can achieve probably being something around 56 kilometres per hour (35 miles per hour). Sometimes makos even land in the fishing boat itself, where a quarter of a tonne of fighting fury can do immense damage or cause serious injury to the crew by virtue of its sheer weight. Makos have also been known to attack the hulls of boats, especially if the keel is painted white, and their distinctive teeth are subsequently found embedded in the timber planking.

Like *Carcharodon*, the mako sharks have a long fossil record dating back to the Age of Dinosaurs, their characteristic dentition being found from North America and the West Indies to Europe and Africa, and from South America to Australasia. Some of these teeth, from 20 million-year-old rocks of Miocene age, suggest creatures 6 metres (20 feet) in length weighing nearly 2 tonnes (4,400 pounds).

Usually a solitary creature, the true mackerel shark, *Isurus oxyrinchus*, is often to be found swimming just below the surface with only its big dorsal fin showing. There is one major world-wide species of this genus, the numerous other forms that have been described being simply growth stages of the same animal. The first dorsal fin, for example, is short, broad and round-tipped in juveniles but tall, slender and sharp-pointed in adults, although this feature has been used in the past to distinguish a number of different species. There is, however, a relatively rare species in the Pacific and Indian Oceans with disproportionately long pectoral fins (*Isurus alatus*).

Porbeagles (*Lamna*) also run up to perhaps 4 metres (12 feet) in length, but they are much more heavily built and offer far less exciting sport than makos, never jumping when hooked and tending to become just sluggishly resistant. With their power and weight, they are nonetheless immensely strong and will sometimes take over 300 metres (1,000 feet) of line off a reel, requiring more than an hour of sheer back-breaking effort to play and eventually land. Porbeagles have a pointed snout overhanging the crescentic mouth, which is armed with slender awl-shaped teeth, often exhibiting small subsidiary cusps at the base of the crown; three or four rows of dentition are functional at any one time, this formidable array being designed to capture the fish upon which porbeagles principally feed – herring, cod, whiting, sardines, pilchards, john dory, hake, mackerel, flounders, or dogfish, with squid and cuttlefish also readily taken when the opportunity presents itself. A distinctive feature of *Lamna* is its wide external gill slits, while the first dorsal fin is located well forward on the back (about opposite the rear margin of the pectoral fins) and the characteristic mackerel-like keels on either side of the tail are supplemented by a pair of similar secondary keels situated below the primary pair.

Essentially a denizen of boreal or warm temperate seas, the porbeagles do not occur in the tropics. They are quite common off British and North American coasts, often appearing in loose groups of perhaps twenty individuals in an area of 130 hectares (a half-mile square), although hunting alone rather than in concert. Quite frequently, they will give the impression of playing with floating objects, such as a baulk of timber or even seaweed.

In summer months, porbeagles will come quite close inshore, sometimes into less than 9 metres (30 feet) of water, and very large specimens measuring nearly 3 metres (10 feet) have been caught only a kilometre or so off popular British south coast bathing beaches, notably along the Devon or Cornish coasts and around Ventnor and Sandown in the Isle of Wight. Porbeagles must be regarded as dangerous to bathers and, occasionally, a fisherman who has accidentally caught one in his nets gets bitten when the shark is unexpectedly hauled in.

The North Atlantic porbeagle, *Lamna nasus*, is dark bluish grey above, changing abruptly to white below. Juveniles are very large at birth, a 9 kilogram (20 pound) embryo having been found in a 3 metre (10 foot) female caught in the Gulf of Maine. The embryos absorb their yolk sacs and umbilical cords *in utero* at a very early stage of development (while still retaining external gills and measuring no more than 6 centimetres/$2\frac{1}{2}$ inches in length) and subsequently live by swallowing unfertilised eggs lying adjacent to them in the uterus of the mother, the stomach becoming enormously distended while the throat is expanded.

Pacific species include *Lamna ditropis* in the northern hemisphere and *Lamna philippii* in the south, with *Lamna whitleyi* occurring around Australia and New Zealand. Porbeagles are, if anything, even more venerable than great whites or makos, their fossil teeth being present in rocks as old as the Lower Cretaceous, some 135 million years ago, some of these specimens suggesting the early stage of evolution that might be expected so far back in time.

Several genera of mackerel sharks seem to have become extinct since the Cretaceous, notably *Carcharoides* (known from South America and Australia), *Leptostyrax* from Kansas, *Paraisurus* (reported from Europe, North America and Africa), and *Pseudocorax* from Europe, North America and North Africa, while another alleged isurid, *Squalicorax*, is represented in museum collections by low, triangular-shaped or hook-like teeth, exhibiting serrated edges, from deposits dating back to the Lower Jurassic.

Research indicates that these massive isurid sharks have acquired a means of maintaining their swimming muscles at a consistently higher temperature than that of the surrounding water. The dark muscle tissue that these great fish use to maintain their almost ceaseless swimming runs along the trunk deep in the body, adjacent to the spinal column. Other fish, without the same requirement for continual forward movement, have this muscle more superficially located. Even when isurids are in water as cool as 6°C (42.8°F), this muscle retains a temperature of over 13°C (55.4°F); in water at 11°C (51.8°F), an internal muscle temperature of 20.2°C (68.4°F) is maintained and water at 21.2°C (70.2°F) enables an isurid shark to keep its muscles at 27.2°C (81°F).

Since the power available from vertebrate muscle increases perhaps threefold for every 10°C (24°F) rise in temperature, the need for an endlessly-moving isurid to keep its muscle temperatures as high as possible becomes apparent. The dorsal aorta in these sharks, normally the major vessel carrying oxygenated blood back to the body, is much reduced and the main blood supply to the muscle is via a series of greatly enlarged cutaneous vessels running longitudinally just beneath the outer surface of the body; small vessels originating from the cutaneous artery and vein intermingle to form a network of veins and arteries (densely concentrated in the mako, more diffuse in the porbeagle and great white) running deep into the body and supplying the dark muscle tissue all along the length of the shark from the front of the pectoral fins to the level of the second dorsal. Even the white muscle of these sharks is supplied principally by blood carried in cutaneous vessels that form segmental vascular bands, comprising alternately arranged arteries and veins penetrating into the tissue. Thus the white muscles also conserve heat, having largely lost the supply of blood that originally, in more primitive sharks, was carried from the gills by the dorsal aorta.

Chapter 6
Lesser Killers and Their Kin

Not all the big predatory sharks are isurids, the family to which the great white, the porbeagles and the makos belong. That group is in some ways rather conservative, its members being notable principally for their very large size, but other dangerous sharks have become considerably more advanced in their structure than the isurids and are sometimes very nearly as massive.

None are more curious or pose a greater enigma than the extraordinary hammerheads (Sphyrnidae), whose common name so aptly describes the head which is expanded sideways and flattened dorso-ventrally, with the eyes and nostrils carried at the extremities of this remarkable evolutionary freak (Fig. 6.1).

Apart from their hammerheaded skulls, these sharks are quite normally proportioned, with two dorsal fins (the first of which is the larger and has a narrow triangular shape) and a caudal fin exhibiting a well developed sub-terminal notch and an antero-ventral lobe. Reproduction is viviparous, the yolk-sac placenta being inextricably interdigitated with the uterine wall while in some (but not all) species the umbilical cord possesses numerous finger-like projections (appendiculae) believed to have a respiratory function. All the hammerheads are coloured a deep olive or brownish grey above, becoming paler below, and the larger members of this genus may reach up to 6 metres (20 feet) in length – a size which makes them decidedly dangerous.

The shovel-head or bonnet shark (*Sphyrna tiburo*) is a small species, measuring only some 1.5 metres (5 feet) when full grown, in which the distinctive broadening of the head is only incipiently developed to give a

Fig. 6.1. The heads, in ventral view, of (left) the relatively conservative *Sphyrna tiburo*, known as the bonnet shark, and (right) the highly specialised great hammerhead (*Sphyrna blochii*), in which the expanded cranium of this family achieves its most extreme development.

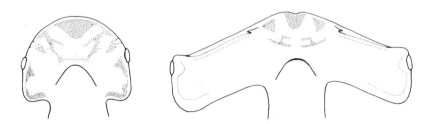

kidney-shaped structure. A denizen of shallow water in the western Atlantic and eastern Pacific, the shovel-head often enters bays or estuaries where it feeds principally on small fish and various invertebrates (crabs, shrimps, isopods, bivalves, squid etc.). Closely allied to *Sphyrna tiburo* is the much larger great hammerhead (*Sphyrna tudes*) of the Atlantic, which sometimes measures 4.5 metres (15 feet) overall, *Sphyrna media* from the eastern Pacific, the southern Caribbean and the southwest Atlantic, and *Sphyrna corona* from the Pacific (Colombia to southern Mexico).

The typical hammerheads include *Sphyrna zygaena*, the common species of temperate seas in both hemispheres (it is apparently absent from the tropics) which occurs in summer around the southern coasts of Britain and Newfoundland and runs up to 4.5 metres (15 feet) in length, as well as several purely tropical forms: the arched hammerhead (*Sphyrna mokarran*) that seems to have a preference for the waters of isolated oceanic islands, the yellow or scalloped hammerhead (*Sphyrna lewini*) and a west African species (*Sphyrna couardi*) with distinctive white-tipped pectoral fins.

Observations of scalloped hammerheads in the Gulf of California indicate that, during the daytime, this species congregates in large polarised schools of twenty to one hundred fish, all the individuals swimming in approximately the same direction, apparently following the sharks in the leading ranks. Females outnumber males by anything up to four to one in these schools, the purpose of which is still obscure. They may possibly provide opportunities for mating, as suggested by some behaviour patterns involving erratic swimming, although actual copulation has not been observed; grouping for defence seems unlikely as the scalloped hammerhead has no known enemies in the Gulf of California. Hunting does not take place during the daytime, so there is no reason for these sharks to congregate as a means of more effectively catching prey. In fact, evidence from individuals tagged with telemetry transmitters indicates that, at night, the schools break up as members go their separate ways in quest of food.

The most extreme degree of specialisation is seen in *Sphyrna blochii* (sometimes assigned to a separate subgenus, *Eusphyra*), which has a grotesquely widened head (Fig. 6.1) and a reduced number of vertebrae. This bizarre shark is restricted to the Indo-Pacific area (northern Australia, the southern Philippines, the Persian Gulf).

The function of the broadened skull, with its greatly expanded olfactory and orbital region, has never been explained. The position of the eyes and nostrils at the extremities of the hammerhead structure might perhaps give these sharks a greater facility in gauging the distances that separate them from prospective prey, sensed either by vision or by smell. The broad, flat wings of the head may possibly act as hydrofoils, making hammerheads more efficient swimmers with enhanced manoeuvrability. Alternatively, the abundant provision of electrically sensitive ampullae of Lorenzini across the broad head of *Sphyrna* may enable this shark to use its hammer-like cranial region as a detector for picking up bio-electricity emanating from the sting rays, upon which the shark preys, as they lie buried in the sandy sea floor; obviously the transversely expanded head would enable the widest possible area to be scanned for prospective prey.

No one knows why the hammerheads, alone among sharks, have evolved this distinctive structure, but whatever its purpose, the group has enjoyed a long and successful career, their fossil teeth being present as early as the Eocene in the northern hemisphere as well as occurring in the Miocene of Africa and Australia and the Pliocene of the East Indies and South America.

Still fished commercially to some extent for skins and liver oil, hammerheads are powerful adversaries for game fishermen and often fight ferociously until they have been pulled right alongside the boat for gaffing. They are widely regarded as being very unreliable – sometimes sluggish and torpid, on other occasions reacting with uncompromising viciousness. The extent of their potential ferocity may be gauged from the unrelenting way in which they chase sting rays across sandbanks, eating this prickly prey with relish and apparently ignoring the spines that frequently become embedded in their mouths, occasionally injuring the area where replacement teeth form, so that a whole series of malformed teeth are generated.

Some of the most beautiful of all sharks are numbered amongst the Carcharhinidae, a large family that includes the supremely elegant grey sharks (*Carcharhinus*), the powerful, but equally sleek, great blue (*Prionace*) and the rather more heavily built tiger shark (*Galeocerdo*), as well as a number of lesser types.

They are known popularly as réquin or requiem sharks, names apparently coined by French and Portuguese seamen over 300 years ago. In his *History of Caribbean Islands*, published in 1666, J. Davies wrote that the 'shark fish' was known as the requiem '. . . that is to say Rest, haply because he is wont to appear in fair weather'.

All of the carcharhinids, large or small, are slim, sinuous swimmers, characterised by elongate, streamlined bodies with pointed, depressed snouts and unkeeled heterocercal tails. The eye is provided with a nictitating membrane and the last one or two gill slits on each side are

Fig. 6.2. Teeth of the lesser killers. Dentition, upper jaw above and lower jaw below, of a) the oceanic white-tip (*Carcharhinus longimanus*), b) the common hammerhead (*Sphyrna zygaena*), c) the tiger shark (*Galeocerdo cuvier*), d) the great blue shark (*Prionace glauca*), e) the thresher shark (*Alopias vulpinus*) and f) the sand shark (*Odontaspis taurus*).

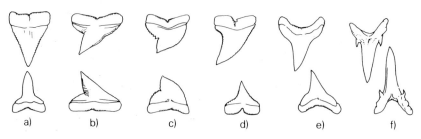

located above the base of the long pectoral fin, but there are no grooves connecting the nostrils to the crescentic mouth, a feature possessed by many other groups of sharks. Along the jaws, there are multiple rows of wickedly efficient, single-cusped, blade-like teeth (Fig. 6.2), designed to act in concert as a fearful sawing mechanism that will slice whole mouthfuls of flesh from a victim.

Carcharhinus itself is represented by around twenty-five valid living species occurring in tropical and warm temperate seas throughout the world, although in excess of a hundred allegedly different species have been published. The first dorsal fin of *Carcharhinus* is set rather far back, which enhances the impression of streamlined speed that characterises grey sharks, while the second dorsal fin and the anal fin are dispro-portionately small. The tail fin has a clearly defined lower lobe, the pelvics are of quadrilateral shape, with no elongation of the inner corners, and the pectoral fins are elongate and gracefully curved. Males have a fan-like cartilaginous structure within their claspers that apparently expands to anchor this intromittent organ within the female's oviduct during copula-tion. In *Carcharhinus* (as in *Prionace*, *Hemigaleus* and *Scoliodon*), the female, after mating, stores the male's sperm in the shell gland of her uterus until the spring of the following year, when ovulation takes place and fertilisa-tion can be accomplished. A yolk-sac placenta is developed, the gestation period ranging from 8–12 months, and there are around fourteen young in a litter. Juveniles measure 40–60 centimetres (16–24 inches) at birth, grow to over 80 centimetres (32 inches) within a year, and become sexually mature at 2 years.

Among the more familiar representatives of *Carcharhinus* are the brown or sandbar sharks (*Carcharhinus plumbeus*), which have markedly ridged backs and occur in shallow water almost worldwide, the smalltail shark (*Carcharhinus porosus*), which only grows to a length of around 1.2 metres (4 feet), the silky shark (*Carcharhinus falciformis*), with notably small, flat denticles that make its hide feel silky to the touch, the powerful *Carchar-hinus longimanus* (the oceanic whitetip) of the Atlantic and Mediterranean, growing to a length of 3.6 metres (12 feet) or more, the black-nosed shark (*Carcharhinus acronotus*), which rarely exceeds 2 metres (6 feet) and ranges the western Atlantic from Rio de Janeiro to North Carolina, and the small blacktip (*Carcharhinus limbatus*). The blacktipped reef shark (*Carcharhinus melanopterus*) is common in lagoons or along reefs in the shallows of the Indian and Pacific Oceans, the massive dusky shark (*Carcharhinus obscurus*) of the Atlantic, Pacific and Indian Oceans measures as much as 3.75 metres (12 feet), and *Carcharhinus gangeticus* is a 2.1 metre (7 foot) species that prowls the bathing ghats of Calcutta, feeding on partially-burned bodies and occasionally taking a bite at a live one, while the remarkable cub shark or bull shark (*Carcharhinus leucas*) is nominally a denizen of the tropical western Atlantic but also occurs in Lake Nicaragua and its Caribbean outlet, the Rio San Juan, as well as in Lake Yzabal (Guatema-la) and the Rio Dulce system, and has been reported in the Mississippi.

Grey sharks seem to be essentially denizens of shallow waters or the surface layers of the ocean, frequently hunting at night with the aid of

A blackfin reef shark (*Carcharhinus melanopterus*). This rather blunt-nosed species grows to about 1.8 metres (6 feet).

their keenly developed sense of smell. They feed principally on fish but must be regarded as potentially dangerous to Man, a number of attacks by grey sharks having been recorded, while around Lake Nicaragua and along the South African coast fatalities attributable to *Carcharhinus leucas* are well documented so that this species at least must be regarded as a man-eater.

In the case of the Galapagos shark (*Carcharhinus galapagensis*), a suspected inclination to seek human prey was gruesomely confirmed in the Virgin Islands (far from this species' normal eastern Pacific range) during 1963, when Lieutenant John Gibson was savagely mauled by a shark. After his body was dragged ashore, one hand was found to be missing and there were enormous bite marks in his left shoulder and right hip and thigh, the femoral artery having been severed in such a manner that death from haemorrhage would have ensued within 15 seconds. Next day, a shark containing human remains, including a right hand, was caught and proved to be a Galapagos shark. The Zambesi shark (*Carcharhinus leucas*) had demonstrated its lethality 3 years earlier when, on Christmas Eve 1960, an individual of this species seized 25-year-old Petrus Sithole while he was swimming just outside the shark barrier protecting the beach at Margate, near Natal, on South Africa's eastern coast. Sithole was heard to scream and onlookers saw the upper part of his body hurled up out of the water with arms flailing wildly. The wretched man then fell forward without another sound and, shortly afterwards, the waves washed his hideously mutilated body onto the shore. Both his legs had been taken off, the left one at the hip, the right one at the knee.

The grey reef shark or silky shark (*Carcharhinus falciformis*, which includes *Carcharhinus menisorrah*) is also aggressive and notable for the display of so-called 'agonistic' behaviour that it exhibits, apparently as a prelude to attacking. Divers who have approached these sharks (or been approached by them) in their Pacific home waters found that the creatures sometimes adopted an erratic manner of swimming with back arched, snout raised and pectoral fins lowered that resulted in an exaggerated weaving and rolling motion. Seemingly a warning of impending attack, this agonistic display became particularly pronounced if a shark was cornered against a section of reef or rock face and had no obvious means of escape. In March 1961, Jim Stewart, a diver engaged in installing a tidal-wave-recording device at Wake Island, was severely bitten on the arm by a grey reef shark that presaged its onslaught with an agonistic display. Subsequently, in 1976, Shot Miller and ichthyologist John Randall from Honolulu's Bishop Museum, were diving near the deep entrance channel to Enewetok lagoon when a grey reef shark approached Randall from behind in an agonistic posture. Miller struck his SCUBA tank with his powerhead defensive weapon to warn Randall, whereupon the shark turned on Miller, whose powerhead chose this moment to misfire. The shark, about 1.4 metres ($4\frac{1}{2}$ feet) long, slashed the side of Miller's face with its upper jaw, cutting away his face mask and opening up gashes that required twenty-five stitches. Two years later, again in the Enewetok lagoon, laboratory manager Michael deGruy and diving partner Phil Light took a flash photograph of a grey reef shark in agonistic display some 2 metres ($6\frac{1}{2}$ feet) away from them. Instantly the creature attacked, coming in so fast that deGruy had virtually no time to defend himself. Attempting to thrust his camera at the shark, deGruy was seized by the right upper arm, elbow and forearm. Light came to his aid with a shark billy and was himself attacked, sustaining a lacerated left hand. After seizing Light's billy in its jaws and shaking it viciously the shark made off, leaving the two divers to make their escape. Both had to be taken to Honolulu for surgery.

The use of a small two-man submersible at Enewetok in 1971 demonstrated that the local grey reef sharks would not hesitate to attack an adversary of considerably superior size. Marine biologist Walter A. Starck, accompanied by laboratory manager Rhett McNair, followed a shark in agonistic display, only to have it turn and make a head-on attack, its teeth severely scoring the 1.25 centimetre ($\frac{1}{2}$ inch) thick transparent plexiglass hood of the submersible. A specially designed, shark-proof, single-man submersible was taken to Enewetok in 1977 and 1978 by Donald S. Nelson of California State University, Long Beach, and a team of accompanying scientists. Setting out to deliberately provoke agonistic behaviour in grey reef sharks, the submersible pilots sustained ten attacks on their craft by this species, some being double strikes. Usually launched from a distance of about 6 metres (20 feet), the attacks came in with

A grey reef shark (*Carcharhinus amblyrhynchos*), of the Pacific and eastern Indian Ocean, which may reach 2.5 metres (about 8 feet) in length.

stunning rapidity: one shark required only 0.33 seconds to dart in, bite the forward motor and break the propeller, disabling the submersible.

It may be that *Carcharhinus falciformis* is a territorial species and, in these instances, was seeking to warn off interlopers, or perhaps the agonistic display is designed to deter prospective rivals for the local food supply: on one occasion, a grey reef shark was seen to adopt the typical threatening behaviour pattern when approached by a hammerhead of considerably larger size.

The facility with which *Carcharhinus leucas* transits from the salt waters of the Caribbean to the freshwater of Lake Nicaragua has been a source of considerable interest, because sharks are geared to life in a marine environment. Their excretory system is specially adapted to retain nitrogenous waste, largely in the form of urea, in the bloodstream, thus maintaining the animal's total osmotic pressure at a level comparable to that of the surrounding saltwater and preventing dehydration. So what happens when a blue shark leaves the Caribbean and swims up the rapids of the Rio San Juan to Lake Nicaragua? It was once thought that the sharks which hunt the waters of this lake were a separate land-locked species left behind when some former channel leading to the Pacific closed up. In fact, they quite readily negotiate the lake's eastern exit to the Caribbean and the freshwater population is indistinguishable from the offshore grey sharks. They all apparently belong to the same species, *Carcharhinus leucas*.

The Lake Nicaragua sharks, it seems, retain less urea in their blood once they leave the sea and also reduce the level of salts in their body fluids. They can therefore maintain a viable osmotic balance between their bodies and the freshwater of the river system and lake, despite incurring a slightly higher total water content and a smaller ratio of extracellular to intracellular fluids.

One species of grey shark, *Carcharhinus perezii*, the reef shark of the Mexican east coast, is often found in underwater caves such as those at Isla Mujeres, where they lie motionless in a manner entirely at odds with the belief that all sharks have to keep perpetually on the move in order to breathe. Perhaps these dormant specimens, which can be aroused only with difficulty and are too soporific to pose any danger, are making use of freshwater upwellings to loosen parasites infesting their skin, mouths or gills, which remoras busily remove: if this is the case, there may be sufficient movement of oxygen-enriched water to provide them with a respiratory current.

Just as elegantly proportioned as *Carcharhinus*, but of somewhat larger size, the great blue shark (*Prionace glauca*) reaches a length of 4.5 metres (15 feet) and also differs from the other grey sharks in the slightly more posterior location of the first dorsal fin (which is closer to the level of the pelvic fins than to the pectorals). *Prionace* occurs world wide in tropical and warm temperate seas, with small individuals sometimes ranging as far north as the British Isles. Great blues seem equally at home in coastal waters or out in the open ocean, but do not normally dive to any great depth, preferring to swim lazily in the surface waters with the first dorsal fin and the tip of the tail fin projecting clear of the water. This sluggish demeanour changes dramatically when great blues are hunting, surging powerfully in pursuit of herring, mackerel, sardines (in European waters), spiny dogfish, cod, haddock, American pollock, anchovies and (in the tropics) flying fish. Great blues are notorious for the voracity with which they attack whale carcases near whaling ships or whaling stations and, when in the grip of a feeding frenzy, seem totally indifferent to injury from blubber spades wielded by the seamen. Because of this taste for whale meat, *Prionace* is sometimes known as the blue whaler.

Although predominantly blue, as its common name indicates, *Prionace* has a white belly, the dark indigo shade of the back becoming progressively paler down the flanks. Reproduction is viviparous, with a well developed yolk-sac placenta attached to the uterine wall (only the right oviduct is present and functional). Mating occurs in summer, the male thrusting one clasper into the female's cloaca while his rough 'love play' leaves teeth marks gashing the skin of his partner's back. Fortunately the female has skin more than twice as thick as that of the male (in fact deeper than the length of his teeth) so little real harm is done. The sperm are stored in the female's shell gland until the following spring, when ovulation occurs and fertilisation is accomplished, up to 135 embryos being known to develop in a single litter. Gestation requires 9 to 12 months, birth taking place in oceanic areas during the summer. Commercially the great blue is not of any great value, its flesh having an unattractive taste.

Prionace must be regarded as a dangerous species, but even more ill-omened is the closely related tiger shark (*Galeocerdo*). Up to 6 metres (20 feet) in length and bulkily proportioned, with a well nourished, fully mature specimen weighing in at as much as 1,300 kilograms (3,000 pounds), the 'tiger' is a world wide terror of tropical and subtropical seas, taking porpoises, turtles, sea-birds, sea-lions, other weaker sharks, all kinds of fish – including even the formidable sting ray (*Trygon*), whose spines often remain embedded in the shark's jaws or body – crabs, squids, octopus, bivalves, gastropods, horse shoe crabs, lobsters and tunicates – as well as injudicious swimmers or fishermen. *Galeocerdo* has large, flat, sickle-shaped teeth that readily distinguish it from other members of the family, the triangular, pointed crowns projecting obliquely outward with coarsely serrate edges and a deeply notched outer margin.

Reproduction is ovo-viviparous, from ten to eighty-four embryos being present within a single gravid female at any one time (average thirty to fifty); they have no placental connection with the mother and some will be more fully developed than others. The young are born at any time of the year and measure only 0.5 metres (18 inches) when they emerge.

Tiger sharks have been seen to pursue sting rays in only a metre or so of water, but also occur far out to sea. Generally sluggish until stimulated, the tiger can be an exciting game fish that fights hard for some hours. It bites on large objects with a rolling motion, so that the teeth cut rather like a saw, and can easily chew a piece out of a turtle's shell, or hack flesh from other sharks (e.g. those entangled in nets). *Galeocerdo* also takes carrion

Sleekly streamlined for deadly speed, the great blue shark (*Prionace glauca*) may grow to nearly 5 metres (about 16 feet) in length.

(dead sheep, dogs, poultry etc.), and is frequently found to contain such innutritious items as lumps of coal, tin cans and cigarette packets that have been indiscriminately swallowed. In Senegal, in 1948, a native tom-tom 27 centimetres ($10\frac{3}{4}$ inches) high and 25 centimetres ($9\frac{3}{4}$ inches) in diameter and weighing 6 kilograms ($13\frac{1}{2}$ pounds) was found in a 226 kilogram (500 pound) tiger shark, whose stomach had been considerably chafed by this curio. The gastric juices of *Galeocerdo* appear to be mainly strong hydrochloric acid, fully capable of digesting bones, but somehow or other these sharks seem able to keep food items relatively fresh in their stomachs for long periods of time, as well as having a capacity for regurgitating unwanted objects – although for tom-toms it would seem to be a one-way trip!

It is apparently difficult to keep tiger sharks alive in an aquarium for very long, but in April 1935, a 4.2 metre (14 foot) specimen found tangled in a fishing net and placed in the Coogee Aquarium, Australia, survived for a week and acquired instant notoriety by suddenly regurgitating most of the contents of its stomach: a smelly brown scum in which floated the remains of a rat, a dead sea-bird – and a human arm with a piece of rope round its wrist. The still largely undigested limb bore a tattoo of two

Readily identified by its bluntly rounded nose, the deadly tiger shark (*Galeocerdo cuvier*) is one of the most powerful carcharhinids.

boxers and had belonged to a well known member of the Sydney underworld, James Smith, who had mysteriously disappeared. It had evidently been severed before the shark swallowed it and, when the unfortunate tiger died 3 days later, it was opened up to see if it contained any other grisly evidence of what was obviously a gangland killing, but the stomach proved to be empty.

In a subsequent court case, it was alleged that Smith, a former amateur boxer, had been involved with Patrick Brady and Reginald Holmes in murder threats, forgery and conspiracy to defraud an insurance company by wrecking a yacht (the *Pathfinder*). The scheme misfired, villains fell out and Smith 'disappeared'. His body was supposed to have been dismembered and stuffed in a tin box, which was then dropped in the sea – all except for the arm, which would not go in and was simply heaved overboard with a weight attached to it by rope, eventually providing a wandering tiger shark with an unexpected snack. Holmes agreed to give evidence for the prosecution but committed suicide – at the second attempt – and without his testimony the crown case was eventually thrown out.

The largest known authenticated specimen of a tiger shark, measuring 6.23 metres (20 feet 9 inches) and weighing 792 kilograms (1,760 pounds), was caught off Taboga, Gulf of Panama, in 1922; a 5.4 metre (18 foot) example caught in a net at Newcastle, New South Wales, early in 1954 weighed 1,512 kilograms (3,360 pounds).

Attacks on human beings attributable to tiger sharks include the double fatality at Kirra Beach, Coolangatta, Australia on 12 October 1937, when Norman Girvan was seized 100 metres from the beach and would-be rescuer Jack Brinkley sustained such a severe mauling that he died after being rushed to hospital. A 382.5 kilogram (850 pound) female tiger was caught next day and, on opening the stomach, various pieces of human legs and arms were discovered, including a right hand, identified by a characteristic scar as Girvan's. In the United States, Claude Ormond was lost in a shipwreck off the Florida coast on 20 October 1943, gruesome evidence of his fate being disclosed when a forearm, leg and pelvis were found in a 4.2 metre (14 foot) tiger taken at Baker's Haulover, near Miami Beach.

Fiercely voracious, the tope (*Galeorhinus galeus*) is common in the eastern Atlantic and the Pacific. Up to 2 metres ($6\frac{1}{2}$ feet) long, it is a bottom-dweller preying on small fishes, crustaceans, starfish and shellfish, as well as scavenging.

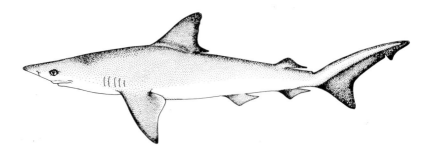

Fig. 6.3. The sharp-nosed shark (*Rhizoprionodon terraenovae*) of eastern North America. A carcharhinid about 1 metre (3¼ feet) in length.

Billy Weaver, the son of a well known Honolulu restaurant owner, met his death in the jaws of a tiger shark on 13 December 1958, while surfing on an air mattress off Lanikai, on Oahu's east coast. Young Billy's death triggered a purge on sharks in Oahu waters that resulted in a 1959 catch of over 500 individuals, seventy-one being tigers – a remarkably high proportion that indicates the presence of a substantial *Galeocerdo* population off the island. In Jurien Bay, Western Australia, during August 1967, spearfisherman Bob Bartle was seized round the waist by a tiger shark with a jaw a metre wide that bit him in two when diving companion Lee Warner buried a spear in the creature's head in an attempt to pierce its brain. 'It hit with a solid clunk,' recalled Warner, 'but it didn't seem to affect it.'

Powerful and vicious, the tiger is probably responsible for at least some of the killings and maulings attributed to great whites. Commercially, the species has a limited value for its skin and for liver oil.

Galeocerdo makes its first authenticated appearance in the fossil record during Eocene times and was probably descended from *Galeorhinus* (the tope), which is of somewhat older origin and represents a more structurally conservative level of evolution. Of slender proportions and brownish or dusky grey hue, topes measure 2 metres (6½ feet) or more in length and hunt along the sea bottom at depths of 40–400 metres (130–1,300 feet) for small fish, crustaceans, starfish and shellfish, as well as scavenging when the opportunity presents itself. The modern species, *Galeorhinus galeus*, is common in the eastern Atlantic and Mediterranean, as well as occurring in the Pacific, the East Indies and Australasia, but is apparently inexplicably absent from the western Atlantic; fossil species occur throughout the Cenozoic after first appearing in the Paleocene, some 60 million years ago.

Other carcharhinids include *Aprionodon*, with slender symmetrical teeth (*Aprionodon isodon*, the round-nosed shark of the Atlantic), *Scoliodon* from the Pacific and Indian Oceans, (notable for the very small size of its eggs, which measure only 1 millimetre/$\frac{3}{100}$ inch when mature), *Hypoprion* (a close relative of *Scoliodon* that includes *Hypoprion palasorrah*, the lesser blue shark), *Loxodon* (common in the Indian Ocean and around the Philippines) and *Rhizoprionodon* (Fig. 6.3) which is of world wide occurrence in warm shallow seas.

A frequently encountered form off the Florida coast is the lemon shark (*Negaprion brevirostris*), a blunt-snouted species which owes its common name to a yellowish brown colouration, fading to yellow on the belly. The lemon shark occurs from New Jersey south to northern Brazil, ranging across the Caribbean where it is particularly numerous on the Bahamas banks. Essentially an inshore species attaining a length of 3.3 metres (11 feet), it is usually found at a depth of about 36 metres (120 feet) but may occur as deep as 400 metres (1,300 feet), although the relatively small eyes are apparently not designed for vision in poorly illuminated depths. Experiments have demonstrated that the eyes of lemon sharks compensate rapidly for bright light by constriction of the pupil. Dark adaptation, however, is a slower process, involving withdrawal of melanin from the melanophores shielding the tapetum as well as dilation of the pupil, which requires a total of 85 minutes to achieve maximum aperture (the pupillary area doubles in the first 2 minutes, then doubles once more in 5 to 7 minutes and again in 40 to 45 minutes).

Lemon sharks sometimes occur in loose schools of twenty or so individuals, often segregated by sex. Mating seems to take place in spring and early summer (and has once been witnessed in an aquarium at the Mote Marine Laboratory, Miami), with gestation lasting about 12 months. The ovarian eggs are up to 4 centimetres ($1\frac{1}{2}$ inches) in diameter and invested by a golden-brown cellophane-like material twisted at each end to form long crimped cords that are bunched up and deeply embedded in the uterine wall. By the time the egg yolk is consumed, a pseudoplacenta has formed and, at birth, the five to seventeen young in the litter are about 60 centimetres (2 feet) long, requiring just over 7 years to reach sexual maturity at a length of 2.4 metres (8 feet). In adolescent males, the claspers initially project only slightly beyond the pelvic fins but grow very rapidly although remaining flexible; ultimately calcification imparts rigidity, which is a better measure of sexual adulthood than maturation of the testes.

The food of *Negaprion brevirostris* includes fish – among them sting rays, (whose spines are often found embedded in the jaws of lemon sharks), guitar fish and cowfish – sea-birds, crustaceans and octopuses. Other species of the genus (*Negaprion sitankaiensis* from the Sulu archipelago, *Negaprion fronto* from the Pacific coasts of Mexico and Costa Rica, *Negaprion acutidens*, the sharp-toothed shark of the Indian and Pacific Oceans) presumably have a similar diet.

Work by Samuel H. Gruber of the University of Miami indicates that young lemon sharks, which are born in shallow-water grass flats or lagoons, tend to remain within quite a small home area of perhaps only 6–8 square kilometres (3.6–4.8 square miles), gradually extending their range until, in late adolescence, they are encompassing a territory of around 300 square kilometres (180 square miles). Once full maturity is achieved, they venture out along reefs to deep offshore waters and may undertake long migrations.

A favourite subject for aquarium behavioural experiments, the elegant lemon shark (*Negaprion*) is one of the carcharhinid group and grows to about 3.5 metres (about $11\frac{1}{2}$ feet).

Measurements of the lemon shark's metabolic rate – the manner in which it converts food into energy – indicate that young individuals (fully grown specimens are too large for laboratory observation) consume about 200 milligrams of oxygen per kilogram of body weight per hour, which means they burn around 1.2 kilocalories every hour. These are mean values for a 24-hour period, however, and lemon sharks have a higher metabolic rate at night than during the day: they are particularly active at sunset and sunrise and probably do much of their hunting during the hours of darkness.

The blood of lemon sharks has an astonishingly high affinity for oxygen, becoming completely saturated at a partial pressure some 200 per cent. less than that of most other fish. When pursuing its prey (or fleeing from a greater predator), these creatures can temporarily boost the amount of oxygen available for instant energy production by drawing off most of the blood-bound oxygen on the arterial side of their circulation and, at the same time, opening up an extra 20 per cent. of gill surface to augment oxygen exchange from the surrounding water.

Commercially, lemon sharks yield a heavy hide that makes excellent leather, large fins for the Chinese trade and good quality meat, while the liver oil yields an abundance of Vitamin A. *Negaprion* is very tolerant of high water temperatures (e.g. 29°C/85°F) and restriction of movement – specimens hooked during the night on set lines will still be alive the following morning, a time interval sufficient to kill most species of shark if they are unable to move and hence keep water flowing through their gills. In fact, lemon sharks can, if they wish, rest on the sea bed, passively pumping water over their gills, but in doing so they consume 9 per cent. more energy than they would if they simply kept swimming.

Fossil teeth of carcharhinids occur fairly commonly in Tertiary marine deposits all over the world, but reports of the group in rocks of Mesozoic age are relatively rare and usually none too well documented. Possibly these sleek sharks represent a later stage of evolution than the massive isurids, which were evidently becoming widespread while dinosaurs still roamed the Earth: grey sharks are exceedingly abundant today and evidently enjoy considerable success as oceanic predators, so it is at least arguable that they constitute the ultimate structural refinement of the basic lamniform type.

One notably small oceanic lamniform is *Pseudocarcharias*, the crocodile shark, which only reaches about a metre ($3\frac{1}{4}$ feet) in length and has highly protrusible jaws with slender, hook-like teeth. It is usually assigned to its own special family, the Pseudocarchariidae, but seems to be a rather phylogenetically isolated creature, with no other close living relatives and no known fossil ancestors. Few specimens have ever been caught, but that does not necessarily signify extreme rarity. The diminutive size of *Pseudocarcharias* would make it liable to be overlooked in a large catch – just another small shark to be casually dismissed – and it might quite easily exist in some numbers in deep, inaccessible parts of the ocean. In the meantime, it remains something of an oddity among lamniforms, a seemingly quite specialised genus of unusually modest dimensions whose habits and way of life are to all intents and purposes quite unknown.

Distinguished primarily by the inordinate length of their huge tails, the thresher sharks (Alopiidae) are probably more closely related to the great whites, makos and porbeagles than to grey sharks or hammerheads. They are not really unduly big, although considerably larger than the little crocodile shark. They are nonetheless powerful enough to be potentially dangerous if encountered in the water and deserve   considerable circumspection when still alive after being caught and landed.

Known also as the thrasher, whip-tailed shark, fox shark, swingletail or swiveltail, *Alopias* does not normally weigh more than perhaps 450 kilograms (1,000 pounds), despite an overall length that may be as much as 6 metres (20 feet). The greatly elongate upper lobe of the tail will contribute as much as half of this measurement, the sleek dark brown, violet or black body with its white belly being relatively small.

Threshers live primarily on fish, notably herring, shad, mackerel and pilchard in temperate latitudes, and it is generally believed that the extraordinary tail is used to 'thrash' a school of frightened, milling fish into a compact mass, so that the shark can then charge in with mouth agape, readily seizing victims with its small , flattened, triangular teeth. Accurate, authenticated observations of this alleged practice are hard to find, however, and this suggested explanation for the thresher's long tail must be regarded as somewhat speculative. Perhaps, after all, it is a physical aberration that simply developed because it had no deleterious effect on its owner's survival prospects and serves no particular specialised purpose requiring explanation.

Alopias occurs virtually worldwide in tropical and temperate seas, the common form being *Alopias vulpinus*. In the western Atlantic, there is a species (*Alopias superciliosus*, the large-eyed thresher) with disproportionately large eyes, fewer teeth than its more usually encountered relative and the dorsal fin located well back along the body which may perhaps be a denizen of deep water where the light is very dim, while other species have been described from Formosa (*Alopias pelagicus*, *Alopias profundus*) and Australasia (*Alopias caudatus*).

Threshers reproduce ovo-viviparously, two to four young, measuring from 1.2–1.6 metres (4–5¼ feet) in length, being born in a litter. They are exciting fish to catch, jumping repeatedly when hooked, but their flailing tails can cause severe injuries to fishemen when they are being gaffed and hauled aboard a boat if due care is not taken. It has been suggested that these sharks really do use their tails as offensive weapons under such circumstances, although the alleged ability of threshers to stun or kill a single fish by aiming a blow at it with this exaggerated caudal appendage seems unlikely. If the thresher can get as near as that to its intended victim, then a quick snap of the jaws would seem to be an easier, surer method of securing a meal. Even more improbable is the proposal that sightings of the so-called 'Loch Ness monster' are attributable to a thresher shark's long, curved tail projecting above the water like a serpent's curved neck. Threshers have not been reported anywhere from freshwater but this does not mean that they cannot survive in lakes or rivers – the grey sharks of Lake Nicaragua manage without difficulty: it is also conceivable that a shark could follow a fishing boat into the Caledonian Canal from the Moray Firth and through the various locks that lead to Loch Ness. Conceivable, but not perhaps very likely.

Fossil thresher shark teeth are not particularly common, although examples as old as the Eocene indicate that this family has been in existence for at least 50 million years.

Very different from the elegant, streamlined carcharhinids and threshers are the nurse or carpet sharks (orectolobids), an ancient group dating back to the early Jurassic, 190 million years ago, that some scientists regard as comprising half a dozen separate families grouped in a single order.

Essentially sea-floor-dwellers of tropical and subtropical oceans, sometimes occurring at considerable depths, these rather sluggish creatures spend much of their time lying on the bottom, occasionally bestirring themselves sufficiently to catch small fish or search for invertebrates (squid, cuttlefish, shrimps, lobsters, crabs, sea-urchins, shellfish etc.), as well as engaging in scavenging forays. They do not normally attack people, although bathers have sometimes unwittingly stepped on a resting nurse or carpet shark, even in one or two instances placing a foot right in the creature's mouth. Not caring for this treatment, the shark is wont to take a defensive bite at the disturber of its repose and a hastily withdrawn leg has been known to emerge from the water with the shark securely fastened thereto by its teeth. Such self-protective antagonism is not likely to have serious consequences for the unfortunate bather, the wound inflicted usually being trivial: a bad fright is normally the worst consequence of such injudicious paddling. More culpable are the heroes who acquire a local reputation for bravery as 'shark-baiters' by catching hold of nurse sharks or otherwise teasing them. Onlookers frequently cannot distinguish a really dangerous shark from a torpid orectolobid and will be suitably impressed. Sooner or later these brave characters are likely to pick on a nurse shark suffering from a bad attack of indigestion or some similar disincentive to benevolence and, when teased, the animal will take a snap at its tormentor before moving off to find a quieter spot for its daily siesta. If the shark has been severely provoked and is really bad-tempered the resulting wound can be quite unpleasant, because the common nurse shark (*Ginglymostoma cirratum*) grows to 3.6 metres (12 feet) in length and has an ample complement of sharp teeth in its jaws: indeed, the name 'nurse' (from the fifteenth-century 'nusse') simply means 'a large fish'. Unfortunately, the sand shark (*Odontaspis taurus*) is known as the grey nurse in Australia (often with the scientific name *Odontaspis arenarius*) but this species is not a true nurse shark.

In general appearance, *Ginglymostoma* is in fact very similar to the closely related sand sharks (Odontaspidae), but like all orectolobids is distinguished by the presence of a groove on each side of the snout running between the nostril and the mouth. Its eyes are small, the caudal fin is long and asymmetrical, and the teeth each bear three or more cusps with the central point being the longest. Reproduction is ovo-viviparous, the mature eggs being of enormous size, sometimes measuring as much as 100 millimetres (4 inches). The common nurse of the Florida Keys and the Caribbean (*Ginglymostoma cirratum*) is a uniformly brownish colour with scattered small black spots occurring in young individuals. Other species include the rusty shark (*Ginglymostoma ferrugineum*) of the western tropical Pacific, the Indian Ocean, Malaysia and the Red Sea, and *Ginglymostoma brevicaudatum*, from Zanzibar and the Seychelles, while fossil examples of the genus occur as far back as the Upper Cretaceous.

Even more sluggish is *Orectolobus* itself, the carpet shark of Australasia (where the native name of *wobbegong* is customarily applied to it), Japan and China. Up to perhaps 2.4 metres (8 feet) in length, with a flattened body, broad depressed head and blunt snout, *Orectolobus* is yellowish, grey or a brown hue with spots, bars and stripes to camouflage it as it lies half-buried on the bottom waiting to snatch at passing fish or crustaceans. The wide, almost straight mouth is nearly terminal in position and tassels of skin line the sides of the head, sometimes extending onto the chin. The dentition comprises slender, single-pointed, medial teeth and smaller, multi-cusped, lateral teeth. Several different species of *Orectolobus* have been described from Australasia, as well as *Orectolobus japonicus* from China and Japan and a small fossil species measuring 17.5 centimetres (7 inches) from the Upper Jurassic of Bavaria that is some 150 million years old.

Less familiar orectolobids include *Brachaelurus* from Australia (the speckled cat shark or blind shark, which can in fact see, although its eyes are very small), *Chiloscyllium* (the lip sharks, dating back to the Upper Cretaceous), *Cirrhoscyllium* from the western Pacific, *Eucrossorhinus* from the East Indies, *Hemiscyllium* (the epaulette shark , with muscular paired fins to assist movement across reefs), *Nebrius* (the tawny shark of the Red Sea, the Malay Peninsula and Australasia, with blade-like teeth), *Neoparascyllium* (the Tasmanian spotted shark), *Parascyllium* (the collared cat shark, the rusty cat shark and the varied cat shark of Australia), *Stegostoma* (the zebra shark, young examples of which bear a saddle-stripe marking which eventually breaks up into spots), *Sutorectus* (the cobbler carpet shark of Australia) and *Synchismus* (the ridge-back shark of the Indian Ocean and the western Pacific), as well as a number of fossil genera. Among these

A sluggish nurse shark (*Ginglymostoma cirratum*) resting at the bottom.

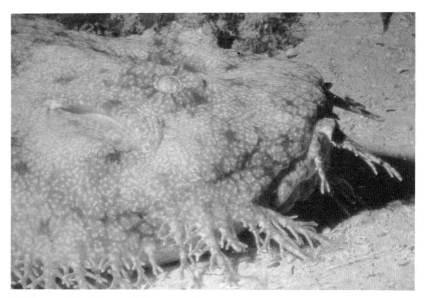

With tassel-like fringes of skin around its mouth, a wobbegong or carpet shark (*Orectolobus*) is almost indistinguishable from a seaweed-encrusted rock as it waits for its prey – usually a small fish or crustacean, which is sucked powerlessly into the wobbegong's maw as the shark opens its jaws.

extinct forms are *Agaleus* from the Lower Jurassic of Lyme Regis, Dorset, represented by teeth about 7 mm ($\frac{1}{4}$ inch) high that are around 190 million years old, and *Palaeocarcharias*, a slender shark about 1 metre ($3\frac{1}{4}$ feet) long from the Upper Jurassic of Eichstatt, Bavaria, with a blunt rounded snout, a large subterminal mouth, two dorsal fins (the second larger than the first), and a rather short caudal – the teeth at the front of

The handsome zebra shark (*Stegostoma fasciatum*) is a member of the carpet shark group. Common in the tropical Indian Ocean, it is largely nocturnal and quite harmless, preying mostly on shellfish and crustaceans.

the jaws were slender and single-cusped, suggesting to some scientists that *Palaeocarcharias* may be an orectolobid close to the ancestry of the mighty isurids.

Bearing a strong resemblance to the nurse sharks, but rather more active and less averse to leaving the sea floor, the family Odontaspidae includes the sand sharks and perhaps also the elfin sharks. They lack the keels on either side of the tail that are so typical of the fast-swimming mackerel sharks to which they are related, their eyes have no nictitating membrane and no grooves connect the nostrils with the large, crescent-shaped mouth, but their slender, awl-like teeth are of proportionately large size with smooth edges and usually one or two subsidiary cusps either side of the central cone. With two large dorsal fins and a long, flattened, asymmetrical tail, they are active denizens of warm seas, often

The sand tiger (*Odontaspis taurus*), up to 3 metres (about 10 feet) in length, with slender pointed teeth, is not normally regarded as dangerous save in Australia, where it has a bad reputation (probably unjustified) for attacking bathers.

occurring in coastal waters; because some species run up to several metres (a dozen feet) in length they can constitute a very real danger to bathers and fishermen, having acquired a particularly unsavoury reputation in Australia. At least one mauling on the United States east coast has also been attributed to a sand shark: in 1961, Bruno Junker was seized by the leg while swimming at Hart Island in Long Island Sound and, from tooth fragments left in the wound, his attacker could be positively identified.

On the other hand, the natives of the West Indies (e.g. Dominica) who make a little cash on the side by wrestling with sharks for the benefit of tourists will choose small sand sharks as adversaries because of their relative docility.

The common sand shark (*Odontaspis taurus*) of the Atlantic, Mediterranean, Australian and South African coasts is a yellowish grey shark of notorious voracity that feeds on small fish (up to 45 kilograms/100 pounds of fish, including small sharks, have been found in the stomach of a single sand shark), cephalopods, lobsters and crabs. *Odontaspis* can apparently fill its stomach with air to serve as a swim bladder.

Although females containing numerous eggs are taken early in the breeding season (April to July in the northern hemisphere), it seems likely that only two young, about a metre ($3\frac{1}{4}$ feet) long, are born from a single litter, this pair having systematically consumed all the other eggs or embryos within the mother's body. Indeed, embryos with their stomachs distended by egg yolk have been recovered from pregnant females, with around them numerous egg capsules, each containing an average of nineteen ova. A weak fighter if hooked, the sand shark is a poor subject for a sport-fisherman's skill.

A number of other living species of *Odontaspis* have been described, one of which may represent a separate genus, *Eugomphodon* (*E. ferox*), as well as a profusion of fossil forms extending back to the early Cretaceous.

Also usually included in the Odontaspidae, but possibly justifying a family of its own, is the bizarre-looking elfin or goblin shark (*Scapanorhynchus*), with a rod-like extension of the snout above a highly protrusible mouth. The fossil dentition of this shark had been known since the middle of the nineteenth century from rocks dating back to the Lower Cretaceous and occurred in localities as far apart as southern England, peninsular India, and New Zealand. Originally the teeth were ascribed to the isurid genus *Lamna*, but in 1887, these thorn-like smooth-edged fangs were assigned to a separate genus, *Rhinognathus*, which was, of course, believed to be extinct. Unfortunately, this name had already been used to describe a beetle, so *Scapanorhynchus* was substituted for it 2 years later.

Imagine the astonishment of everyone therefore, when, within a few years, a shark of outlandish appearance that had been fished up from deep water near Yokohama, Japan, proved to have teeth apparently identical with the fossil ones known under the name *Scapanorhynchus*. Professor Kakichi Mitsukuri had taken this specimen to the United States in 1897 so that it could be scientifically described by Professor David S. Jordan of Stanford Junior University, California, who accorded it the name *Mitsukurina* and assigned it to its own special family, the Mitsukurinidae. Once

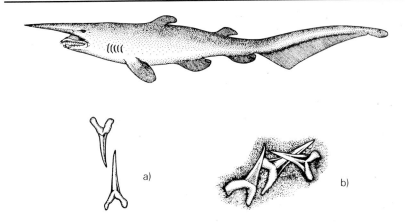

Fig. 6.4. The elfin shark, with teeth of a) the living *Scapanorhynchus owstoni* and b) the extinct *Scapanorhynchus lewisi* from the Upper Cretaceous of Mount Lebanon, Syria.

the commonality of its dentition with *Scapanorhynchus* fossil teeth (Fig. 6.4) was established, however, this new name had perforce to lapse into synonymy as the earlier publication possessed taxonomic priority by 9 years.

Professor Mitsukuri's original specimen was eventually returned to Tokyo University, but living examples of *Scapanorhynchus* were subsequently obtained from the Indian Ocean and off Portugal, as well as being the subject of a report from Australia. The bizarre appearance of this creature quickly led to it becoming known as the goblin or elfin shark, the curious head structure probably being an adaptation to bottom-feeding. The body and fins of this greyish brown shark are, in fact, unremarkable in their proportions, although the two dorsal fins are both rather small and the lower lobe of the tail fin is poorly developed. Attaining a length of 4.2 metres (14 feet), *Scapanorhynchus* remains an enigmatic creature of the depths, but at least its existence as a living species instead of an extinct fossil has been established.

If the carcharhinid sharks represent the most advanced level of evolution attained by the typical lamniforms (the apparently even more specialised hammerheads can scarcely be regarded as 'typical'), then their structural origins are possibly represented by the Triakidae, a family of small sharks that inhabit the shoals and moderate depths of tropical and temperate seas throughout the world. Known collectively as the smooth dogfish or smooth hounds, the triakids have small, rounded teeth, each bearing three or four separate cusps, two dorsal fins and an only moderately elongate caudal fin. This assemblage should perhaps really be split up into a number of smaller families to take account of the quite wide variation to be found among these modestly dimensioned sharks and some scientists do, in fact, recognise various separate groupings to accommodate some of the more markedly divergent types.

Known as the leopard shark down the western seaboard of the USA, *Triakis felis* occurs from Oregon in the north to Magdalena Bay in Baja California.

The so-called stellate smooth hound (*Mustelus asterias*) from the Mediterranean and eastern Atlantic, measuring up to 2 metres ($6\frac{1}{2}$ feet) in length.

The white-tip reef shark (*Triaenodon obesus*) is about 1.5 metres (approximately 5 feet) long and can be readily distinguished by its white-tipped first dorsal fin.

Triakis itself has an especially well developed spiracle and, on the North American west coast, is known as the leopard shark (*Triakis felis*), other species occurring in the western Pacific (*Triakis leucoperiptera* from the Philippines, *Triakis scyllia*, *Triakis venusta*), off Peru (*Triakis maculata*) and in Californian waters.

The most common member of the family is, however, *Mustelus* and, at one time, the group was in consequence known as the Mustelidae, until it was realised that this name had long been employed to designate the mammalian family to which the weasels (*Mustela*) belong. Along the continental shelf of the western Atlantic, from Cape Cod to Uruguay, the smooth dogfish itself (*Mustelus canis*) is abundant, ranging up to 1.5 metres (5 feet) in length and feeding on crabs, lobsters and bottom-dwelling fish. The skin incorporates melanophores that can be expanded or contracted to change the creature's colouration from dark grey to a translucent pearly tint, transition to the palest hue requiring 2 days. Its relative on the opposite side of the Atlantic, the smooth hound proper (*Mustelus mustelus*) does not exceed 1.6 metres ($5\frac{1}{4}$ feet) in length and is active mainly at night in coastal waters of 40–100 metres (130–325 feet) depth.

An abundance of lesser species of *Mustelus* has been described from all over the world, other notable members of the genus including the Florida dogfish (*Mustelus norrisi*), the sicklefin smooth hound (*Mustelus lunulatus*) of southern California to Colombia, the striped dogfish (*Mustelus fasciatus*), of eastern South America, the stellate smooth hound (*Mustelus asterias*) of the eastern Atlantic and Mediterranean, with its unusual white-spotted grey colouration, and the diminutive *Mustelus schmitti* from southern Brazil, Uruguay and northern Argentina that does not even attain a metre ($3\frac{1}{4}$ feet) in length.

The spiracle is only of moderate size in *Mustelus* and, although the eyes lack a nictitating membrane (as do all the sharks of this family), there is a pronounced sub-ocular fold. Usually ten to twenty (rarely up to forty) embryos of varying ages develop within the female at any one time, so they will not all be born at once after their 10-month gestation period is complete and in at least some species there is a placental attachment between mother and embryo.

Several other less well know genera are also referable to the Triakidae. Among them is *Triaenodon* which is widespread from the Red Sea through the Indian Ocean and right across the Pacific, the sedentary, essentially-nocturnal *Triaenodon obesus* with a distinctive white spot on its first dorsal fin being the common form that attains 1.5 metres (nearly 5 feet) in length and is sometimes found 'sleeping' in underwater caves off Japan, while *Triaenodon apicalis* (the whitetip shark) occurs off Queensland, Australia. *Scylliogaleus* and *Neotriakis* are restricted to South Africa, *Proscyllium* comes from Formosa, the Andaman Sea and the Bay of Bengal, *Emissola* and *Furgaleus* are of Australasian origin, *Leptocharias* was described from West Africa, *Iago* from the Arabian sea measures only 0.5 metres (18 inches) with males barely 60 per cent. the length of females, and *Eridacnis* hails from the Philippines. *Gogolia* is a long-snouted form known only from a single specimen 74 centimetres (29 inches) long caught in Astrolabe Bay,

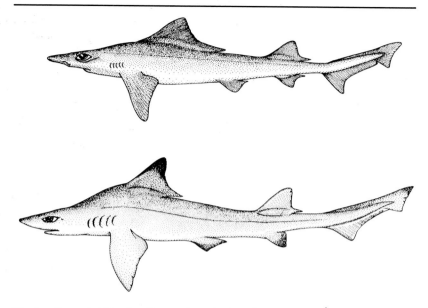

Fig. 6.5. Rare triakids. *Iago* (bottom) attains less than a metre ($3\frac{1}{4}$ feet) in length and occurs in the Arabian Sea and the Western Pacific. *Gogolia* (top) is of similar size and comes from New Guinea.

off the Gogol River in New Guinea, *Ctenacis* has a remarkably broad, depressed head, and the oddly named *Gollum*, about 1 metre ($3\frac{1}{4}$ feet) long from New Zealand, has an extraordinarily wide, flattened nose – its identification is derived from one of the less lovable characters in J.R.R. Tolkien's famous fable *The Lord of the Rings*, apparently because this shark supposedly both looks like and behaves like the Gollum in the story!

From its name, *Pseudotriakis* would seem likely to be another member of the triakid group, but in fact this so-called false cat shark is a large, slender-bodied fish with a pointed snout and a long, low, first dorsal fin that belongs to a separate family of its own and is apparently more akin to the relatively conservative scyliorhinids – a group close to the central stem of the lamniforms as a whole. *Pseudotriakis* is quite a rare shark, brownish grey in colour, that grows to perhaps 3 metres ($9\frac{3}{4}$ feet) in length. It lives in the deep waters of the North Atlantic and the Indian Ocean and also occurs off Japan, feeding on the bottom at depths of 300–1,500 metres (975–5,625 feet), preying mostly on crustaceans and fish. Some tiny fossil teeth less than 1.5 millimetres ($\frac{1}{20}$ inch) in height described from the Upper Cretaceous of Montana under the name of *Archaeotriakis* may be attributable to an early ancestor of the false cat shark.

The scyliorhinids are perhaps the most unspecialised of living lamniform sharks, probably not greatly advanced over the ancient ancestors of this group that must have lived in Mesozoic seas but still remain essentially unknown. The group includes the cat sharks and dogfish, few of which exceed 1 metre ($3\frac{1}{4}$ feet) in length, and most are deep-water

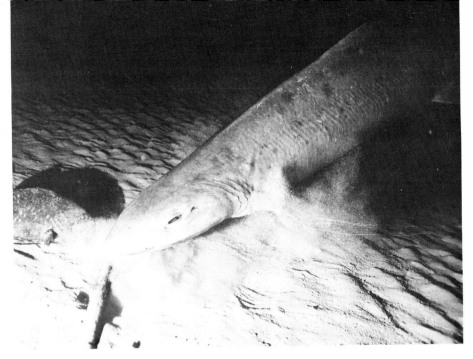

Searching the sea bed 640 metres (1,936 feet) down off Aldabra Island in the Indian Ocean, this false cat shark (*Pseudotriakis*) has located the bait put out to bring it within camera range.

bottom-dwellers, some species having been obtained from water over 1,500 metres (5,625 feet) deep.

Quite slimly proportioned but not really powerful swimmers or fast-moving fish, the scyliorhinids usually have two dorsal fins (one species with only a single dorsal is known) and unkeeled tails. Their eyes lack a nictitating membrane and the dentition comprises several functional rows of small teeth with subsidiary lateral denticles either side of the main cusp. The relative primitiveness of the family is demonstrated by the remarkable similarity of their teeth to the anterior dentition of the extinct hybodonts, although those ancient Mesozoic sharks had not yet developed teeth with bifurcated roots such as the scyliorhinids possess.

Crustaceans, crabs, small fish, worms and other small animals of the benthic fauna constitute the main diet of scyliorhinids, which tend on the whole to be relatively sluggish. Because of the considerable depth at which these small sharks feed, many of them remain obscure forms whose way of life is largely a mystery. Quite often, even their method of reproduction is unknown and some genera seem to include species that lay eggs as well as species that give birth to live young. Undoubtedly many of the temperate-latitude scyliorhinids undertake seasonal migrations, but precise details are limited, and it is likely that at least some of them forage along the sea floor in large groups.

On the other hand, the Scyliorhinidae does include some very common small sharks. *Galeus*, with its long attenuate snout and a crest of dermal denticles running along the top of the tail fin, includes the familiar

A lesser spotted dogfish (*Scyliorhinus caniculus*), a common small shark of the eastern Atlantic ranging up to about 1 metre ($3\frac{1}{4}$ feet) in length.

Scyliorhinus stellaris, the greater spotted dogfish of the eastern North Atlantic and the Mediterranean, which attains a length of about 1.5 metres ($4\frac{3}{4}$ feet).

black-mouthed dogfish (*Galeus melastomus*) of the eastern North Atlantic and the Mediterranean, which lives at depths of 250–900 metres (800–2,900 feet), feeding chiefly on crabs, cephalopods and small fish, the females laying two, four or eight eggs (without securing filaments) at a time. Other species of *Galeus* apparently give birth to live young (*Galeus arae*, the marbled or roughtail catfish of the Caribbean/Gulf of Mexico region, and *Galeus polli* from the Senegal coast), while a number of poorly known forms have been described from such widely-separated areas as Iceland, Japan, Australia and California.

Scyliorhinus itself comprises primarily the lesser spotted dogfish (*Scyliorhinus caniculus*), which does not normally exceed 1 metre ($3\frac{1}{4}$ feet) in length, and its larger relative the greater spotted dogfish (*Scyliorhinus stellaris*) that sometimes reaches 1.5 metres (nearly 5 feet). Both are found in the eastern Atlantic and Mediterranean, feeding on molluscs, worms, crustaceans and small fish at depths of anything from 40–800 metres (130–2,600 feet). The males copulate by wrapping their tails laterally round the females, who subsequently lay clutches of eighteen to twenty eggs in the form of rectangular horny capsules measuring 4–6 by 10–12 centimetres ($1\frac{1}{2}$–2 inches by 4–$4\frac{3}{4}$ inches). Females swim among seaweeds, gorgonians, sponges or other branched structures while laying and the egg cases become attached to these projections by means of 1 metre

($3\frac{1}{4}$ feet) long filaments that arise from each corner and spiral down to a length of only 15 centimetres (6 inches). Development requires 8–9 months, the embryo being attached to a large yolk sac but nonetheless making swimming movements that pump a flow of water through the permeable membrane of the transparent capsule to facilitate respiration. When hatched, the young are 9–10 centimetres ($3\frac{1}{2}$–4 inches) long and bear dark diagonal stripes that eventually break up into spots. Elsewhere in the world, *Scyliorhinus* occurs in the Indian Ocean (the lazy shark, *Scyliorhinus capensis*), Japan and Korea (*Scyliorhinus torazame*), the East Indies (*Scyliorhinus garmani*, known only from a single female 24 centimetres ($9\frac{1}{2}$ inches) in length), off Brazil (*Scyliorhinus haeckelii*, *Scyliorhinus boa*), Cuba (*Scyliorhinus torrei*) and the United States eastern seaboard (*Scyliorhinus retifer*).

The extraordinary swell sharks (*Cephaloscyllium*) are nocturnal bottom-dwellers that lie up during the day in sheltered rocky caverns or crevices. Only about a metre ($3\frac{1}{4}$ feet) long, they have the ability to distend their stomachs with air or water so that they swell up to appear twice their normal size (Fig. 6.6). When thus inflated, a swell shark is exceedingly difficult to dislodge from its daytime underwater retreat, since the small lanceolate dermal denticles of its skin catch on the sides of the crevice and

Capable of grotesquely inflating itself when alarmed, this swell shark (*Cephaloscyllium ventriosum*) is reposing peacefully on the bottom of Monterey Bay, California.

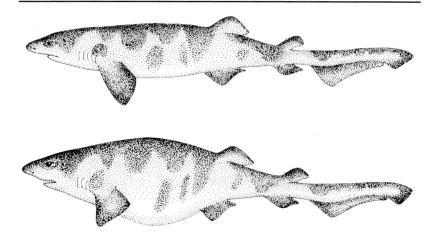

Fig. 6.6. The swell shark (*Cephaloscyllium*) in its normal relaxed habitus (top) and distended (bottom). Length about 1 metre ($3\frac{1}{4}$ feet).

keep it firmly anchored. Newborn individuals exhibit a row of enlarged denticles along the upper flanks and these are thought to assist the embryo in emerging from its egg case: the hooked blades would provide a purchase on the ruptured edge of the case as the emergent juvenile wriggled to free itself.

Apristurus is normally only found very deep, somewhere beyond the 900 metre (3,000 feet) mark. Most of the species of the genus are small, not exceeding about 0.5 metres (18 inches) in length, but they occur virtually worldwide: one of them, *Apristurus riveri* from Cuba, is notable because adult males have single-cusped teeth twice the size of the flattened three- to five-cusped dentition found in females and immature males. *Atelomycterus* includes a Sumatran species (*Atelomycterus marmoratus*) that is known as the marbled cat shark (an unfortunate duplication of common names with *Galeus arae*), *Aulohalaelurus* is the black-spotted cat shark of Australia, *Cephalurus* is from the Gulf of California and the Mexican west coast, and *Halaelurus* is a widely distributed but none too well known genus.

Among other scyliorhinids that remain somewhat obscure, largely because of their deep-water bottom-dwelling habits, are *Haploblepharus* (the banded cat shark of South Africa), *Holohalaelurus* (a distinctively marked South African genus covered in variegated dark spots that alter in pattern as adulthood is attained, the males of this form being – unusually for sharks – larger than the females), *Juncrus* from South Australia, *Parapristurus* from Hawaii, and *Poroderma* from South Africa, which includes the striped cat shark (*Poroderma africanum*) and the lazy or ocellate shark (*Poroderma pantherinum*).

Schroederichthys, up to 70 centimetres (28 inches) in length, occurs off South America and is another form in which the males have much larger teeth than the females, while *Pentanchus* is known only from a solitary specimen – a male 50 centimetres (18 inches) long caught at 1,069 metres (3,974 feet) in the Sea of Mindanao before World War 1 – and has only a single dorsal fin, which initially led scientists to suspect that the specimen had been mutilated, either during or after capture: however, careful examination of the preserved specimen suggests that it is indeed a unique scyliorhinid with only one dorsal fin. *Parmaturus* from the western Atlantic and the North Pacific has rather soft, loosely-arranged dermal denticles that give the skin a velvety texture and, for a scyliorhinid, also incorporates an unusually large amount of the low-specific-gravity component squalene in its liver oil – possibly an adaptation to a mid-water habitat, although *Parmaturus* has been seen on the sea floor at the bottom of the Santa Barbara basin off southern California feeding on moribund myctophids (lantern fish) that had apparently wandered unwittingly into these oxygen-deficient depths. The sharks seemed to have no respiratory problems.

Since the scyliorhinids are such a conservative family, it is not surprising that they have a long fossil history, with extinct forms, barely (if at all) distinguishable from living genera, present in the Upper Cretaceous and somewhat older, more primitive types occurring as early as the Upper Jurassic (the long-tailed *Macrurogaleus* and *Palaeoscyllium*).

Perhaps forming a connecting link between the scyliorhinids and the original central lamniform stock are the Orthacodontidae, an extinct family known only from teeth occurring in Jurassic, Cretaceous and early Cenozoic rocks that have slender compressed crowns but simple, primitive roots of a broad, depressed type. *Orthacodus* itself goes right back to the European Lower Jurassic, *Eychlaodus* is a Cretaceous genus from Scandinavia. Possibly extending this line even further back is *Palaeospinax* from the Lower Jurassic of Lyme Regis, in southern England – an ancient genus which already had its dentition specialised into a number of prehensile anterior teeth and more abundant low-crowned posterior elements (alternatively *Palaeospinax* may be related to the bullhead sharks).

Chapter 7
Gentle Giants

Huge, docile and entirely harmless, placidly cruising the oceans gulping plankton, the basking sharks, the whale sharks and the megamouth sharks are all lamniforms and thus members of the same general group as the lethally dangerous isurids and all the other big voracious sharks. There could hardly be a greater contrast between these gentle giants and their deadly cousins, but it is not known how these krill-eaters originated, or why they abandoned the predatory way of life that is characteristic of sharks in general.

Despite the similarity of whale sharks and basking sharks, both in appearance and in habits, they do not seem to be closely related and have been assigned to two different families, which were apparently going their separate ways early in the Tertiary, some 50 or so million years ago.

The basking shark, *Cetorhinus maximus*, is by far the better known of the two. Attaining a length of at least 9 metres (30 feet) and possibly longer, with a gross weight exceeding 4 tonnes, this monstrous creature is a denizen of temperate seas in both the northern and the southern hemispheres. Coloured bluish grey, greyish brown or sometimes nearly black on its upper surfaces, but becoming paler-hued below, the basking shark has enormous gill clefts almost completely encircling the neck. The nostrils are widely separated from the mouth, there are two dorsal fins (the first being much the larger) and the tail fin is lunate (half-moon shaped).

A bluntly pointed snout overhangs the cavernous mouth which can take in up to 9,000 litres (2,000 gallons) of water an hour while cruising at 2

With mouth agape and gill slits fully open, a basking shark (*Cetorhinus maximus*) feeds on plankton off the British coast.

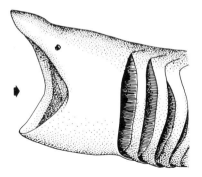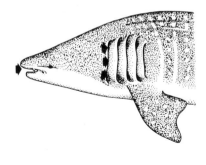

Fig. 7.1. Filter-feeding sharks: (left) basking shark (*Cetorhinus*); (right) whale shark (*Rhincodon*). These sharks ingest plankton and strain it from the water through their large flaring gill openings. Whale sharks are also known to swallow fish, whether by accident or design is unknown, as well as such indigestible items as old shoes, leather belts and even, in one instance, a piece of oak pole 30 centimetres (1 foot) in length.

knots with the jaws fully open and the gills and pharyngeal region greatly expanded. The incoming current is strained for planktonic food (e.g. fish eggs, copepods, cirripedes and decapod larvae) by a thousand or more gill rakers, each about 10 centimetres (4 inches) long, that are borne on the hoop-like gill arches in the wall of the gullet. When the mouth is opened, these rakers are erected by muscle strands connecting their bases with the branchial cartilages. Upon closure of the mouth, elastic fibres return them to a resting position, lying flat on the gill arches. Mucus secreted by the epithelium at the base of the rakers traps planktonic organisms and, when the mouth closes, these are probably squeezed into the mouth cavity by the collapsing rakers. Teeth are still present, but they are of very reduced size and represent simple modifications of the placoid scales present in the skin, with lateral expansions that appear to be vestigial cusps. During feeding, respiration continues simultaneously and automatically.

The brain of *Cetorhinus* is diminutive, even by the modest standards of sharks, and much of the skull's brain cavity is, in fact, filled by numerous fine strands of supporting tissue. There is, however, a substantial proportional development of the thalamencephalon (or diencephalon). The hypothalamus and thalamus of this co-ordinating centre for sensory inputs is of cardinal importance in the brains of all vertebrates – in fish, if the thalamus should be destroyed, they become incapable of spontaneous activity.

Basking sharks always sink when dead, as do sharks in general, because their density (in the absence of a swim bladder) is greater than that of the water. It was once believed that a substantial deposit of oil existed beneath the skin of these fish, which would reduce the relative density of the creature and make it more buoyant. This proved not to be the case, as investigation of captured specimens disclosed that the hide is in fact bound tightly to the fascia covering the muscles by only a thin layer of connective tissue. However, the liver is of enormous size and contains an immense amount of oil, rich in Vitamin A and including up to nearly 50 per cent. of low specific gravity squalene, that will effectively increase a basking shark's buoyancy.

In male individuals, the pelvic fins incorporate claspers with horn-shaped spines, examples of which occur as fossils in the Pliocene of England and Belgium. The body slime of the basking shark is notoriously heavy and rots fishing nets very rapidly: it endows the creature with a highly offensive smell that has been likened to rotting weed.

This sluggish and inoffensive shark is frequently seen lying motionless in the surface waters with its back awash and the dorsal fin, the tip of the snout and the caudal fin exposed as if 'basking' in the sun, hence its common name (fishermen in Wales and western Ireland also know it as the sun fish). Allegedly they will lie on their backs to sun the belly and are said to occasionally jump clear of the water, perhaps to remove ectoparasites which include lampreys (usually attached dorso-laterally behind the shoulders or else on the flanks) and copepods on the skin and gills. The hide of the basking shark incorporates simple placoid scales with an irregularly oval base measuring 1.3 by 0.9 millimetres ($\frac{5}{100}$ by $\frac{3}{100}$ of an inch) wide and a spine projecting sharply upwards and backwards; this dermal protection is apparently too tough for the rasping tongue of a lamprey to penetrate and the presence of these parasites is indicated only by external marking of the shark's skin. Evidently lampreys utilise basking sharks purely to provide transportation – whales, for example, sometimes have quite large lumps chewed from their superficial tissues by these parasites. Internally, the basking shark's intestine is populated by cestodes, which are present in the spiral valve.

Although normally relatively slow-moving, basking sharks exhibit evident adaptations for sustained powerful swimming and can in fact move quite rapidly if necessary: the strongly calcified skeleton, firm muscles, stiff fins, dense skin, tough connective tissue, huge oily liver, lunate tail fin and strong caudal keels all indicate a quite high potential level of activity, while the enormous gill cavities, with long external clefts and smooth, slender gill rakers are clearly intended to sustain a high through-put of water.

Sometimes solitary, but usually seen in twos and threes, *Cetorhinus* occasionally occurs in shoals of sixty to a hundred individuals, with enormous schools reported off the Welsh coast in 1776 and subsequent summers and off Norway in 1800 and 1880 (although rare in this area in the early eighteenth century and in 1840).

What happens to basking sharks in winter time is something of a mystery. As the water chills with the coming of autumn in the temperate latitudes they frequent, these great creatures apparently vanish. Just occasionally an isolated individual is caught or found stranded during the winter months, and these stragglers usually prove to be without gill rakers, although careful dissection reveals that under the skin of the gill arches a new set of rakers is in the process of development.

During the summer there is a lush burgeoning of plankton in the surface waters of the temperate oceans. The basking sharks engulf this ultra-nutritious 'soup' by the gallon and grow fat. But in winter the plankton dwindles to a mere fraction of its former abundance. A 7 metre (23 foot) basking shark, feeding at a swimming speed of 2 knots requires 0.33 hp to propel its bulk through the water, even at this modest pace, and, if its muscles are 40 per cent. efficient and its tail is 80 per cent. efficient (probably optimistic estimates), it will consume over 600 calories an hour. Plankton-rich summer seas can provide enough food to more than balance this nutritional equation, but the depleted 'soup' of winter could at most provide only perhaps 400 calories an hour. So it seems that, when winter comes, basking sharks sink to the sea floor and hibernate, lying on the bottom orientated so that the deep oceanic currents provide a flow of water through their gills. There they presumably shed their gill rakers, regenerating a fresh set for the coming spring, and are thus the only sharks known to have an annual moult of any sort.

Basking sharks are presumably either ovo-viviparous or viviparous. The lower part of the male genital duct on each side comprises a large ampulla where sperm are gathered together in small masses around which a firm, transparent, gristly envelope develops. These structures, known as spermatophores, have a core about 1 centimetre ($\frac{2}{5}$ of an inch) across but possess an overall diameter of up to 5 centimetres (2 inches); stored in each of the two ampullae are 19–27 litres (5 to 6 gallons) of watery fluid in which the spermatophores float. Mating occurs in May in the North Atlantic, the uterine secretion of the female dissolving the spermatophore envelope to release the sperm. Something like 6 million eggs 0.5–5.0 millimetres ($\frac{1}{50}$ to $\frac{1}{5}$ of an inch) in diameter are produced by each ovary, but the nidamentary (shell) gland is vestigial, while the oviduct is richly endowed with small, tag-like projections (trophonemata) for nourishing developing embryos. The evidence thus indicates that basking sharks do not lay eggs, but give birth to fully formed young, although why in this case the females produce such a huge number of eggs is unknown, unless the embryos consume unfertilised eggs during their gestation period.

It may be deduced that the young are about 2 metres (6 feet) long at birth (an embryo 30 centimetres/1 foot in length has allegedly been taken from a female, according to the eighteenth-century naturalist Thomas Pennant in Volume 3 of his *British Zoology*, published in 1776), and immature individuals 3–4.5 metres (10–15 feet) long possess a thick, pointed fleshy snout with the tip produced into a soft curved hook; sexual maturity is attained at 4.5–6 metres (15–20 feet), with small claspers present in males 3.3 metres (11 feet) in length and well developed claspers in 7.5 metre (25 foot) individuals. Very young juveniles have not been identified and may remain in deep water until well grown.

Beached carcases are often mistaken for 'sea monsters' because disintegration as a result of decay or the buffeting of the waves causes the bulky jaws and gill arches to separate from the rest of the corpse, along with the pectoral and pelvic fins, leaving only the backbone and the box-like cranium. An example was the 9 metre (30 foot) 'unknown marine animal' washed up near Scituate, Massachusetts, in November 1970 that was described as being like 'a camel without legs', while the scientific name *Halsydrus pontoppidiani* was bestowed on the partially decayed carcase of a basking shark, found at Stronsay in the Orkneys, early in the nineteenth century, that was believed to be a hitherto undiscovered sea monster.

A good-sized basking shark would be about 9 metres (30 feet) in length, but there are records of much larger specimens, such as the 10.8 metre (36 foot) example washed up at Brighton, Sussex, in 1806, a 9.85 metre (32 foot 10 inch) individual captured near Brown's Point, Raritan Bay, New Jersey, in 1821, a 12 metre ($40\frac{1}{4}$ foot) specimen trapped in a herring gill net in Musquash Harbour, New Brunswick in 1851, a 12 metre (40 footer) taken at Povoa de Varzim, Portugal, in 1865, a 10.5 metre (35 foot) specimen stranded at Eastport, Maine, in 1868, and examples obtained on the Norwegian coast between 1884 and 1905 measuring 13.7 metres (45 feet, the largest on record), 12 metres (40 feet), 10.9 metres (36 feet) and 9.7 metres (32 feet).

Basking sharks are totally harmless, although boats have been wrecked and their crews drowned by these massive fish either colliding with them or jumping on them.

Fishing for such a huge fish with rod-and-line is wildly impractical and harpooning is the only logical way to capture one. They offer no kind of sport, however, merely plunging stolidly through the ocean in an effort to escape, and, because of their size, they can easily tow a small boat out to sea or even drag it below the surface if the line is not cut in time, quite apart from the danger of so a large creature wrecking the insubstantial hull of such a vessel should an accidental collision take place.

Much less well known than the basking shark, but even larger, the whale shark (*Rhincodon typus*) is a denizen of tropical seas. It easily attains a length of 12 metres (40 feet) with a weight of 20 tonnes (44,800 pounds) and allegedly much more – estimates exceeding 18 metres (60 feet) have been made for specimens seen but not actually landed and measured. Known by a variety of names around its circum-tropical range (it is called the *chagrin* in the Seychelles, the *tiburon ballenas* in Spanish-speaking California, the *tintoreva* in the Gulf of Panama, the *chacon* in the Philippines and the *mhor* in Karachi), the whale shark is sometimes found in groups lying on the surface ('basking') but probably spends much of its time in the deeps of the open ocean, following currents that carry the plankton on which it feeds. By day, under the intense light of the tropical sun, this teeming community of microscopic life may retreat to depths of 600 metres (2,000 feet), where the whale sharks doubtless spend the daylight hours feeding, normally only coming to the surface at night when plankton rises to shallower levels.

World famous Australian diving champion Valerie Taylor hitches a free ride by clinging to the vast flattened head of a gigantic whale shark (*Rhincodon typus*).

Rhincodon has a broad, blunt head and an almost cylindrical body with two or three lateral keels or ridges running along the upper part of each side and a single median ridge. The vast straight mouth, located at the end of the snout, contains numerous very small teeth, forming a rasp-like dentition that is not designed for tearing flesh but can, nonetheless, cause quite severe bruising and minor lacerations if a diver should accidentally allow an arm or leg to become caught in the creature's maw while playing with this giant of the deeps – normally a safe enough practice as whale sharks are of an entirely pacific disposition.

The five pairs of large external gill clefts provide an exit for the flow of water that pours in through the mouth while the creature is cruising at its 2 or 3 knot feeding speed. Internally, the gill arches are connected by numerous cartilaginous bars supporting soft spongy masses of tissue that develop from modified denticles to form a sieve of minute meshes 2–3 millimetres ($\frac{7}{100}-\frac{11}{100}$ of an inch) across. In addition, the oesophagus is lined with prominent papillae covered with denticles, this whole remarkable straining mechanism being designed to filter out the diminutive copepods, fish larvae and other nutritious components of the rich planktonic 'soup'. Whale sharks allegedly sometimes feed while vertical in the water and will swallow anchovies, sardines, albacores and small squid, so they have obviously not fully abandoned the fish-eating habits that their ancestors in the distant past presumably still practised.

Two dorsal fins are present, the front one (located in advance of the pelvic fins) being the larger and standing 1.2 metres (4 feet) tall with a base 1.2 metres (4 feet) in length. The anal fin is located immediately beneath the second dorsal and remains entirely separate from the huge, almost symmetrical tail fin, which has a well developed lower lobe.

Whale sharks are brownish or greyish in colour, becoming paler ventrally, with round white or yellow spots closely spaced on the head but separated by narrow vertical streaks of the same colour on the body.

Compared with the basking shark, *Rhincodon* has a less fusiform body, flattened anteriorly, with a shorter body cavity, smaller liver and less extensive external gill openings. Its filtering apparatus of cartilage-cored parallel plates bridges the internal gill openings transversely in paired dorsal and ventral series, the lobulated pharyngeal margins forming a dense grid that constitutes a very efficient filtration mechanism but one incapable of passing a large volume of water. Probably the short, wide mouth cavity, the long, low, broad pharynx and the relatively small external gill slits enable the whale shark to employ a combination of suction-feeding and filter-feeding in order to ingest larger prey than the plankton upon which basking sharks subsist, even when the creature's rate of forward movement is low. It is not known whether *Rhincodon* can filter out organisms as small as copepods.

The first whale shark to be scientifically described was harpooned in Table Bay, South Africa, in April 1828, by fishermen who noticed its unusual greenish grey colour with white spots. Dr Andrew Smith, a military surgeon with the British garrison in Cape Town, published a brief description of it in 1829, followed by a fuller one in 1849; this particular whale shark was only 4.95 metres ($16\frac{1}{2}$ feet) long, and its dried skin (for which Smith paid £6) is now in the Musée d'Histoire Naturelle, Paris.

Forty years passed before the whale shark was heard of again. Then, in 1868, a young Irish naturalist, E.P. Wright, spent 6 months in the Seychelles and heard of the *chagrin*. He offered a reward of $12 for the first example harpooned and brought to him. As a result, two, measuring 5.48 and 6.09 metres (18 feet and 20 feet) were secured, photographed and dissected. Swinburne Ward, the civil administrator of the islands, told Wright that he had measured a whale shark 13.71 metres (45 feet) in length.

Since then about a hundred whale sharks have been reported, including a number that have been rammed by ships or found stranded, but few of them have been scientifically examined.

A huge fish caught for a week during 1919 in a bamboo-stake trap in 15 metres (50 feet) of water at Koh Chik (Chick Island) in the eastern Gulf of Siam was probably a whale shark. It was ultimately killed by rifle fire, but proved too big to drag ashore, apparently measuring 10 wa (Siamese fathoms) in length. Originally 1 wa represented the span of a man's outstretched arms (about 1.7 metres or $5\frac{1}{2}$ feet), but this unit is now regularised at 2 metres (6 feet $6\frac{3}{4}$ inches): the Koh Chik fish was therefore about 17–20 metres (55 feet 9 inches–65 feet 7 inches) long.

In May 1912, an 11.4 metre (38 foot) whale shark was caught by Captain Charles Thompson and some local fishermen just below Knight's Key, southern Florida. It was beached after a 9 hour battle and eventually had to be killed by cutting a piece out of its head with a hatchet and piercing the brain with a knife on a long pole. The carcase was towed to Miami and loaded on a railroad flat car, which promptly collapsed, but subsequently it was skinned and stuffed (several months' work) and taken on tour round the United States.

In June 1923 it took 54 hours to land a 9.45 metre (31½ foot) whale shark at the appropriately named Marathon, on the Florida Keys and, in the summer of 1926, the movie pioneer, Mack Sennett, tried out a newly invented underwater camera in Los Frales Bay, in the Gulf of California, and filmed a whale shark estimated to be 19.5 metres (65 feet) long and 3 metres (10 feet) across.

During September 1934, the liner *Maurganui* collided with a whale shark 96 kilometres (60 miles) north-northeast of Tikehau atoll in the south Pacific and impaled its body on the bows with 4.5 metres (15 feet) on one side and 12 metres (40 feet) on the other.

The reproductive process of whale sharks was essentially unknown until, on 2 July 1953, an egg was fished up by Captain Odell Freeze of the shrimp trawler *Doris* some 208 kilometres (130 miles) south of Port Isabel, Texas, on the 'Twenty-Four Ten Bank' from a depth of 56 metres (186 feet). The case measured 30.4 by 13.9 by 8.8 centimetres (12 by 5½ by 3½ inches), and contained an embryo 35 centimetres (13¾ inches) long, which fell out when the egg was opened. The diminutive juvenile was unmistakably a whale shark in miniature. A pregnant female containing eight egg capsules has also been caught, the developing embryos all having the characteristic shape and colouration of adults.

Aloof, mysterious, harmless to Man and of no commercial importance, whale sharks are enigmatic giants of the deep tropical oceans. They will readily tolerate divers playing around them and catching hold of their fins to obtain a free ride, regarding these interlopers from an alien terrestrial world with apparent interest through their alert, rounded, slightly slanted eyes. When they tire of these inquisitive human interlopers, whale sharks simply dive straight down into the depths, sounding in the manner of a baleen whale rather than adopting the oblique diving path common to sharks in general.

Basking sharks and whale sharks seem to be parallel evolutionary developments from separate ancestors in the remote past. If anything, whale sharks are allied to the orectolobid sharks like *Ginglymostoma* (the nurse shark) and some tiny fossil teeth from the early Cenozoic of southern England and Belgium described under the name of *Palaeorhincodon* may indicate its line of descent, but the basking shark has no obvious near-relations, although it is usually classified among the lamniforms.

It seems incredible that another type of giant plankton-eating shark could have been lurking unknown in the deep waters of the tropics until as late as 1976. But on 15 November of that year, the United States research vessel *AFB*-14 hauled in a parachute anchor some 42 kilometres (26 miles) north west of Oahu and found entangled in it a huge shark resembling nothing that any of those on board had ever seen before. Realising the potential significance of their unexpected catch, the crew succeeded in pulling it aboard the research vessel, not without considerable difficulty, and brought it into the Kaneohe Bay facility of the Naval Undersea Center, where it was tied alongside the dock overnight.

The following morning, Leighton R. Taylor of Waikiki Aquarium, came down to view the prize. It did not take him long to realise that this shark was something totally new to science and should be preserved intact for study. A U.S. Navy crane was used to winch the huge fish out of the water by its tail, an operation that nearly proved disastrous, as the caudal fin broke off and the shark fell back into the sea. A naval diving team was hurriedly mobilised and succeeded in retrieving the carcase, which was rushed to Hawaiian Tuna Packers of Honolulu for quick freezing while an enormous preservation tank was constructed. On 29 November, 2 weeks after being caught, the shark was taken to the Kewalo dock-site of the National Maritime Fisheries Service for thawing and injection with formalin as a preservative.

Now proper scientific examination could begin. It immediately became apparent that the newly discovered shark, 4.46 metres ($14\frac{1}{2}$ feet) in length and weighing 750 kilograms (1,653 pounds), was a plankton-eater. The cavernous, broadly arched mouth that glowed with silvery luminescence for some time after the fish was caught quickly led the local press to christen it the megamouth shark, and it was found that the long jaws were protrusible and could provide an enormous gape. An abundance of very small teeth in multiple rows ran along the sides of the mouth, although there were edentulous gaps at the symphysial region both above and below, and the interior gill openings had rows of gill-raker papillae lining their anterior and posterior edges for filtering out the euphausiid shrimps (*Thysanopoda pectinata*) and other tiny life forms upon which this huge shark subsists.

The skeleton is poorly calcified, with elongate radials supporting the supple pectoral fins, rather small pelvics incorporating slender claspers (the specimen is a male), a large but rather rubbery first dorsal fin, a low second dorsal and a small anal fin, and a very flexible asymmetric caudal fin, incorporating a long, broad upper lobe and only a short lower lobe.

The stoutly proportioned body is loosely covered by a smooth-textured skin studded with very small flattened denticles, the underlying musculature and connective tissue being remarkably flabby.

It took nearly 7 years to complete the initial scientific study of this first known example of the megamouth shark (Fig. 7.2), which was given the scientific name of *Megachasma pelagios* and assigned to a special family of its own (the Megachasmidae).

Fig. 7.2. The megamouth shark (*Megachasma*). Length 4.5 metres (15 feet).

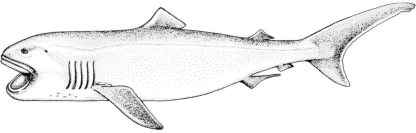

With its dark grey or blue-black body, shading to light grey below, *Megachasma* is, it seems, a creature of the tropical deep sea, a habitat relatively impoverished in nutrients compared to the more prolific seas of inshore areas. A low specific gravity is indicated by the megamouth shark's poorly calcified skeleton, soft loose skin, and flabby connective tissue and muscles. Furthermore, the flexibility of its fins, lack of keels on the caudal peduncle (such as mackerel sharks possess) and asymmetric caudal fin indicate that *Megachasma* is a weak swimmer. (Similar reduced levels of tissue development and low activity levels are seen in open-ocean teleosts living in nutrient-poor environments, to which these adaptations may be a response.) The megamouth shark probably feeds by cruising through shoals of euphausiids with its jaws protruded to scoop up the planktonic 'soup', occasionally closing its mouth and contracting the pharynx to expel water and concentrate the trapped shrimps on its gill rakers before swallowing them. Its origins are obscure, although a few fossil teeth of Miocene age obtained from a road-cutting in California, and some even older ones from the Eocene of southern England and Argentina, may indicate its prehistoric ancestry.

Late in 1984 another example of this rare and mysterious shark was caught in the Pacific. Taken off the south California coast, this specimen measured 4.3 metres (just over 14 feet) in length and weighed more than a tonne; it was taken to the Los Angeles Museum of Natural History for intensive study by shark specialists. A third specimen of *Megachasma* materialised in 1988, when an example 4 metres (13 feet) long was washed ashore near Mandurah, a holiday resort to the south of Perth, in Western Australia.

Chapter 8
Sharks of the Ocean Floor

The second major group of living sharks are the squaliforms (Fig. 8.1), which are far less spectacular than the lamniforms and rarely achieve even moderately large dimensions, although the assemblage does include one or two species of considerable size.

Fig. 8.1. Representative members of the Squalidae, all about 1 metre ($3\frac{1}{4}$ feet) in length. a) *Scymnodon*, b) *Centrophorus*, c) *Oxynotus*, the humantin or prickly dogfish, frequently referred to a separate family of its own, and d) *Centroscymnus*.

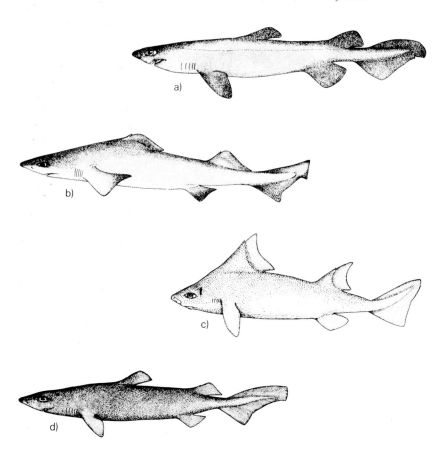

Fig. 8.2. The skull of a squaliform shark
(*Squalus*) showing the single rostral
cartilage (1), the orbital process of the
palatoquadrate (2), the hyomandibular
(3) and the nasal capsules (4).

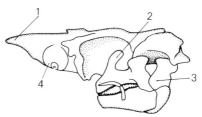

Most squaliforms seem to be bottom-dwellers, sometimes of abyssal depths. Their snouts are only slightly elongate and incorporate but a single supporting rostral cartilage (compared to the three cartilages present in lamniforms), while the upper jaw has a sliding articulation with the narrow basicranium via a large orbital process on the palatoquadrate, the hyomandibular arch forming an additional brace (Fig. 8.2). The jaws of squaliforms do not extend as far forward as the nasal capsules (which they always do in lamniforms), nor are they ever produced posteriorly beyond the level of the occiput. There are five pairs of gill slits and spiracles are present, but the eyes never have protective nictitating membranes.

The trunk is normally subcylindrical and the pelvic fins each have two basal elements articulating with the pelvis (there is only one basal forming this joint in lamniforms). A fully segmented vertebral column has been developed, the axial canal being constricted within the well differentiated centra (which incorporate calcareous lamellae in a ring round a central axis, Fig. 8.3) but dilated between vertebrae. There are two dorsal fins, each usually (although not invariably) preceded by a projecting spine – apparently a notably primitive feature – and all living squaliforms lack an anal fin.

There can be little doubt that squaliforms have pursued a separate evolutionary path from the lamniforms for many millions of years and the structural differences between the two groups, although small, are nonetheless significant. *Squalus* itself occurs as early as the Upper Jurassic, and teeth identified by the name *Pseudodalatias* from Upper Triassic

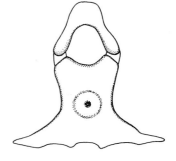

Fig. 8.3. Cross section of a squaliform vertebra showing calcareous lamellae in a ring around the central axis.

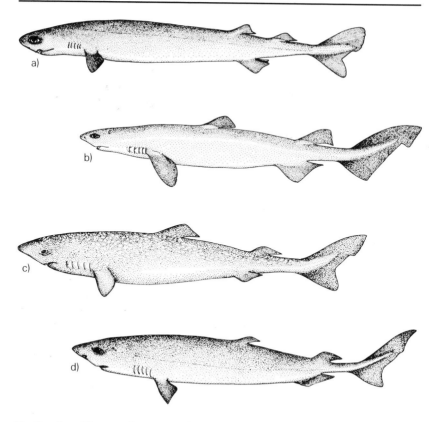

Fig. 8.4. Squaliform variety; examples of the Scymnorhinidae. a) *Isistius*, the cookie-cutter shark, about 50 centimetres (20 inches) in length; b) *Scymnorhinus*, the darkie charlie, about 1.8 metres (6 feet) in length; c) *Somniosus*, the sleeper shark, up to 6.5 metres (20 feet) in length; d) *Euprotomicrus*, about 23.5 centimetres ($9\frac{1}{2}$ inches) in length.

deposits in the English Midlands and Lombardy, in Italy, carry the history of the squaliform sharks back 200 million years.

By the end of the Age of Reptiles, 65 million years ago, squaliforms apparently indistinguishable from surviving genera (Fig. 8.4), were to be found in the late Mesozoic seas. The Squalidae (spined sharks) were well represented in these ancient oceans, with fossil teeth of *Squalus* itself reported from Cretaceous rocks in Asia and Europe. Today, this genus includes the familiar spiny dogfish, spur dog or piked dogfish (*Squalus acanthias*), a white-spotted, slate-coloured species, sometimes tinged with brown, which ranges from the temperate to subarctic Atlantic (in water of 4.4°–15.5°C or 40°–60°F), the northern Pacific (south to California, Japan, northern China and Hawaii), the Mediterranean and the Black Sea, and a similar longitudinal belt in the South Atlantic, southern Pacific, Indian Ocean and around South Africa. These fish

The lantern shark (*Etmopterus spinax*), a member of the Squalidae up to 45 centimetres (18 inches) in length which has small light organs embedded in its belly and lives in the eastern Atlantic at depths down to 2,000 metres (6,500 feet), feeding on crustaceans and squid.

undertake substantial seasonal migrations to keep within their optimum water temperature, western Atlantic populations in the northern hemisphere appearing off the United States east coast in the spring, then moving north to the cooler coastal waters of Newfoundland and Labrador for the summer, returning to New England in the fall. The winter months are apparently spent on the offshore banks of Newfoundland and Labrador, where breeding takes place. In addition, one specimen tagged off Washington in 1944 was recovered 8 years later some 8,000 kilometres (5,000 miles) away in Honshu, so spiny dogfish evidently travel very large distances, quite apart from seasonal migrations.

Attaining a length of just over a metre ($3\frac{1}{4}$ feet), *Squalus acanthias* is a neritic form, feeding voraciously on such fast-moving fish as capelin, herring, menhaden, mackerel, scup, hake, cod, haddock, pollack, blennies, croakers etc., as well as taking crustaceans and other invertebrates (worms, lobsters, jellyfish), and even consuming red, brown or green algae. Reproduction is ovo-viviparous, with two to six embryos developing initially in a large common egg capsule (or candle) within each uterus during a 22–24 month gestation period (the longest known in any vertebrate) and hatching inside the mother; the pups are born during autumn or winter and each measures 20–24 centimetres ($8-9\frac{1}{2}$ inches). Individual fish may attain an age of up to 30 years, judging from alternating light and dark growth rings developed in the second dorsal spine.

When hooked, the spiny dogfish puts up little resistance, but should be removed from the line with care as the dorsal spines incorporate poison glands at their bases which, when activated, transmit venom through a tract of white tissue to the point of the spine. Although not likely to be fatal, the victim may be incapacitated for some days. The meat of *Squalus acanthias* is sold in Germany as 'marine eel' and in Britain as 'rock eel', the annual European catch totalling some 46,000 tonnes.

Closely related species include the Cuban dogfish (*Squalus cubensis*), a slightly smaller fish than *Squalus acanthias*, the circum-polar southern hemisphere form (*Squalus fernandinus*) that is dark grey or brown in colour and attains a length of about a metre ($3\frac{1}{4}$ feet), and *Squalus megalops* from Australia and Japan.

Centrophorus (Fig. 8.1) is a slender squalid of widespread occurrence (the eastern Atlantic, the Mediterranean, South Africa, Japan, New Zealand and Australia), while *Centroscyllium*, another slimly proportioned genus, includes the black dogfish (*Centroscyllium fabricii*) of the North Atlantic as well as representatives in the Arabian Gulf, the Pacific, the Indian Ocean and the Falkland Islands.

Centroscymnus coelolepis, the dark chocolate-brown-coloured Portuguese shark (Fig. 8.1), grows to over a metre (nearly 4 feet) in length, has been recorded as deep as 2,718 metres (8,917 feet) and possesses dissimilar dentition in the upper and lower jaws, the superior teeth each bearing a single lanceolate cusp while the lower teeth are approximately quadrate with deeply notched, smooth-edged outer margins and set obliquely to form a continuous cutting edge. *Scymnodon* (Fig. 8.1), from the eastern Atlantic and Japan, is another squalid with differentiated upper and lower dentitions, and *Cirrhigaleus* from Japanese waters is distinguished by the possession of a prominent barbel extending from the anterior margin of the nostril past the corner of the mouth. In *Deania*, the teeth are all single-cusped but those of males are more erect in the jaws than those of females: this genus occurs in the eastern Atlantic, off South Africa and Japan, around the Philippines, and in Australasia (it includes '*Nasisqualus*' *profundorum*, a small dark brown species only 60 centimetres/2 feet long that has been found in deep water – 550 to 1830 metres/1,800 to 6,000 feet – around the Philippines).

One of the most obscure members of the Squalidae is little *Etmopterus*, which never grows more than 70 centimetres ($2\frac{1}{4}$ feet) in length, some of the smaller species of this genus measuring less than 30 centimetres (1 foot) when fully mature. Occurring as far down as 2,000 metres (6,500 feet), this diminutive dark-coloured shark has very prominent spines in front of its dorsal fins (of which the first is the larger) as well as the large eyes so frequently found in deep-water fish, while some species have luminous photophores (light-emitting organs) along the flanks that may help individuals to orientate themselves within hunting packs as they range across the lightless sea floor of abyssal depths in search of prey. The upper teeth are multi-cusped, those of the lower jaw being of a totally different single-cusped pattern, deeply notched outwardly and obliquely set to form a continuous cutting edge.

Etmopterus virens, the green dogfish (Fig. 1.5), occurs at around 350–400 metres (1,150–1,300 feet) in the Gulf of Mexico and, from the stomach contents of individuals caught in trawls, it is evident that they feed largely on squid and octopus. Even a full-grown green dogfish is only about 25 centimetres (10 inches) long, however, and cephalopod beaks and eyes found inside them have been so large that the fish must have had the greatest difficulty in swallowing them. To overcome such substantial prey, these voracious midgets must presumably hunt in packs.

Another phosphorescent species of the genus, the lantern shark (*Etmopterus spinax*) occurs as deep as 2,000 metres (6,500 feet) on the edge of the eastern Atlantic's continental shelf and also enters the Mediterranean. Up to 45 centimetres (18 inches) in length, it feeds on crustaceans and small squid. Reproduction is ovo-viviparous, eight to twenty-four young being born in each litter during the summer months. *Etmopterus hillianus*, some 30 centimetres (12 inches) in length, is found at depths of 360–730 metres (1,200–2,400 feet) in the West Indies, off southern Florida and Bermuda and in Chesapeake Bay, and a number of other species extend the range of *Etmopterus* to the southwest coast of South America, the Straits of Magellan, Japan, Australia, West Africa, the Hawaiian Islands and Madeira. Fossil remains carry the history of this elegant little shark back to the Upper Cretaceous, at least 65 million years ago.

Also usually numbered among the Squalidae (although sometimes assigned to a separate family of their own) are the angular rough sharks (*Oxynotus*, Fig. 8.1), with short stout bodies of rectangular cross-section, spined dorsal fins, high backs and longitudinal ridges located low down on the flanks. *Oxynotus centrina*, the humantin or prickly dogfish of the eastern Atlantic and Mediterranean, is the best known of these rough-skinned little sharks, which only grow to about a metre ($3\frac{1}{4}$ feet) in length and live on the bottom at depths of 30–500 metres (100–1,650 feet), preying on hard-shelled invertebrates. The upper teeth are arranged in a triangular patch on the roof of the mouth, with only two or three teeth in the first series and a greater number in each of the six or so succeeding rows, while the lower teeth are blade-like, arranged in a single series, and point backwards. The mouth is surrounded by thick spongy lips with a complex series of cross-folds and the dermal denticles that cover the skin are large and prominent, endowing *Oxynotus* with the rough-textured integument from which the common name of the genus is derived. Reproduction is ovo-viviparous, pregnant females containing three to twenty-three large eggs or embryos. Other species of rough sharks include *Oxynotus bruniensis* (the prickly dogfish) from Tasmania and *Oxynotus paradoxus* (the eastern Atlantic, from Ireland to Morocco and the Gulf of Gascony), while fossils referable to the genus have been found in the late Tertiary of Italy.

The spineless dogfishes or sleeper sharks (Scymnorhinidae) include squaliform sharks that typically lack spines in front of their dorsal fins (one genus still has a spine in front of its first dorsal, although this is largely or wholly buried in the skin) and possess single-cusped teeth, those of the upper jaw being narrow and conical while the lower series are widely expanded laterally to form a cutting edge.

Scymnorhinus (Fig. 8.4) itself (formerly called *Dalatias* and still often referred to by that name) is a moderate-sized shark some 2 metres ($6\frac{1}{2}$ feet) in length that is variously known as the black shark, black jack or darkie charlie (it is in fact dark brown). Present in the eastern Atlantic, the western Mediterranean, off South Africa and Japan, and in Australasian waters, it is an ovo-viviparous species normally frequenting depths of 100–1,000 metres (325–3,250 feet). Its fossil remains occur in rocks as old as the Upper Cretaceous.

Little *Isistius* (Fig. 8.4) is a short-snouted genus that barely reaches 50 centimetres (20 inches) in length and has slender, thorn-like upper teeth opposed by a widely spaced lower series of triangular teeth each with a smooth-edged or only partly serrate cusp originating from a quadrate base. Replacement apparently occurs a whole row at a time, specimens having been taken with both the new series and the old one in place together. The occurrence of numerous mandibular teeth in the stomach (twenty-seven in one example that displayed no gaps in its functional dentition) suggests that they were swallowed with food when they became loose, the basal interconnections between them being broken up, partly by the act of biting and partly by the effect of the processes of digestion.

The teeth of *Isistius*, which have led to it becoming known as the cookie-cutter shark, are so sharp that it is a very difficult form to catch in a trawl, as it quickly chews through the net and releases itself. It attacks tuna, porpoises, whales, squid and other sharks, from which small round cores of flesh are taken. Possibly *Isistius* approaches its victim head-on, secures a brief purchase with its sucker-like lips (aided by a tongue-created vacuum) and then, as the flow of water swivels the creature around, it removes a disc of meat with its extraordinary teeth. Lesions apparently due to the depredations of *Isistius* have been reported in whales, porpoises and tuna, as well as on the throat and body of the massive filter-feeding shark *Megachasma*, while the neoprene sonar dome shields of American nuclear submarines have also been damaged.

An array of brilliant photophores covers the ventral surface of *Isistius* and extends in gradually diminishing numbers up the flanks (there are almost none on the back). Individuals vary as to the degree of illumination of which they are capable, but a really switched-on specimen glows an incredibly vivid green colour.

Isistius brasiliensis is found not only off Brazil, as its name implies, but also throughout the tropical and subtropical Atlantic and Pacific, as well as in the East Indies and around Australasia, while *Isistius plutodus* is a slightly larger species with even more disproportionately large lower teeth from the Gulf of Mexico and the Riu-Kiu trench off Okinawa. The genus is normally found at depths of less than 600 metres (2,000 feet).

Even smaller than *Isistius* is *Euprotomicrus* (Fig. 8.4), a shark with a smooth-skinned, subcylindrical body and a blunt snout, the head making up something like 25 per cent. of its total length. *Euprotomicrus* has slender, symmetrical, slightly recurved upper teeth, the lower series being outwardly directed so that the inner edges make an angle of about 45° with the jaw. The only known species is *Euprotomicrus bispinatus*, which seems to prefer mid-oceanic waters, occurring in the Indian Ocean near Mauritius, in the north Pacific between Hawaii and California, and around Australia and New Zealand. It grows to about 27 centimetres ($10\frac{1}{2}$ inches) in length and is strongly luminescent, photophores concentrated along the belly and lower regions of the flanks generating a pale greenish light that flares up when the fish moves and then dies down as it becomes quiescent again.

But sharks still smaller than *Euprotomicrus* have been found. *Squaliolus* (Fig. 1.1) is the most minute living shark that is known to science, so diminutive it could be held in the palm of a man's hand. This tiny creature looks very like *Euprotomicrus*, but has a proportionately longer, more posteriorly located first dorsal fin that is stiffened by a spine (a unique exception to the general rule that scymnorhinids are spineless), as well as a pointed snout. The head makes up about a third of the overall length and the concave crowns of the dermal denticles give the integument a pebbly texture.

Squaliolus laticaudus, commonly known as the midwater or dwarf shark, was the first species of the genus to be described. This jet black, cigar-shaped mini-shark with white fins was discovered living nearly 180 metres (600 feet) deep in the waters of the Philippines: an adult male and a mature female scarcely 15 centimetres (6 inches) long that had been caught in Batangas Bay, Luzon, were described in the scientific press in 1912. Nearly half a century later, on 2 June 1961, some Japanese shrimp fishermen caught five more examples of what they called *tsuranagakobito-zame* ('the dwarf shark with a long face') in Suruga Bay, Honshu, none of which exceeded 13 centimetres (5 inches) in length.

Marginally larger than *Squaliolus laticaudus* is *Squaliolus sarmenti*, the first known specimen of which was a female taken off Madeira during the 1920s, on lines reaching down to 1,400 metres (4,600 feet) for the capture of black swordfish (*Aphanopus carbo*). This species, which grows to 24.6 centimetres ($9\frac{3}{4}$ inches) is blackish brown above and slaty black below, with a fine shagreen of small quadrangular tubercles each bearing four ridges. A second example of *Squaliolus sarmenti* was obtained in April 1935, but surprisingly this came from quite shallow water: it was taken among eel grass near Arcachon, on the Bay of Biscay.

Another tiny scymnorhinid was identified in 1966 among a catch trawled off Cape Town by the fishing vessel *Arum*. Very similar to *Euprotomicrus*, but with a more robustly proportioned body, more or less equal-sized dorsal fins, and larger gill openings, the solitary specimen so far known (a male 17.6 centimetres/7 inches long with a brown body darkening to black on the belly) has been described as *Euprotomicroides zantedeschia*, the specific name being derived from the Latin name for the South African arum lily (*Zantedeschia*), in recognition of the part played by the crew of the *Arum* in securing this unique specimen.

Euprotomicroides was caught at a depth of 450–550 metres (1,500–1,800 feet), and it seems likely that these tiny sharks are essentially creatures of the deeps, despite their presence in shallow waters along the Bay of Biscay, but how they live and where their ancestors came from is totally unknown.

The Scymnorhinidae includes not only the smallest of all sharks, but also the largest of all squaliforms – *Somniosus*, the sleeper shark (Fig. 8.4), which regularly reaches a length of 2.4–3.6 metres (8–12 feet) and may occasionally measure up to 6 metres (20 feet). Rather stoutly proportioned, with a small head, a bluntly rounded snout, small external gill clefts and a prominent spiracle, *Somniosus* has a large first dorsal fin with a rounded apex, a short, deep and very wide caudal fin, incorporating a notched subterminal margin, and round-tipped pectoral fins. The upper teeth are small, narrow, conical and widely spaced in several rows, while the lower dentition is markedly asymmetrical with unserrated, outwardly-directed cusps and notched outer margins. Conical or thorn-like dermal denticles cover the skin.

Somniosus microcephalus, the Greenland or gurry shark, is the common northern hemisphere species. A slaty grey or black-coloured shark, with pale underparts, this sluggish bottom-dweller occurs in Arctic and northern seas where water temperatures may be as low as 0.6°C (33°F). Southward it ranges down to Cape Cod and the Gulf of Maine in the west, France and Portugal in the east, as well as cruising in Pacific waters as far south as Oregon, California and Japan, where sea temperatures may be 12°C (53.6°F) – the name *Somniosus pacificus* is sometimes assigned to these Pacific representatives of the genus.

The Greenland shark lives extensively on carrion, but also preys on seals, porpoises, fish and crabs. It feeds voraciously on offal in the vicinity of salmon canneries, whaling stations or seal-hunting areas, a predilection that has earned it the name of gurry shark on the New England coast (*gurry* is refuse derived from the processing of carcases at a whaling station), and there are ancient accounts of Greenland sharks penetrating far up the fjords of Iceland to feed on the carcases of horses that had ventured out on thin ice, fallen through and drowned. The greater part of a reindeer was found in the stomach of one Greenland shark, but stories of these creatures attacking Eskimos in their kayaks seem to have been exaggerated, as do accounts of them setting about living whales. That they gorge themselves to stupefied repletion on whale carcases is indisputable, however, and while engaged in this repast they seem almost insensible to blows from clubs or thrusts from knives or lances intended to drive them off.

The eyes of *Somniosus microcephalus* are infested by small parasitic crustaceans that may act as lures to the fish on which it preys. In spring, young Greenland sharks come inshore, followed a little later by the adults, and they do not return to deep water until September. Reproduction is ovo-viviparous, a 4.8 metre (16 foot) female having been caught near the Faroe Islands in 1954 containing ten embryos, while other females have been found nurturing great numbers of soft eggs without horny capsules (up to the size of a goose egg). There is some evidence that Greenland sharks are individually long-lived.

A single liver from a Greenland shark can provide up to 3 barrels (105 gallons/477 litres) of economically valuable oil, and the flesh is used in Iceland and Greenland as food for dogs or, occasionally, for human consumption. The meat of Greenland sharks must only be eaten dried or semi-putrid, however, as when fresh it produces an intoxicant poisoning, both in Man and dogs. The Eskimos make footwear out of the skin and, in Greenland, where there is (or was) a taboo on using an iron utensil to cut children's hair, special knives made from the teeth of this species were employed instead.

Traditionally, the Eskimos used to catch Greenland sharks through holes in the ice during the winter, using the entrails of a seal or some similar putrid delicacy as a bait. A shark rising to the opening in the ice would simply be gaffed with an iron hook and hauled out on the ice. Alternatively, a light was sometimes employed as a lure, or ordinary baited fish hooks on long-lines of common twine let down to the bottom would be used, this simple tackle being quite sufficient to haul in one of these sluggish creatures. During the summer months, Greenland sharks were hunted from small wooden boats, or even from frail kayaks constructed of watertight skins stretched over a light framework.

A small species, *Somniosus rostratus*, that only reaches a metre ($3\frac{1}{4}$ feet) in length has been reported from the Mediterranean and may be the same as *Somniosus longus* from Japan, while a southern hemisphere form, *Somniosus antarcticus*, occurs off the Macquarie Islands, about 1,600 kilometres (1,000 miles) south west of New Zealand.

Somniosus is known to descend into very deep water, and has been photographed on the bottom of the Pacific 1,890 metres (6,200 feet) down off Oahu, so it is conceivable that the northern and southern hemisphere populations do in fact interchange with each other but traverse the tropics at considerable depths where water temperatures are low enough to be acceptable to this native of icy seas.

Fossil teeth of sleeper sharks (*Somniosus crenulatus*) have been found in the Eocene of Morocco, so these lethargic creatures have evidently enjoyed a long and successful history.

The bramble or spinous shark (*Echinorhinus*) has been assigned to a family of its own, the Echinorhinidae, and is an offshoot of the squaliform assemblage that takes its name from the scattered, round, button-like

A sleeper shark (*Somniosus*) filmed at 2,008 metres (6,588 feet) off Baja California.

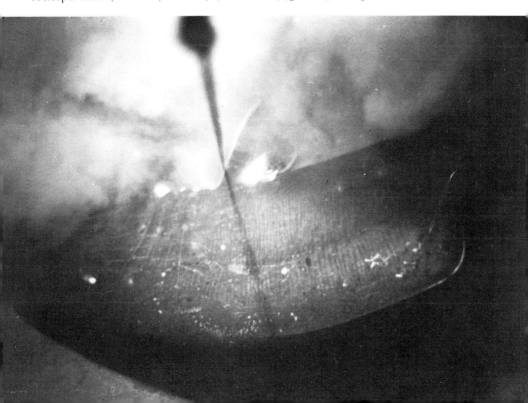

denticles studding the skin, some of which are surmounted by a tuft of small prickles resembling those of a bramble. The sole living species. *Echinorhinus brucus*, runs to 3 metres (10 feet) in length and is found in the eastern Atlantic, the Mediterranean and the Pacific, as well as occasionally appearing in the western Atlantic and as far south as Argentina and South Africa.

Dark brown in colour, sometimes with dark spots, the undersurfaces being paler-hued, the bramble shark has multi-cusped teeth in both the upper and the lower jaw, spineless dorsal fins, proportionately large external gill slits and minute spiracles.

A deep-water shark usually found near the bottom at depths of 400–900 metres (1,300–3,000 feet), *Echinorhinus* preys largely on fish (including spiny dogfish) and crustaceans.

That the squaliform assemblage as a whole includes so many bottom-living species may well be significant, taken together with the undeniably primitive retention in many of them of spined dorsal fins. The Mesozoic hybodont sharks were apparently largely bottom-dwellers as well, often with broad crushing teeth for breaking hard-shelled food, and also had prominent spines in front of their dorsal fins. Possibly the squaliforms are a less progressive group than the more dynamic lamniforms, retaining a preference for a benthic habitat as well as ancient anatomical characteristics. In contrast, the lamniforms have, to a large extent, left the bottom waters, acquired the more active life style of out-and-out hunters and, in the process, lost most of their more conservative structural features, as well as becoming in many cases substantially larger than all but a few of their squaliform cousins.

Chapter 9
Experiments in Evolution

There are two groups of undoubted sharks that have a most conspicuously unshark-like appearance, do not fit readily into any straightforward classification and are therefore usually assigned to separate orders of their own. These are the angel sharks or monk fishes (Squatiniformes), which look superficially more like skates than sharks, and the saw sharks (Pristiophoriformes), which resemble the sawfishes of the batoid assemblage (skates and rays).

Initial impressions can be misleading, however, and careful examination of these fishes makes it evident that they really are true sharks which have evolved similar specialisations to certain families of rays through pursuing a similar way of life. They are examples of parallel evolution, members of different – though distantly related – groups that went their separate ways many millions of years ago but have since acquired comparable structural adaptations to cope with the same sort of life styles and thus appear superficially very similar.

In the case of the squatiniforms, the original divergence of this stock evidently took place at a very early point in shark evolution because fossil examples of this order have been found in rocks of Triassic age which are some 200 million years old. These curiously flattened sharks are evidently bottom-dwellers, which explains their skate-like configuration. The pectoral fins are greatly expanded, with the front edge carried forward to an abruptly angled point that provides a fancied resemblance to an angel's wings. Unlike the skates, however, this anterior edge of the pectoral fins remains separated from the side of the head and the five pairs of gill slits are definitely on the sides of the throat and not ventrally located as in skates. The pelvic fins are also well developed and expanded, but most of the swimming effort is generated, shark-fashion, by the slimly proportioned, oar-like tail fin, which is used to scull the creature along (in contrast to sharks in general, the lower lobe is larger than the upper lobe). There is no anal fin, suggesting squaliform affinities, since one of the features that distinguishes the squaliforms from the lamniforms is the absence of this ventral median fin. There are, however, two small unspined dorsals set well back along the tail behind the level of the pelvic fins.

The head of squatiniforms is depressed, with a short, blunt snout and small, dorsally located eyes lacking nictitating membranes. The mouth is terminally situated, without the overhanging pointed nose of active predatory sharks, the nostrils are near the front edge of the upper jaw and have variously lobed barbels originating from their anterior edges, and the

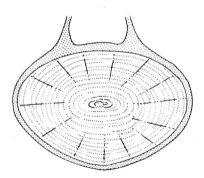

Fig. 9.1. Cross section of a squatiniform vertebra, showing multiple concentric arc-shaped lamellae.

large, crescentic spiracles are positioned close behind the eyes. No differentiation of upper and lower dentition is evident, the teeth all having a single horn-like cusp surmounting a broad base, with three or perhaps four series simultaneously in wear. The dermal denticles of the upper surfaces are spiky, possibly to deter would-be aggressors from above, but on the belly they become flat and scale-like, presumably to provide protection from rough obstacles or obstructions on the sea floor as the creature glides along close to the bottom in search of the flatfish (such as flounders or skates), shellfish and crustaceans on which it feeds.

The vertebrae of squatiniforms exhibit a characteristic pattern of calcification when transversely sectioned, with multiple, concentric, arc-shaped lamellae (Fig. 9.1) split by irregular divisions and the axial canal greatly constricted within each centrum. In the heart, there are six or

Fig. 9.2. The angel shark (*Squatina*), which grows to a length of 1.5 to 2.4 metres (5 to 8 feet), and its teeth.

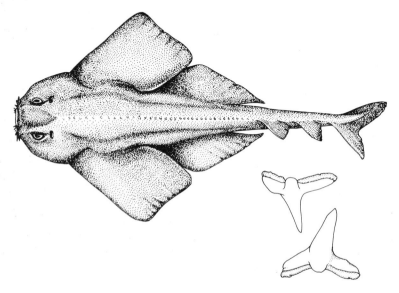

seven rows of valves – a number more typical of skates or rays than sharks, which normally have only perhaps three or four rows.

Reproduction is ovo-viviparous, the young each being provided with a large yolk sac, and breeding takes place inshore during the summer months when up to twenty-five juveniles are born in each litter.

Squatina itself (Fig. 9.2) quite a large fish, the common species (*Squatina squatina*) attaining a length of 2.4 metres (8 feet) and a weight of 77 kilograms (170 pounds). Known also as the monk fish (from a monk-like cowl on its head) or fiddle fish (its broad body, wide paired fins and long narrow caudal region recall a stringed musical instrument in shape), this form occurs in the eastern Atlantic and the Mediterranean. The coloration is normally grey or brown on the back (exceptionally varying from yellowish to nearly black) with dark spots or blotches, sometimes accompanied by white lines and spots, while the belly is white.

A rather smaller species, *Squatina dumeril*, measuring up to 1.5 metres (5 feet), is present in the western Atlantic at depths of 1,260 metres (4,000 feet) or more. This form attains sexual maturity at a length of about a metre ($3-3\frac{1}{2}$ feet) and usually has a greyish upper surface, tinted with red on the head and the margins of the fins, and reddish spots on the throat, abdomen and ventral part of the tail, the lower surfaces otherwise being white.

Other species of *Squatina* include *Squatina africana* (from South Africa), *Squatina armata* (from Chile and Peru), *Squatina argentina* (from the temperate western Atlantic), *Squatina californica* (the eastern Pacific from southern Alaska to Mexico), *Squatina australis* and *Squatina tergocellata* (from Australia and Tasmania) and *Squatina japonica* (from Japan and Korea).

Considering that angel sharks are by no means uncommon, it is surprising how little is known about their way of life. In an attempt to find out more concerning their habits, E.A. Standora and D.R. Nelson of California State University undertook to tag some of these sluggish sharks with ultrasonic transmitters. Around Santa Catalina Island, some 48 kilometres (30 miles) off Long Beach, California, there is a substantial colony of Pacific angel sharks. Standora and Nelson took out there a number of single- or multi-channel transmitters 15 centimetres (6 inches) long and 3.5 centimetres ($1\frac{1}{2}$ inches) in diameter that would emit 10 msec sonic pulses at 40 kHz, recording the fish's swimming speed, the depth at which it was located, the depth and temperature of the water, and the light conditions, as well as providing a tracking facility, the maximum range of the equipment being 5 kilometres (3 miles).

The attachment of these transmitters was effected by two SCUBA divers, who went down early in the afternoon to seek out the largely nocturnal angel sharks while they were resting on the bottom through the daylight hours. After an individual had been measured and its sex determined by checking to see whether or not it had the pelvic claspers characteristic of male sharks, an applicator pole was used to drive a stainless steel dart beneath the skin close alongside the mid-dorsal line, thus securing the transmitter. After an initial panicky flurry of swimming activity when the dart was thrust home, the angel sharks seemed largely to disregard the quite bulky transmitter, the only exception being an individual that was tagged too far back and ended up with the equipment trailing behind it. Not surprisingly impeded by this unwanted appurtenance, the fish declined to move more than about 600 metres (2,000 feet) in the entire 20 hours that it was under surveillance.

Those that had been successfully tagged were tracked from a 7 metre (23 foot) powerboat, which had on board receivers to pick up the eight information channels being used by the transmitters. Half-hourly sensor-data recordings were made, with the locations of the subjects plotted every hour when this was possible.

Five males and four females were tagged and it was found that, by and large, these creatures were nocturnal, bestirring themselves from the sand and mud of the sea floor as the light intensity fell off at sunset and demonstrating maximum activity levels at dusk and around midnight. The transmitters had a life of up to a week, but trackings were in fact limited to between 13 and 25 hours. During this period of time, it was found that the tagged angel sharks moved an average of 4 kilometres or $2\frac{1}{2}$ miles (a range of 2–9 kilometres, 1.2–5.6 miles), with a mean maximum rate of progression of 490 metres (1,600 feet) per hour. They swam at depths of 27–100 metres (90–325 feet), ignored sea-water temperature gradients in their foraging expeditions, and seemed to be territorial creatures with a home area of about 150 hectares (375 acres).

Recovery of the transmitters was undertaken either by SCUBA divers or through the medium of a magnesium break-away link that corroded through after a predetermined time in the sea, allowing the unit to bob to the surface buoyed up by a foam float.

While engaged in this exercise, divers found two angel sharks lying on top of the sand in an alert attitude during daylight hours, when most of their kith and kin were resting. One of these individuals was speared for examination and, on opening the stomach, it was found to have recently swallowed four blacksmith ranging from 11–15 centimetres ($4\frac{1}{4}$–6 inches) in length, the remains of these unfortunate fish being still essentially intact. Evidently angel sharks are sometimes active by day, although the night is their usual time for hunting. It was also found that, during the winter months, there was a sharp fall in the angel shark population at Santa Catalina island. By March, as the springtime became established, the numbers had begun to increase again, although individuals of rather small size were preponderant, and the June–July period produced the greatest abundance, most of these summer residents being fully grown adults.

Angel sharks are of little commercial value nowadays, although there was once a market for their rather coarse flesh in European fried-fish shops. The skin was formerly quite widely used for polishing wood and ivory and folklore held that the dried meat was 'a sovereign remedy for the itch'.

Successful sharks today, if their wide geographical range is any criterion, the squatiniforms trace their lineage back to the early days of the dinosaurs. Fossil representatives of the group are usually assigned to a separate genus, *Phorcynis*, which includes a number of species represented by excellently preserved specimens from the famous lithographic stone of southern Europe. This deposit, of Upper Jurassic age, dates back some 150 million years and was formed from fine sediment settling out in a tropical lagoon. It was widely used by nineteenth century lithographic printers (hence its name) and is a very fine-grained stone capable of preserving fossils in astonishing detail.

The saw sharks (Pristiophoriformes) are a good deal less ancient than the angel fish, making their first appearance in the Upper Cretaceous, about 75 million years ago. Their most conspicuous distinguishing characteristic is a greatly elongate blade- or beak-like rostrum, armed laterally with sharp, transverse tooth-like structures, giving these forms more than a passing resemblance to the sawfishes (a group of rays). Unlike rays, however, the saw sharks do not have the origins of their pectoral fins extended forward along the sides of the head and posses free upper eyelids, while the five or six pairs of gill openings are lateral rather than ventral in position – features that indicate membership of the shark assemblage. The two dorsal fins lack spines, there is no anal fin (an absence typically diagnostic of squaliform sharks to whcih the pristiophorids may be related) and the oral dentition (Fig. 9.3) comprises small, single-cusped teeth arranged in several functional series. Three rows of heart valves are present and the vertebral column is completely segmented with the notochord restricted by the centra.

Not of any great size, the pristiophorids grow only to about 1.2 metres (4 feet) in length, including the curious-looking rostrum with its pair of long sensory barbels trailing downwards. Manifestly bottom-dwellers of

Fig. 9.3. The saw shark (*Pristiophorus*), which reaches a length of about 1.2 metres (4 feet), and its teeth.

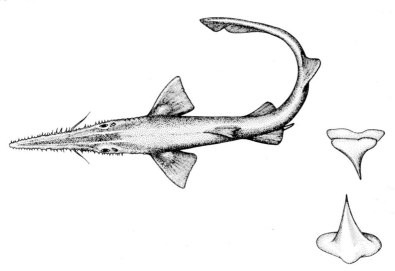

the continental shelves and upper slopes at depths of 18–950 metres (60–3,000 feet), they allegedly plough this saw-like structure along the sea floor between algae and seaweeds in search of prey and possibly also use it to disable small fishes and crustaceans after the manner of the true saw fishes. Reproduction is ovo-viviparous, the 'teeth' of the rostrum lying flat against the snout in the unborn young to avoid damaging the walls of the birth passage and becoming erect only after the juvenile has emerged.

Pristiophorus itself, the five-gilled saw shark, occurs in the seas of Australasia where an extensive fishery for them exists off the south Australian coast, in the Philippines and around Japan and Korea. The six-gilled saw shark (*Pliotrema*) has, as its common name indicates, an additional pair of gill slits over and above the normal complement of five customarily found in sharks. In modern seas, it is known only from South Africa.

Extinct pristiophorids occur in North America, Europe, southern Africa, New Zealand and Australia, but in no case is the material older than the Cretaceous period (e.g. *Propristiophorus* from the Upper Cretaceous of Lebanon) and much of it is considerably younger. *Ikamauius*, from the Cenozoic of New Zealand, ranges from the Upper Eocene to the Lower Pleistocene and is distinguished by rostral teeth that are barbed along both their front and back margins, *Pristiophorus*, in contrast, has unbarbed rostral teeth, and *Pliotrema* is intermediate in this respect with rostral teeth barbed only on their posterior edge.

Chapter 10
Ancestors from Ancient Seas

Today the nearest ocean to Ohio is 480 kilometres (300 miles) away – the Atlantic coast of New Jersey. But in Upper Devonian times, 350 million years ago, a broad incursion of the sea extended southwest from the St Lawrence region across the Great Lakes down to Arkansas and the waters of an ancient ocean rolled over what are now the rich farmlands of America's buckeye state.

In those waters swam some of the earliest known sharks. Already sleek, streamlined predators sometimes as much as 2 metres ($6\frac{1}{2}$ feet) in length, with fierce-looking teeth, each comprising a large central cusp and various numbers of lateral denticles on a horizontally expanded base, these archaic sharks were fast-moving killers that lived on the myriads of small fish flourishing in the Devonian seas. Like all sharks, living and extinct, their skeletons were almost entirely cartilaginous, but remarkable conditions of fossilisation in the deep, soft sediment of the ancient ocean floor led to some specimens being so beautifully preserved that not only is the soft cartilaginous skeleton still discernible but there is even evidence of gill filaments, muscle structure, the kidneys (with their tubules) and the contents of the digestive tract. Today the bodies of these Devonian sharks are found in concretions up to 2 metres ($6\frac{1}{2}$ feet) in length that weather out of the soft shale along the steep banks of Ohio's Rocky River, or become exposed in the waterway bed. Sometimes a complete fish is found inside, sometimes only a part of one, but usually the specimen is belly uppermost having sunk quickly after death and settled deep into the thick sand and mud of the sea floor, subsequently becoming inverted by gaseous accumulation in the digestive tract as decomposition set in.

The fossil sharks of Ohio were first investigated in detail by Bashford Dean, the young New York scientist whose studies in Japan disclosed so much information about one of the most conservative of all living sharks, *Chlamydoselachus*. In 1894, Dean formally named the commonest of the extinct Ohio sharks *Cladoselache* (Fig 10.1). With its slender body and powerful heterocercal tail, it must have been quite a rapid swimmer – in some specimens, the intestines contain the fossil remains of agile little palaeoniscid fish that had been caught and eaten – but although evidently capable of a quick straight-line dash, its overall manoeuvrability was probably rather restricted. The pectoral fins were proportionately large but constituted little more than broad-based flaps with a row of basal cartilages from which unjointed cartilaginous radials extended right out to the edge of the blade; some degree of flexibility near the hinder margin was apparently provided by short subsidiary rays. The pelvic fins,

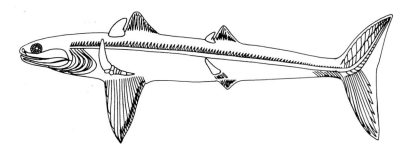

Fig. 10.1. The skeleton of the common Upper Devonian shark *Cladoselache*, about 2.5 metres ($6\frac{1}{2}$ feet) long.

likewise broad-based, were in addition very small, and neither the pectoral nor the pelvic girdle was fused in the mid-line to provide the firm point of origin for the paired fins seen in modern sharks. No anal fin is evident, but two dorsal fins occurred, again supported by cartilaginous radials, and each preceded by a short, antero-posteriorly broad spine that had only a shallow insertion in the muscles of the back so that it may not have been the evolutionary precursor of the slender, pointed spines present in many later fossil sharks and a number of living ones. There were five pairs of gill slits, as is customary (but not universal) in sharks, and the eye was very large, anteriorly situated and surrounded by a ring of small, thin, irregularly quadrangular plates arranged in several series. It seems possible that this apparent emphasis on vision means that *Cladoselache* hunted its palaeoniscid prey either in deep, poorly lit water or else at night. The upper jaw (the palatoquadrate) was articulated with the braincase posteriorly via a large post-orbital ramus that contacted a post-orbital process of the cranium, while further forward it was tied to the suborbital shelf by ligaments and possessed an anterior articulation in the otic region; the hyomandibular element was moderately well developed as a supporting prop in the primitive amphistylic manner.

   No proper vertebral centra had developed in the spinal column, the principal structure still being the notochord, but just in front of the caudal fin a pair of small lateral keels were present on either side – probably an indication of a fast swimmer as similar structures are present in modern mackerel sharks.

Fig. 10.2. Fossil sharks' teeth of the 'Cladodus' type, common in the Devonian and the Carboniferous.

Cladoselache had teeth of a type known as cladodont (because they were first described under the scientific name *Cladodus*) that are fairly abundant in Palaeozoic rocks but usually occur in isolation and, in most cases, cannot readily be ascribed to any particular shark – lots of these ancient sharks had virtually identical teeth of this sort (Fig. 10.2). There was a large central cusp flanked by varying numbers of subsidiary lateral denticles surmounting a horizontally expanded base, the teeth towards the front of the mouth being larger than those at the back.

Despite its great antiquity, it seems likely that *Cladoselache* was not in fact the ancestor of all later sharks. More probably, it was a somewhat specialised side-branch of shark evolution that enjoyed a brief early prosperity and, hence, became very numerous in Devonian seas, with the result that its fossil remains occur in some abundance.

There were other sharks lurking beneath the ocean waves that rolled over eastern North America 350 million years ago. *Cladolepis*, *Ohiolepis* and *Deirolepis* are known from dermal denticles and *Tamiobatis* is represented by a fossil neurocranium from Kentucky (a state also inundated by the Devonian sea). In one particular respect, all of these genera were still very unprogressive: the males lacked the copulatory claspers that are universally present in modern sharks and also occur in every known fossil species save *Cladoselache* and its allies. But living alongside the cladoselachians were a few small sharks that, while of otherwise archaic appearance, had nonetheless managed to take a step further along the evolutionary road – by developing claspers. They were the coronodonts, the best known example of this family being *Diademodus* (Fig. 10.3), an elongate, slender-bodied form with a prominently pointed snout and rather small eyes that may not have been a particularly accomplished swimmer, to judge from its rather inefficient-looking fins. Possibly it was a scavenging bottom-dweller, although fossil gut contents found in particularly well preserved specimens include sharks' teeth and the scales of bony fish, so perhaps *Diademodus* was more agile than appearances suggest and capable of catching some of its less wary contemporaries. *Coronodus* itself is based only on detached teeth and these early progressive sharks are not very well known, but they evidently represent a structural advance – albeit only a small one – over the cladoselachians.

Where these first known sharks came from is still a mystery. The best candidates for shark ancestry may be the placoderms, the first group of

Fig. 10.3. *Diademodus* equally as ancient as *Cladoselache* but more advanced in the possession of pelvic 'claspers' (the presence of a second dorsal fin is speculative). About 40 centimetres (16 inches) long.

fishes (or indeed vertebrates) to have jaws. They made their debut late in the Silurian period, about 400 million years ago, and all but one line of placoderm evolution was extinguished during the transition from Devonian to Carboniferous time; only the little acanthodians persisted longer, these so-called 'spiny sharks' enduring for another 140 million years until the Permian – and it is not certain that they were really placoderms at all. Some authorities regard the acanthodians as an entirely separate subclass more closely related to the bony fishes than to the cartilaginous ones. Although placoderms had successfully modified their most anterior gill arches to form upper and lower jaws, this structural re-arrangement was still imperfect and whether sharks (along with their allies, the chimaeras) are really of placoderm derivation, or whether all three groups – sharks, chimaeras, placoderms – trace back independently to some unknown ancestral group now lost in the mists of early Palaeozoic time, is a matter for speculation. The origin of sharks is a mystery and will probably always remain one. *Cladoselache* and its relatives appear in the fossil record as fully evolved sharks with no known antecedents.

The next step forward from the cladoselachians and coronodonts is represented by the ctenacanthids, which still looked very much like the primitive sharks of Ohio's Devonian sea but now had typical, deeply inserted, shark-like spines acting as cutwaters in front of the two dorsal fins, while their pectoral fins had only three basal elements articulating with the shoulder girdle, thus offering a potentially somewhat more flexible joint, although the fin apparently still retained a broad union along the flank.

Dorsal fin spines are the most frequently-encountered evidence of ctenacanth sharks, body impressions or remains of their skeletons being rare. Readily identified by their longitudinal ribbing, these spines occur in deposits extending from the Upper Devonian through the Carboniferous and the Permian, with a few specimens still turning up in the Triassic. On this evidence, ctenacanths were present in the Devonian seas of eastern North America alongside *Cladoselache*, but their heyday was undoubtedly the Carboniferous – the Age of Coal Forests, when vast low-lying swamps along the edges of the continents supported a luxuriant tropical vegetation which rotted down eventually to become coal.

The ctenacanths had cladodont-type teeth, amphistylic skulls with the upper jaw braced by the hyomandibular element as well as being articulated to the auditory capsule of the braincase, and strongly-heterocercal tails. *Goodrichthys* (Fig. 10.4) is one of the best known members of the group, this species being represented by a specimen over 2 metres ($6\frac{1}{2}$ feet) long discovered in Carboniferous rocks at Glencartholm, Eskdale, Scotland; unfortunately the fossil is contained in nearly 200 separate pieces of rock and is therefore not easy to interpret. *Ctenacanthus* itself includes a vast collection of species established in most cases only on fin spines, while *Phoebodus* is, if anything, even more obscurely known.

A temporarily quite successful off-shoot from the early shark stock was the xenacanth line (Fig. 10.5), which comprised freshwater forms that

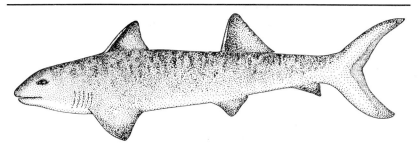

Fig. 10.4. *Goodrichthys*, a ctenacanth shark from the Lower Carboniferous of Scotland. Length approximately 2.3 metres ($7\frac{1}{2}$ feet).

prospered from late Devonian times until the early Permian and persisted into the Triassic in Australia. They were elongate, slim-bodied sharks with a posteriorly projecting spine at the back of the skull, a single continuous dorsal fin extending right the way along the back, and a diphycercal tail (with the spinal chord running through it almost straight and long upper and lower fin webs, the ventral one being rather weakly developed). The anal fin was a curious double structure, the paired fins had supporting rays arising from either side of a central axis (the pelvics of males incorporated claspers), and the teeth were of a characteristic twin-cusped type with a small median denticle. Aberrantly specialised in all these features, the xenacanths still had a primitive amphistylic jaw articulation and were ill-equipped to cope with the challenge posed by newly arisen groups of bony fish that began to make their appearance both in freshwater and in the seas as the Palaeozoic era waned. Their final extinction took place early in the Mesozoic.

By Permian times, however, sharks were on the brink of a major step forward in their evolutionary advance. The first hybodonts had arrived.

The peculiar *Trystychius* (Fig. 10.6), a Coal Age genus that may be an early hybodont, was something of an aberration that did not long survive. It had its external gill openings covered by an opercular flap – a structure unknown in any other shark, living or extinct – and the pectoral fins articulated with the shoulder girdle through only two basal elements (all other sharks have at least three), while the dentition consisted entirely of flattened crushing teeth.

Fig. 10.5. The extinct freshwater shark *Xenacanthus*, about 75 centimetres ($2\frac{1}{2}$ feet) long.

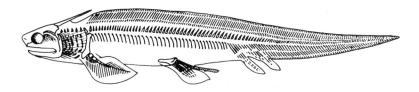

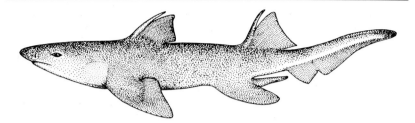

Fig. 10.6. *Trystychius*, an early hybodont unusual in possessing external gill covers supported by hyoid rays. About 60 centimetres (2 feet) long.

Typical hybodonts first appear in the Carboniferous and subsequently became the dominant Mesozoic sharks – common denizens of the seas throughout the Age of Dinosaurs. These successful but still comparatively unspecialised sharks began to exhibit substantial shortening of the cranium as they approached the level of structural sophistication seen in modern sharks, but an amphistylic jaw articulation was retained. However, there was a progressive tendency for the upper jaw element (the palatoquadrate) to lose its post-orbital articulation with the braincase, despite the fact that the jaws still remained elongate and extended to the tip of the snout. It has, in any case, been found that in those modern sharks which still retain the supposedly primitive post-orbital articulation, the joint is held together only loosely by skin, connective tissue, ligaments and tendons. It is readily disarticulated to provide additional freedom of movement for the upper jaw, and a similar arrangement possibly existed in fossil species that are regarded as primitive because they apparently possess a firmly interlocked post-orbital articulation. The teeth of hybodonts were arranged in multiple functional rows, those at the front of the mouth usually being sharp-cusped while at the back they were often low-crowned and blunt, suggesting a diet that included a substantial proportion of hard-shelled food such as molluscs. It seems likely, therefore, that the hybodonts spent much of their time cruising the sea floor and their rather heavily built bodies certainly lack the streamlining that makes modern oceanic sharks such superbly beautiful creatures.

The fins of hybodonts also indicate a somewhat less accomplished level of swimming ability than that of their successors in today's seas, although they nevertheless represent a substantial advance over the cladoselachians. In the pectoral fins, there was a narrow basal articulation, as in modern sharks, and the radial cartilages were frequently segmented, terminating some distance from the edge of the fin but with flexible ceratotrichia extending support towards the margin of the web, the entire structure being far more flexible and freely movable than in Devonian sharks. The two dorsal fins were each preceded by a spinous cutwater, while an anal fin was now present, located well to the rear in close proximity to the initially equilobate tail fin (advanced hybodont species have a reduced lower lobe, the upper lobe becoming endowed with enhanced flexibility due to the incorporation of jointed radials).

Along the spinal column, the notochord was persistent, surmounted by elongate neural arches, and the dermal denticles covering the skin were either single- or multi-cusped. Male hybodonts had pelvic claspers as well as one or two pairs of curious hooked spines located above each eye that may have served as additional coupling accessories during copulation.

Although fossil fragments dating back to the Devonian have been rather questionably identified as hybodontoid, one of the oldest undoubted members of the group is *Arctacanthus*, which is known from spines and teeth occurring in the Upper Permian of east Greenland and Wyoming – regions that 250 million years ago enjoyed a much warmer climate than they do today.

Hybodus itself (Fig. 10.7) is the typical Mesozoic genus, occurring worldwide from the Triassic to the end of the Cretaceous. A blunt-snouted shark with a moderately elongate body, it grew to at least 2.5 metres ($7\frac{1}{2}$ feet) in length and was quite slenderly built for a hybodont. Its more anterior teeth were sharp-cusped structures with a large central crown and one or more pairs of lateral denticles, which reduce in size progressively towards the back of the jaws, possibly indicating that *Hybodus* actively pursued some of its prey instead of relying entirely on sessile shellfish for food.

Acrodus (Triassic to Cretaceous) was very similar to *Hybodus* but with a dentition incorporating round, non-cuspidate teeth; *Dicrenodus* and *Hybocladodus* from the Carboniferous, with large, thick-crowned teeth, may be early hybodonts and *Asteracanthus* (Triassic to Cretaceous) had flattened dentition forming a grinding pavement, while *Carinacanthus* (from the Triassic of Pennsylvania) was a tiny shark only 15 centimetres (6 inches) long. *Hybodonchus* and *Nemacanthus* are known from fin spines of Triassic and Jurassic age, *Lissodus* (Lower Triassic of South Africa) and *Lonchidion* (Cretaceous of England, Spain and the United States) were small hybodonts not more than perhaps 50 centimetres (20 inches) in length, and *Wodnika* was an unusual almost fusiform genus with large crushing teeth and a weakly calcified skeleton that occurs in the Upper Permian of Thuringia.

Poorly known early probable representatives of the hybodont assem-

Fig. 10.7. *Hybodus*, the typical early and mid-Mesozoic shark. Up to about 2.3 metres ($7\frac{1}{2}$ feet) in length.

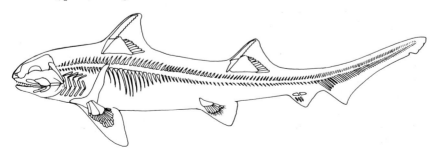

blage include such Carboniferous forms as *Trichorhipis*, *Styracodus*, *Sphenacanthus*, *Scoliorhiza* (also present in the Upper Triassic), *Petrodus*, *Onychoselache*, *Moyacanthus*, *Mesodmodus*, *Lambdodus*, *Holmsella* and *Echinodus*, while later genera that have never been adequately described include *Pristacanthus* (Jurassic of England), *Priohybodus*, *Palaeobates*, *Doratodus*, and *Bdellodus* (Lower Jurassic of Wuerttemberg).

During the Cretaceous period, the fortunes of the hybodonts declined precipitately. Many early lamniform sharks had now appeared and, at the same time, the old fish faunas of the Triassic and Jurassic, among which the hybodonts had flourished, were being displaced by an influx of new types – teleosts, the most advanced of all bony fishes, which swarm in uncounted millions in today's seas, providing the staple diet of modern sharks. In Cretaceous times, the teleosts were already represented by large species related to tarpons and herrings. In addition, oceanic invertebrate life was undergoing a revolution, with such formerly abundant shellfish as the ammonites becoming extinct mystifyingly abruptly. It was a changing world 65 million years ago, and the hybodonts had become out-dated relics of an earlier age. Unable to compete with the new generations of sharks, deprived of their food supply by widespread extinctions among prey species (both vertebrate and invertebrate), they vanished from the scene.

The Carboniferous and Permian also witnessed the flourishing of innumerable shark-like cartilaginous fish that apparently became totally dependent on hard-shelled prey picked from the sea floor. Some of these species persisted into the Triassic and early examples have been reported from deposits as old as the Devonian, but whether any of them should be included among the sharks proper is arguable. There are grounds for believing that some at least are more closely akin to the chimaeras.

Edestus, from the Carboniferous of North America, England and Europe, is a typical example of this problematical assemblage and, like virtually all of them, is very poorly known. The available fossil material consists essentially only of teeth – and what teeth! At the junction of the two halves of the lower jaw (the mandibular symphysis), there was a great semi-circular whorl of laterally-compressed, sharp-crested teeth, continuously erupting from the inner end of the series while worn out teeth were shed at the front. What sort of teeth *Edestus* had along the margins of its jaws is unknown, but the related *Sarcoprion* (Fig. 10.8) had a flattened lateral dentition forming a grinding pavement, the snout being prolonged into a greatly elongate rostrum.

Edestus and its allies, assigned to the family Edestidae, had disproportionately large eyes and the upper jaw (the palatoquadrate) was fused to the braincase in holostylic fashion. How they lived, and what they lived on, is problematical: some fifteen or so genera are known, possibly including *Ornithoprion* which still retained an almost free palatoquadrate, had a peculiar anterior prolongation of the lower jaw which projected even further forward than the extended snout, and possessed mandibular teeth that lacked the tubular dentine found in edestids generally, the crowns being of trabecular dentine with a thin layer of orthodentine.

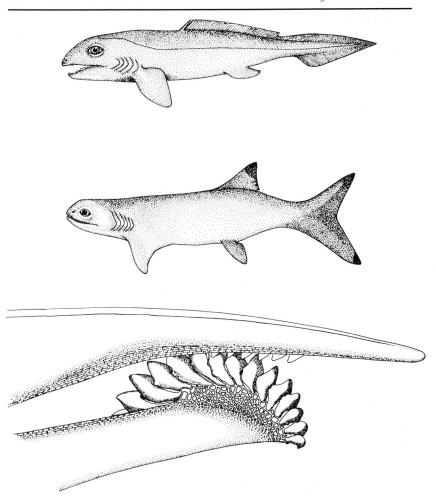

Fig. 10.8. (Top) The desmiodont *Heteropetalus* from the Lower Carboniferous of Montana (length 12 centimetres/$4\frac{3}{4}$ inches). (Centre) *Symmorium* from the Carboniferous of Illinois and Scotland (length 3 metres/$9\frac{3}{4}$ feet). (Bottom) the anterior of the skull and the symphysial region of the edestid *Sarcoprion* from the Permian of East Greenland, showing the tooth whorl rotating newly erupted teeth forwards into wear.

Somewhat similar to the edestids, but with their symphysial teeth transversely crested instead of laterally compressed, were the Caseodontidae, which still had their greatly reduced palatoquadrate elements articulated to the braincase at the front (by hook-shaped joints) and behind the eye socket. Again, the lateral teeth form a crushing pavement and, in one genus (*Fadenia*), the fossilised stomach contents consisted

165

almost entirely of brachiopods – precisely the sort of hard-shelled invertebrate which these small sharks might be expected to have eaten. *Campodus*, *Caseodus*, *Chiastodus* and *Romerodus* are from the Carboniferous and *Erikodus* and *Fadenia* date from the Permian; all of them come from North America or Europe.

Possibly assignable to another separate family (the Desmiodontidae) are *Desmiodus* and *Heteropetalus* (Fig. 10.8), both from the North American Carboniferous; these lacked a symphysial tooth whorl but had blunt-crowned crushing dentition, while the Eugeneodontidae (*Bobbodus*, *Eugeneodus* and *Gilliodus*, all of Carboniferous age and North American origin) had a pavement-like dentition that nonetheless still retained cutting edges.

The Symmoriidae include a number of short-nosed North American Carboniferous and Permian sharks with single dorsal fins, deeply forked tails, no anal fins and cladodont teeth. *Cobelodus*, *Denaea* and *Symmorium* (Fig. 10.8) are typical members of this group, but *Stethacanthus* (Fig. 10.9), sometimes included with them, may belong to a separate family. In *Stethacanthus* the structure above the pectoral fins is not a proper dorsal but an extraordinary wedge-shaped device bearing on its broad summit a battery of forward-inclined tooth-like denticles which bears a superficial resemblance to a brush. On top of the head is another

Fig. 10.9. *Stethacanthus*, from the Late Palaeozoic of North America, was about a metre ($3\frac{1}{4}$ feet) long and had an erectile dorsal appendage of brush-like appearance bearing forward-projecting dermal denticles that may have interacted with a patch of backward-projecting denticles on the head when the muscles connecting the 'brush' to the cervical vertebrae were contracted (lower illustration). The function of these features is unknown but they might have enabled *Stethacanthus* to take a grip on a passing larger fish, like the sucker of the living remora.

area of similar, though slightly smaller, denticles that are inclined backwards. The dorsal 'brush' seems to have had musculature extending forwards from an integral supporting spine in front of it to the cervical (neck) vertebrae, indicating the likelihood that it could be drawn forward at the same time as the head was pulled back, thus bringing the two patches of tooth-like denticles – on the summit of the 'brush' and the top of the head – into something approaching jaw-like opposition.

American fossil shark expert Rainer Zangerl suggests that *Stethacanthus* may have used these structures to simulate a large, heavily toothed mouth which would scare off would-be predators. On the other hand the patch of denticles on top of the head recalls the sucker similarly positioned on the head of remoras (sharksuckers) – living bony fish which have their first dorsal fin modified to form a double series of rough-edged transverse lamellae with which these curious creatures attach themselves by suction to sharks, barracudas or other large fish.

Could *Stethacanthus* have used its 'brush' and its head denticles to clamp a hold on larger fish to hitch a ride and perhaps share leftovers from its benefactor's meals? Certainly this metre-long Palaeozoic elasmobranch was an indifferent swimmer, with relatively weak fins, quite apart from the substantial drag that the 'brush' must have offered to the water, so hitch-hiking might have been its favoured means of getting around.

The elongate *Orodus* is assigned to a family of its own. This blunt-snouted genus from the Carboniferous of North America, the British Isles and Europe is distinguished by its proportionately small fins (the dorsal is unspined) and pavement-like crushing dentition, one group of teeth in each jaw ramus being greatly enlarged.

The ultimate in tooth specialisation among these enigmatic shark-like forms is to be found in *Helicoprion* (Fig. 10.10). Practically nothing is known of this genus except for its extraordinary dentition, which took the form of an enormous symphysical spiral, erupting continuously from the back forwards but without any facility for losing old teeth; instead, worn-out teeth were rotated up inside the structure of the lower jaw and retained there in a special chamber throughout the rest of the animal's life. Superficially this arrangement resembles that seen in edestids, except for the retention of spent teeth, but in *Helicoprion* the structure of the dentition is very different: there is no tubular dentine, such as occurs in edestids, and the outermost layer is of an enamel-like substance.

Helicoprion occurs in the Carboniferous and Permian of North America and in the Permian of Asia, Europe, the East Indies, Australia and Japan, but its origins and relationships are totally unknown. It is not even certain that it is an elasmobranch, although it is customarily placed in its own special family within this group of cartilaginous fishes.

The end of the Palaeozoic era, 230 million years ago, brought with it a massive wave of extinctions that decimated the life of land and sea alike. Sharks suffered no less than other groups and all of the curious forms with flattened, crushing dentition and bizarre whorls of symphysial teeth succumbed, either then or very early in the Mesozoic – the edestids and their allies, the enigmatic *Helicoprion*, all vanished. Why? Various reasons can be postulated. They must obviously have lived on some sort of hard-shelled prey and by far the most abundant hard-shelled animals of Palaeozoic seas were brachiopods – sessile bivalves filtering food from the water by means of a ciliated structure (the lophophore) which has the 'mouth' at its centre. Unlike molluscs, the shells of brachiopods comprise an upper and a lower valve (instead of a left and a right) and, from humble beginnings in the Cambrian period, these characteristic shells occur in astonishing abundance among the fossil faunas of the Ordovician, Silurian, Devonian, Carboniferous and Permian. Indeed, during Permian times, there were giant brachiopods to be found – the massive, spiny productids with shells 30 centimetres (12 inches) across.

It is inconceivable that the abundance of readily available protein food represented by vast colonies of brachiopods would not have been exploited by predators of some sort – and what better than the burgeoning population of sharks. That some edestids and edestid-like forms did feed on brachiopods has been irrefutably demonstrated by the discovery of fossil brachiopod shells in the stomach region of petrified late Palaeozoic sharks.

Once an animal becomes as specialised as, for example, *Helicoprion* obviously was, it is vulnerable. Adaptability has been irrevocably lost, the mould is too rigidly established. While conditions to which this advanced

Fig. 10.10. The tooth whorl at the apex of the lower jaw in the late Palaeozoic presumed elasmobranch *Helicoprion*. The teeth erupted forwards so that the oldest ones were at the centre of the whorl, retained throughout life in a cavity within the mandibular symphysis. Diameter of whorl about 19 centimetres ($7\frac{1}{2}$ inches).

level of specialisation were a response still prevail, the group will flourish, as the edestids did during the Late Palaeozoic. But change sooner or later is inevitable and, when it comes, the highly specialised species suddenly find themselves ill-suited to the new circumstances and so rigidly committed structurally to their old way of life that they have lost all capacity to adapt. Their structural options, as it were, have been sacrificed for a level of specialisation that gives an immediate evolutionary advantage under specific contemporary conditions but becomes a fatal liability if any change in the environment occurs.

This, it seems, is what happened at the end of the Palaeozoic. The continents, which had been joined together to form a single vast supercontinent called Pangaea, began to break away from each other. A world revolution was in progress. Geography and climate underwent radical transformation, the shallow seas which had hitherto provided such an ideal home for marine life withdrew from the margins of the separating continents until they only occupied about a third of their former extent, and everywhere the more specialised life forms found themselves under environmental pressure.

As major predators, sharks were at the summit of food chains and, in theory, could simply swim around to find more amenable localities where sea temperatures and conditions were to their liking. The relatively unspecialised hybodonts apparently did just this. As they were not irrevocably committed to a narrowly defined life style or food source, they could adapt: to new conditions, to new prey species. For the edestids, however, it was another matter.

In their case, the animals on which they preyed were largely or exclusively sessile invertebrates, like brachiopods, which were incapable of rapid or extensive migration. And at the end of the Palaeozoic, the brachiopods were decimated: they revived in subsequent geological periods, but never again dominated invertebrate marine faunas in the way they had during Palaeozoic days. Also, the replacement stocks were, in the main, radically different from their forerunners and doubtless a good deal less suitable as food for edestid sharks.

Brachiopods were not the only invertebrates to suffer severe reductions as the Palaeozoic era waned. The long-established trilobites – marine arthropods with their bodies longitudinally divided into three lobes – vanished entirely, as did the bactritoid cephalopods (straight-shelled relatives of the nautiloids): both of these groups may also have been food sources for the edestids and their kin.

Without much doubt, these remarkable sharks were the victims of their own advanced specialisation and must be numbered among the casualties of the great Upper Palaeozoic extinctions.

The freshwater xenacanths managed to survive slightly longer, into the Triassic period, but after their demise, the hybodonts became the dominant surviving group of sharks. Eschewing excessive specialisation, they were very successful, too, but early representatives of modern elasmobranch stocks were already present by Jurassic times, having possibly arisen from the ctenacanth group, and the Cretaceous brought

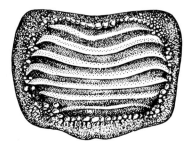

Fig. 10.11 Crushing teeth of the enigmatic *Ptychodus*, from the Cretaceous. (Left) Posterior view. (Right) Crown view.

another flowering of sharks with flattened teeth designed for crushing hard-shelled invertebrates. These were the ptychodonts, known almost exclusively from fossil teeth (Fig. 10.11) and, in consequence, a somewhat obscure assemblage, although evidently quite common (and hence presumably successful) for some 70 million years or so, to judge from the relatively large numbers of these curious flattened tooth plates that have come to light. They are present in Cretaceous marine deposits from North America and Europe to West Africa and eastern Asia, but evidently failed to survive the 'great dying' that took place at the end of the Mesozoic era, bringing the Age of Dinosaurs to a close.

The teeth of ptychodonts were arranged in paired longitudinal rows at the symphysial portion of the upper and lower jaws, with a single median series. In the upper dentition, this median row is composed of very small teeth with the first pair of rows on either side of it formed from proportionately large dental plates, succeeding lateral rows becoming progressively smaller; the lower dentition had a median row of large teeth, with the lateral rows diminishing gradually in size outwards.

What the ptychodonts lived on is problematical. Perhaps it was bivalved molluscs, or gastropods; maybe they preyed on the spectacular ammonites which, like the ptychodonts, all became extinct at the end of the Cretaceous. For one reason or another, however, they died out some 65 million years ago, along with all the hybodonts. The seas of the Cenozoic era, the Age of Mammals in which we are still living today, became the domain of the modern lamniform and squaliform sharks. As early as the Cretaceous period, there were goblin sharks, grey sharks, sand sharks, porbeagles, makos, great whites, nurse sharks, hammerheads, saw sharks and angel sharks, as well as a whole host of the smaller types, loosely referred to as dogfish and cat sharks.

It is not strictly true to describe sharks in general as living fossils or left-overs from prehistoric days. As a race, they are undeniably ancient, but only a few living species seem to be really primitive. Most modern sharks date back less than 100 million years or so – no great time span geologically – and they have now attained a level of structural sophistication far in advance of the extinct cladoselachians and hybodonts.

Chapter 11
A Role to Play

Sharks have few real enemies, save Man himself. A big predatory shark is a match for any other marine hunter, apart from sportsmen and commercial fishermen, so it is scarcely surprising that sharks proliferate wherever conditions are favourable, their numbers governed essentially only by the availability of food.

Small sharks, of course, are vulnerable to bigger sharks, and killer whales are known to attack sharks of quite large size, up to perhaps 3 metres (10 feet). Some species of sharks habitually follow schools of whales or porpoises, probably feeding mostly on left-overs from the meals of these sea-living mammals, but also no doubt preying occasionally on sick or injured animals that lag behind their fellows. Dolphins, however, have been known to attack and kill sharks, driving their bony beaked snouts into the vulnerable gill structure or the soft cloacal region where the weakly suspended intestinal tract is easily ruptured by repeated blows.

By and large, though, sharks are the hunters rather than the hunted and, like all predators, they have a role to play in maintaining the ecological balance of life in the seas. Apart from contributing to the maintenance of strong, healthy stocks of food fishes by catching sick or weakly individuals, the predacious sharks ensure that no one species of fish becomes over-numerous at the expense of other less prolific species, while shark populations are themselves held in check by the availability (or non-availability) of prey species. Without sharks at the pinnacle of the food chain, the numbers game that all species of fishes play would rapidly become unbalanced and chaotic.

Man has also found roles for sharks in his own economy, although, almost inevitably, it is a somewhat one-sided relationship offering negligible benefits to the unfortunate sharks, save perhaps a realisation that at least some of them are worth conserving, even if only to provide food, by-products or sport. Shark stocks are not inexhaustible – no species can withstand prolonged indiscriminate killing by Man and sharks are no exception to this rule.

In some ways, sharks are in fact very vulnerable to over-exploitation as a natural resource. Predatory animals are always in a substantial numerical minority compared with their prey, otherwise they would rapidly consume all the available food and starve to death. The balance of nature prevents this: when predators become too numerous, they are subject to a high mortality rate from food shortage that reduces the stock, while conversely a population explosion among prey species produces a concomitant increase in predator numbers to bring them back under control. Sharks, therefore, are not numberless. They may seem astonishingly abundant in some parts of the tropics, especially where such manifestly well adapted, highly evolved types as the carcharhinids or the hammerheads swarm in vast schools, but compared with the teeming millions of food fishes in the seas, they are in a very small minority.

Furthermore, sharks tend to be slow breeders (Fig. 11.1). Many species have less than a dozen young in a litter, some only two, and a corollary of such parsimonious breeding habits is an often long gestation period that ensures the emergent young, born alive and fully formed, have the optimum chance of individual survival. Even those shark species that do lay eggs tend to produce only a relatively small number and these are lodged in secure places to hatch. This is in marked contrast to other fishes whose breeding strategy is based on the hope that perhaps two or three eggs out of the millions which they strew indiscriminately in the sea will somehow escape being eaten or otherwise destroyed before they hatch. Even then, most of the larvae will be gobbled up by predators long before they develop into recognisable juvenile miniatures of their parents.

Because sharks are such slow breeders, no large-scale commercial shark

Fig. 11.1 Sharks that are ovo-viviparous or viviparous are slow breeders, the young being relatively few in number and born at an advanced stage of development after a long gestation period. (Top) An embryo of the ovo-viviparous porbeagle (*Lamna nasus*) about 18 centimetres (7 inches) long, with the stomach distended from swallowing unfertilised eggs lying adjacent to it in the uterus. (Bottom) An unborn embryo measuring 57.5 centimetres ($22\frac{1}{2}$ inches) of the viviparous oceanic white-tip (*Carcharhinus longimanus*), with an umbilical cord and the placental connection.

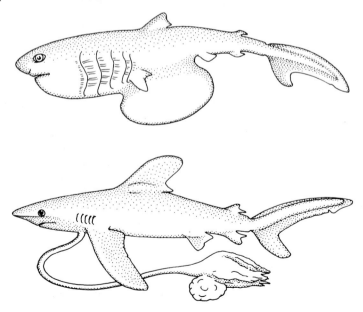

fishery established in any one locality has ever proved viable. In a matter of months, or at best a few years, the shark stocks are fished out and they take decades to regenerate. Small-scale enterprises have more prospects of maintaining themselves, since they make less severe inroads into the available stocks, but financial returns are proportionately much less. Even sport-fishing can seriously deplete shark populations. Off the Australian coast, the popularity of shark-hunting with powerhead weapons, as a means for young men to project the approved macho image, has led to a level of carnage calculated to make dramatic inroads into shark stocks, with the once common grey nurse (*Odontaspis taurus*) becoming scarce or, in some areas, even disappearing altogether. Peter Benchley's novel *Jaws* must be held largely to blame for this situation, especially since it was made into a major movie with two full-length feature film follow-ups, the last of them in 3-D for maximum spine-tingling impact. In United States' waters, the almost legendary Frank Mundus has seen the decline of the shark-fishing game off his Long Island home port. Back in the 1960s, a good day's hunting off Montauk would see his boat, *Cricket II*, sailing home in the afternoon with perhaps ten sharks already hanging from the pole, all hooked before noon. Now one or two sharks represents a reasonable return for a full day's fishing. Mundus himself thinks that a decline in the number of baitfish may be at least partly responsible, the menhaden population having been almost fished out by foreign trawlers, particularly those from Russia. If there is hardly anything to eat, big sharks are not going to hang around Montauk Point any more.

Shark-fishing for sport nonetheless remains a big leisure business in tropical vacation areas like Florida, Australia and the Caribbean. An hour or more fighting to land a 45 kilogram (100 pound) shark with rod-and-line is calculated to leave even a fit, experienced fisherman with his back and arms aching. For an amateur, trying some deep-sea fishing on his annual holiday, it is certainly the thrill of a lifetime, but also a physical ordeal to which his muscles will be ill-atuned.

To attract sharks to the vicinity of a fishing boat, a lure is made up from a smelly mixture of fish bran, offal, guts, fish bones and blood, all secured in a bag that is trailed in the water. This is known as a rubby dubby bag and the odour of blood permeating through the water will normally fetch sharks from a considerable distance, even if they are not really hungry. Once the sharks are circling the boat, they can be brought in even closer by 'chumming' – feeding them rubby dubby scraps over the side. Some fishermen carry a drum of whale oil slung over the stern and leaking into the sea (a practice now curtailed by whale conservation measures) and the Australian Alf Dean, a specialist in great whites, used to drape a dead seal over the transom so that blood oozed into the water.

For baiting the line, a couple of freshly caught mackerel are a favourite choice in North Atlantic waters, where sea temperatures are low, even in summer, and sharks require less food to keep their cold-blooded metabolism ticking over. In warm tropical seas, however, their higher levels of activity are matched by a more voracious appetite and they will take a hook baited with kingfish, salt pork, horse flesh or even rotten meat. One

British army doctor, stationed at Ahwaz, on the Shatt-el-Arab in the Persian Gulf, tried to catch the sharks which infested the waters of this river in the summer months by using ripe appendices extracted in the local military hospital. He seems to have had singularly little success.

Quite often baits will be floated at different levels, with perhaps a shallow line at 9 metres (30 feet), another at 18 metres (60 feet), and a deep bait at 27 metres (90 feet). If the sharks can see the trace, they may be suspicious and circle warily, sniffing in almost dog-like fashion with their sensitive, pointed noses. A skilled fisherman may move the bait away a little, so as to suggest to the shark that its prospective meal is about to escape. This may be enough to persuade the shark to take the bait.

When the shark comes in, it comes fast, and usually from below, braking its forward rush with the large pectoral fins, seizing the bait and then heading down deep with it. The line runs out in a rush from a multiplying reel that turns without the reel handle revolving with it – an out-of-control reel of the old type can break a man's fingers as its handle spins wildly while the line races out. With a multiplying reel, the fish runs against a pre-set drag of, say, 18 kilograms (40 pounds) which will give a 4.5 kilogram (10 pound) margin for the 22.5 kilogram (50 pound) dacron line that is usually quite adequate in temperate northern waters, combined with a 12-0, 14-0 or perhaps 16-0 hook. Some remarkable catches have been made with line a good deal lighter than this: in the summer of 1984, Denis Froud, from Maidstone, Kent, landed a 50 kilograms (110 pounds) porbeagle on a 1.8 kilograms (4 pounds) line after playing it for 2 hours off the Hampshire coast. In the tropics, where bigger, faster sharks can be expected, stainless steel hooks will be required, with a thousand yards or more of 68.5 kilogram (130 pound) line on a 14-0 or 16-0 reel and a huge multiplier.

Sometimes a shark that has taken a bait will swallow it immediately, especially if it is a greedy, voracious tropical specimen. Then it will usually head for deep water, with the line running out so fast that, if it is a really big, powerful fish, water has to be thrown over the reel to cool it.

Alternatively, the shark may seemingly play with the bait for a while, trying to carry it to an area clear of other sharks, then turning it between the jaws to a comfortable position for swallowing. Finally the bait is taken. This time, however, the shark will not immediately race off: the knowledge that it is caught will not as yet have dawned on it. When realisation comes, the shark really goes and then the linesman strikes.

Ideally, the hook should go into the shark's mouth, but it will often instead sink into the gills or gullet, where it will cause massive haemorrhage and rapidly weaken the fish. The clouds of blood leaking out will attract other sharks and the fisherman is quite likely to end up with two sharks on his line if the first one was small enough to be swallowed whole by a bigger fish. Alternatively, when he does pull his catch in, it will have been extensively mutilated by other sharks taking bites out of it.

A shark hooked in the mouth will fight hard and long, sometimes for hours. On occasion, this may be long enough for the hook to work such a large hole in its mouth that the shark breaks free. On other occasions, a

(Left) The hazards of diving with sharks were vividly demonstrated when top underwater photographer Ron Taylor of Australia pictured this white-tip reef shark (*Triaenodon obesus*) biting at his wife, Valerie Taylor. Fortunately, she was wearing an experimental protective suit of chain mail that effectively guarded her against the razor sharp teeth.

(Right) Always a fighter when hooked, the mako is a trophy worthy of any shark fisherman's mettle.

shark will roll when hooked, coiling the line around its body with the result that the sharp denticles studding its skin cut through the polyester fibre, leaving the shark to take off with the hook still in it. Some sharks jump spectacularly when first hooked (makos, threshers, black tips and white tips being notable examples) and sometimes fall back across the line so that it snaps under the sheer weight of the creature's body. An especially long wire leader is usually employed so that, even if the shark rolls in the line, its abrasive skin denticles cannot cut it. Whether a shark will live if it gets away with a hook and trace still in it depends on where and how deeply it was struck. If the hook is embedded in the gills or gullet, it will almost certainly die from haemorrhage, impairment of respiration or inability to swallow.

A big shark is 45 kilograms (100 pounds) or more – much more sometimes – of gristle and hard muscle. Playing it successfully, and getting it alongside the fishing boat, is not a job for boys – even the men frequently have to be strapped into a 'fighting chair' as the line races out and the rod bows under the strain of a really big hammerhead or great white, although a fish up to 2.4 or 3 metres (8 or 10 feet) in length can be brought in by a man standing up.

Not all sharks fight for their lives in spectacular fashion by leaping clear of the water. Great whites or tigers will simply dive deep and throw their weight and strength against the angler's arms, so that the line has to be brought in inch by inch, sometimes giving a little back, but always, in aggregate, gradually moving the shark closer to the boat. If the prospective catch is big enough to go into the record books, it must be landed with no-one but the original angler who made the strike handling the rod and without the rod touching any part of the boat. Only when the shark is at last close enough in for gaffing is the fisherman seeking a record allowed assistance: then someone else is permitted to grab the trace with a gloved hand and bring the fish in.

The best place to gaff a shark is in the belly behind the cartilage of the pectoral girdle. This is likely to precipitate a final desperate flurry as the fish is hauled out of the water, so the gaff rope must be instantly made fast around the transom post or a cleat while a heavy wire loop, like a giant rabbit snare, is dropped over the creature's tail; the frantic lashing of a dying shark's tail can do a lot of damage, not only to the anglers but to their boat as well, and if the catch is a thresher with a 2 metre (6 foot) tail the consequences could be catastrophic.

The shark is pulled aboard tail first and, as a precautionary measure, it is customary to mete out a welt with a suitable club across its surprisingly-sensitive nose to immobilise it. Bringing it over the side usually ruptures its stomach and, sometimes, the stomach is found to be actually everted from the mouth (possibly so that the shark can rid itself of undigested food the better to fight), but there is still a chance of getting a dying bite from the savage jaws or a dangerous blow from the rough-skinned tail. British shark-fishing expert, Trevor Housby, sustained permanent disability to his right leg when a big shark was hauled aboard his boat with a lot of life still left in it and proceeded to lash its massive tail around so much that it wrecked all the seating and the engine cover, as well as Housby's leg.

Commercial shark-fisheries are somewhat limited, although the total tonnage landed world wide in 1976 was still an impressive 307,085 tonnes. The only really important species caught in any numbers by fishermen is the spiny dogfish (*Squalus acanthias*). In Britain, 10,930 tonnes of this small shark were landed in 1982, mostly for marketing as 'rock salmon', the catch being somewhat down on the early 1950s' figure of around 14,000 tonnes per year but an increase on the 5,500 tonnes brought ashore in 1965, when this trade seemed to be in decline due to over-fishing. There is no longer much demand for spiny dogfish on the United States' market, where its oil was once sold in some quantities. Nowadays, the species is merely considered to be a nuisance in the western Atlantic, where it is held to do more damage to fishermen's gear than any other fish and causes considerable interference with commercial fishing activities – allegedly, the spiny dogfish tears nets, attacks netted or hooked fish, bites snoods off long lines and drives away the shoals of food fish.

The hides of some sharks are remarkable for their hard-wearing qualities and attractive markings. Shark skin is used for fashionable footwear, handbags, brief cases and pocket books. The skinning operation itself is particularly difficult because the toughness of the hide (calculated as being up to ten times the strength of ox-hide in the case of the tiger shark) is sufficient to dull rapidly the sharpest knife, while a single careless cut may so damage the skin as to render it almost worthless. Once successfully stripped in one piece from the carcase, the skin is subjected to 'beaming' to remove surplus flesh from the inner side, using a cleaver-like knife. The skin is then soaked for a week in sea water with a good coating of brine applied to the inner surface; a second coating of brine is then added, followed by a further week's soaking, with, 2 weeks later, a third and final brining to complete the curing process. Tanning now dissolves the tissues around the roots of the dermal denticles and also incorporates treatments to soften and finish the final product. Shagreen is the untanned denticulate skin, which is sometimes rubbed down to provide a coarse fancy trimming (for sword grips to prevent them becoming slippery when covered with blood, jewel cases, bookbindings, cigarette lighters, etc.), and is frequently employed as an abrasive or polishing agent by jewellers or cabinet makers (the 'darkie charlie', *Scymnorhinus licha*, used to be caught specifically for this purpose).

Species taken for their hides include the nurse shark (*Ginglymostoma*), tiger shark (*Galeocerdo*), silky shark (*Carcharhinus falciformis*) and lemon shark (*Negaprion*), all of which are caught for this purpose off Florida (the formerly extensive tiger-shark fishery in the Virgin Islands is now largely defunct). In the Azores, there is a substantial leather fishery for the 'darkie charlie', and the skin of the tope (*Galeorhinus*), carpet shark (*Orectolobus*) and zebra shark (*Stegostoma*) are noted for producing an excellent shagreen. Hammerheads are rather thin-skinned but also provide a durable and handsome leather after curing and tanning.

The designation 'shark skin' is also applied to certain synthetic fabrics made of acetate rayon that are used for summer sports clothes and resemble real shark skin in their smooth, shiny appearance, as well as to a two-coloured weave of woollen yarn that looks superficially like the processed hide of a shark.

Hammerheads are caught primarily for the oil from their livers, which is especially rich in Vitamin A, recorded potencies including a figure of 357,000 units of Vitamin A per gram in a 4.2 metre (14 foot) specimen taken off Florida and 55,000 units of Vitamin A per gram in another example. The vitamin content of the oil will depend on how well nourished the individual fish was when hooked. Vitamin D is never

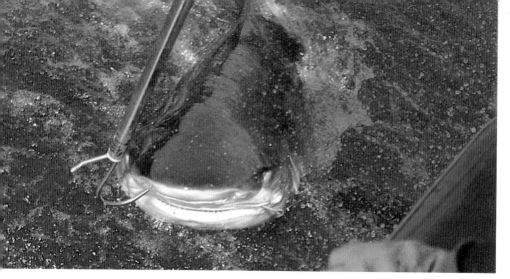

A gaffed bull shark (*Carcharhinus leucas*), with its characteristic bluntly rounded snout, is brought alongside for landing.

abundant in sharks' livers, presumably because this particular vitamin is associated with bone development and sharks have cartilaginous skeletons with only limited calcification and consequently a very small calcium requirement. In this respect, cod liver oil is a superior product, since it is richly endowed with Vitamin D, and, following the advent of synthetic Vitamin A production shortly after World War 2, the demand for sharks as a source of this substance has plummeted: between 1938 and 1945, something like 20 per cent. of the sharks taken by the fisheries along the east coast of Mexico (San José del Cabo, Mazatlan, Isla Maria Madre, Isla Isabela, San Blas) were hammerheads, as much as 4,000 pesos – a good sum at that time – being obtainable for only 18 kilograms ($39\frac{1}{2}$ pounds) of salted liver. Nowadays, these eastern Pacific fisheries are primarily for dried or salted flesh (bacalao), hides and fins; sharks caught on long-lines or hand-lines and in gill-nets and beach-seines include *Carcharhinus*, *Galeocerdo*, *Ginglymostoma*, *Negaprion*, *Rhizoprionodon*, *Sphyrna*, *Triakis* and various representatives of *Mustelus*, with a few of the smaller forms sold as fresh fish in the local markets. Even so, the trade is a declining one, with production of frozen shark fillets at Mexican fisheries falling from 5,877 tonnes in 1979 to 3,920 tonnes in 1981. In India, however, there is still a demand for hammerheads as a source of Vitamin A and embryos taken from pregnant females are considered a beneficial delicacy by nursing mothers as they are so rich in this substance.

An extensive liver-oil fishery for Greenland sharks (*Somniosus*) once existed on the coasts of Greenland, Iceland and Norway, as much as 3 barrels (477 litres or 105 gallons) of oil, representing 50 per cent. of the liver's total volume, being obtainable from a large example of *Somniosus*. This industry apparently originated about 1805 and, by the middle of the nineteenth century, was taking between 2,000 and 3,000 Greenland sharks a year. By 1914, the catch had risen to an astronomical 32,000 sharks in a single year but, subsequently, it declined steeply and is now no longer of major importance. Greenland sharks are still caught using hand-lines or long-lines fished at depths of 180–360 metres (600–1200 feet).

The basking shark (*Cetorhinus*) used to be extensively fished when animal oils were required for lighting purposes. The oil from its liver was regarded as comparable to sperm-whale oil in quality and a large specimen of this monstrous shark might contain 1,800 litres (400 gallons) in its liver. Small-boat harpoon-fisheries grew up during the nineteenth century in Ireland, Iceland, the United States (Massachusetts), Peru and Ecuador, but despite the periodic presence of large schools of up to a hundred strong, its numbers tend to fluctuate and the species is not now the subject of regular commercial exploitation. To a limited extent, it is still taken for oil, fish meal and the manufacture of fishburgers, notably in California and Japan, while the cartilaginous skeleton is made into fertiliser and the fins can be processed for soup.

Another shark once caught for its liver oil is the Atlantic porbeagle (*Lamna nasus*), the liver from a 2.7 metre (9 foot) specimen yielding perhaps 50 litres (11 gallons) of oil. In the early years of the nineteenth century, a major centre of fishing for this species was Provincetown, Cape Cod, the oil being in demand principally for tanning, but by 1850 this Massachusetts industry had largely died out. In the waters around northern Europe, the porbeagle was taken by the Norwegians (on long-lines) and the Germans (using herring-trawls), the flesh being esteemed in Italy, where it was known as *smerglio*, and parts of France. The Norwegian operation, which was taking just over 4 million kilograms (9 million pounds) of porbeagle a year in the early 1960s, eventually declined as the stocks were fished out.

Tiger sharks and lemon sharks also provide good quality liver oil, as does the seven-gilled shark (which is, in fact, known to Japanese fishermen as the *aburazame* or oil shark) and the nurse shark (caught for oil in the islands off the coast of southern Brazil, where the natives once believed its crumbly, limy ear stones possessed diuretic qualities). Japan is now the leading producer of shark-liver oil, processing 146 tonnes in 1978 and 130 tonnes in 1980, but the industry is of very small proportions.

Sharks have a rather limited commercial value for human food, but shark-fin soup is a famous Chinese delicacy: California-based Chinese use the tope to make up this remarkable culinary concoction. Other Chinese communities import the dried fins of grey sharks from Ceylon, the Philippines and elsewhere for this purpose, the cartilaginous fin rays, not the flesh, being the portion used. These rays are pressed into discs about 23 centimetres (9 inches) in diameter and 1.25 centimetres ($\frac{1}{2}$ inch) thick that resemble matted coconut fibres to touch, with a pale yellowish colour and a slightly glossy appearance. They dissolve into a pleasant-tasting gelatine that provides the essential ingredient of the famous shark fin soup. Japan produced 833 tonnes of dried unsalted shark fins in 1980 (compared with 700 tonnes in 1979 and 600 tonnes in 1978); other major sources include the Republic of Korea (115 tonnes in 1980) and the Yemen (82 tonnes in 1979), while India produced 332 tonnes of salted shark fins in 1980 (373 tonnes in 1979, 423 tonnes in 1978).

The flesh of hammerheads has a fine grain that makes it an acceptable item of diet in Japan, where highly regarded fish cakes are still made out of shark meat. The squalene component of liver oil is marketed as a health food useful in preventing heart disease and cancer, as well as promoting longevity. In addition to being sold as a general cure-all at around $1 a capsule under such trade names as 'Marine Gold' (the Japanese will take half-a-dozen or more of these pills a day), squalene is employed for the treatment of burns and as a base for cosmetics and lipsticks. It was even allegedly used as a lubricant in the Kasei radial engines of the World War 2 Mitsubishi J2M Raiden (Thunderbolt) fighters, which were brought into service during 1944 to intercept the high flying USAAF Boeing B-29 Superfortress bombers, operating at altitudes where the air is bitterly cold and lubricating oils need special qualities to function efficiently.

The meat of grey sharks is eaten fresh in the Philippines and elsewhere in the Far East, as well as in South America, where the freshwater-invading *Carcharhinus leucas* of Lake Nicaragua is caught for food. The small grey shark of the tropical eastern Atlantic and the Pacific (*Carcharhinus porosus*) is often to be found for sale as a food fish in the markets of Panama and Colon and, in southern Florida, the fins of lemon sharks are used for food. Shark flesh is, in general, no longer regarded as an acceptable item of diet in western Europe, although the meat of grey sharks was at one time eaten by the poorer classes in Italy and Greek fishermen reputedly used to catch thresher sharks for food.

As a source of curios for sale to tourists, sharks are becoming an increasingly profitable commercial proposition. At the major vacation centres in tropical latitudes, such as the Caribbean, every resort has its souvenir shops selling sharks' teeth (often made up as necklaces or bracelets), sharks' jaws (for nailing up on the wall of study or hobby room) and sometimes walking sticks made from the backbones of sharks.

In former days, however, sharks' teeth were a rather more sinister item of trade and barter. When the Pacific Islands were a centre of almost perpetual inter-tribal war, clubs and swords studded with sharks' teeth constituted terrible weapons, capable of tearing an antagonist to pieces.

Not only is there a great deal still to be discovered about sharks, but it seems very likely that we ourselves have much to learn from them. One of the two great killing diseases of modern Man is cancer (the other is heart disease), but sharks rarely suffer from neoplasms and hardly at all from malignancies, or so it would appear from the paucity of such disease lesions discovered in sharks that have been caught. They are not totally immune, however, although, in most cases, tumours found in sharks have arisen from the mesenchyme tissue (the basis of bone, cartilage, much of the musculature and the circulatory system) rather than the epithelial tissue, which forms the outer surface of the body and lines the digestive tract and is the commonest site of neoplasms in Man and other mammals.

In 1972, a diseased grey shark (*Carcharhinus amblyrhynchos*) nearly 120 centimetres (about 4 feet) long was taken at Enewetok Atoll in the Marshall Islands during a scientific programme designed especially to assess the incidence of disease in the sharks of the area. Just above and slightly in front of its right pectoral fin, there was a large, irregular, convoluted tumour. Careful histological examination showed that it consisted principally of collagen fibres and, deep within them, was a dermal denticle. There was no indication of virus particles being present, necrosis was minimal and none of the changes in cell structure normally associated with a malignant condition were observed. It appears to be a keloid, the first to be reported in any shark and only the second found in a fish of any sort (a comparable tumour was reported on a Spanish mackerel, *Scomberomorus masculatus*, taken off southwest Florida).

Keloids usually appear in human beings as a response to chemical irritation, injury, cauterisation, burns, or even something as simple as an injection. Individuals of African origin seem to be particularly susceptible, but it is not known if *Carcharhinus amblyrhynchos* is specially prone to keloid development or if the victim had been injured previously. Malignant changes do sometimes occur in association with keloids, but in human subjects are usually restricted to the overlying dermis and do not involve the epidermis.

Another benign tumorous condition, an epidermal papilloma, was found growing on the caudal fin of a 94-centimetre (3-foot) smooth dogfish (*Mustelus canis*) trawled off Cape Hatteras, North Carolina, on 25 April 1974. A series of randomly distributed, white, umbilicated, rough-surfaced excrescences varying from 2–10 millimetres ($\frac{1}{10} - \frac{4}{10}$ of an inch) in diameter were present on the right hand side of the fin, occurring singly or in groups of five or six. In Man, and in domestic animals, papillomas are of viral origin, but microscopic section of this affected tail fin failed to demonstrate the presence of any viral particles. On the other hand, the dermis was thickened in the region of the tumour and thrown into finger-like projections with focal areas of dysplasia that, in a mammal, would be regarded as definitive evidence of malignant cancer.

An alleged epithelioma in the oral mucosa of an example of *Scyliorhinus caniculus* is seemingly regarded as a report of questionable validity, but one undoubted malignancy has been recorded in a sandbar shark (*Carcharhinus plumbeus*), which proved to have a reticulum cell sarcoma of the spleen. There is even an instance of a neoplasm in the central nervous system of a shark, a specimen of the spiny dogfish (*Squalus acanthias*) 2 kilograms ($4\frac{1}{2}$ lb) in weight taken in Frenchman's Bay, near Bay Harbor, Maine, proving to have a 3 millimetre (about $\frac{1}{10}$ of an inch) diameter tumour located on the choroid plexus of the brain's fourth ventricle. Analysis demonstrated that the growth was benign, but, although this discovery led to the dissection of over 1,000 dogfish brains over a 5-year period in the early 1970s, not a single additional case came to light. On the other hand, a 1.45 metre (4 ft 8 in) specimen of the same species taken in the Black Sea in 1965 contained a huge mid-intestinal adenocarcinoma weighing 615 grams (22 ounces) exhibiting unmistakable signs of neoplastic spread.

Given that weakly, diseased sharks are unlikely to survive for long in the fiercely competitive undersea world, the known incidence of neoplasms in elasmobranchs is nonetheless astonishingly low. Detailed post-mortem examinations are not very often carried out, of course, but, even so, far more instances of sharks self-evidently suffering from malignant disease would reasonably be expected if tumours were anything like as common in them as they are in higher vertebrates, or even in other fish.

Could there be something about the physiology of sharks that makes these creatures resistant to tumour development and, if so, could anything be learned from them that might help in the conquest of human cancer? In centuries past, products of sharks or extracts from their bodies have been prescribed for a weird and wonderful selection of ailments. For example, the gall bladder of the humantin, *Oxynotus*, was believed to be beneficial for cataract and baked ashes of the same species were once used as a treatment for ringworm. Teething pains in children could allegedly be alleviated by the baked ashes of grey sharks or smooth hounds and the Roman writer Pliny (A.D. 23–79) recommended rubbing the teeth once a year with the cooked brains of a dogfish preserved in olive oil. Dried shark brains become very hard and when ground into powder and added to white wine, are supposed to be invaluable for women in labour and powdered sharks' teeth were held to cure gall stones and arrest haemorrhages.

Modern cancer research is a far cry from this sort of superstitious quackery, but it is undeniable that today's medical science can sometimes profit from a re-appraisal of old-fashioned remedies. It is always possible that there is something about sharks which makes them a good deal less susceptible to cancers than human beings.

To begin with, it has been discovered that sharks possess only one class of antibodies (proteins that combine with toxic antigens to render them harmless) in their blood serum. These antibodies are like the ones produced by human infants which help to protect them from disease; in adults, however, they only occur in comparable quantities when the individual concerned is suffering from certain blood cancers. Serum from adult sharks severely limits the growth of human cancer cells in a tissue culture (serum from young sharks is less effective) and also agglutinates and breaks down the red blood cells of numerous animal species. Shark serum, it seems, either contains a large number of antibodies, each with its own specific target (or small number of targets), or else a limited number of antibodies possessing broad individual specificities.

One type of adenovirus (type 12) will induce the development of tumours if experimentally injected into unborn hamsters. Treatment with shark serum resulted in partial suppression of tumour development. When doses of 100,000 cells from adenovirus tumours were transplanted into adult hamsters, which were then treated 15 days later with shark serum, it was found that these animals never developed neoplasms, whereas in a group of similarly-implanted hamsters that were denied shark serum no less than 75 per cent. had tumours within 60 days. When a massive dose of 1,000,000 tumour cells was transplanted, shark serum only provided limited protection: 70 per cent. of the hamsters that received no shark serum developed tumours, but so also did 50 per cent. of the ones that had been given the serum.

Other viruses and bacteria also seem to be affected by shark serum. Rous sarcoma virus, which causes tumours in chickens, is neutralised by it, the bacterium *Escherichia coli* (a common cause of human urinary tract infections as well as diarrhoea in cattle and babies) is agglutinated and killed, and influenza virus is readily killed by shark serum. It is important, however, to make sure that the serum is from adult sharks, as the product of immature individuals is substantially less effective; heat is also deleterious to its efficiency. Sharks, it seems, have developed substances that provide them with increased resistance to infections of one sort or another.

It would be tragic if any shark species were allowed to disappear from the seas through over-exploitation – not simply because it would represent an unnecessary loss to the environment, but also because medical science might be forever denied information of inestimable value in the treatment of a whole spectrum of diseases and pathological conditions.

In 1983, for example, it was reported that a compound obtained from the fin and vertebral cartilage of basking sharks prevents tumour growth in rabbits by inhibiting the generation of new blood vessels towards implanted carcinomas.

The threat to sharks is a very real one, however. Commercial fisheries, sportsmen, tourist shops (where the jaws of a great white can fetch up to $1,000) and well intentioned public authorities all take their toll. Safety netting to protect bathers off the beaches of Queensland alone killed 20,500 sharks in just 16 years, along with 468 dugongs (an imperilled marine mammal), 317 porpoises, 2,654 sea-turtles, and 10,889 rays – a catastrophic toll of oceanic wildlife in general, quite apart from the sharks.

Even the modern packaging industry, with its cheap but non-degradable throw-away appurtenances, has claimed its victims. Several sharks have been caught that had thrust their snouts through heat-sealed crating-strap loops made of synthetic materials. Unable to back themselves out of these encumbrances once they were looped over their heads (because sharks are incapable of swimming backwards) and prevented from swimming on through them by their projecting dorsal and pectoral fins, the unfortunate creatures found that, as they grew, the straps gradually cut into their flesh. Eventually the tissues even partially healed over the strap, thus incorporating it immovably into the shark's body, but the injuries inflicted by the encircling band were horrific.

A male bull shark (*Carcharhinus leucas*) 2.4 metres (8 feet) long taken off Sarasota, Florida, in September 1975 had a blue-coloured glass-fibre and resin strap, 1.25 centimetres ($\frac{1}{2}$ inch) wide and 115 centimetres (nearly 4 feet) long, so tightly encircling its body that it had cut into the bases of its pectoral fins and the ventral region of the body in between (where healing tissue had enclosed it), while, on the back, the vertebrae in front of the still-exposed strap were deformed into a hump. Taken at the same time and place was a female tiger shark 3.2 metres (over 10 feet) long with a similar band that had partially destroyed the gills on both sides of the throat and chewed 8 centimetres (3 inches) into the basal cartilages of the pectoral fins, leaving an open wound. Just over a month later, in October 1975, the waters of Sarasota yielded a female dusky shark (*Carcharhinus obscurus*) with a strap healed into the bases of its pectoral fins, the three posterior gills on each side having been severely damaged.

A hammerhead (*Sphyrna zygaena*) inextricably entangled in a tuna fishing net. These sharks seem to succumb rapidly when trapped in nets.

All of these sharks must have survived for a considerable period after ensnarement because of the time required for growth to cause the straps to bite through the living tissue. The tiger shark and the dusky shark also exhibited grooved scars where the straps had inflicted deep wounds that had healed as the bands worked back along the growing body.

Two years later, at Pensacola, Florida, two more dusky sharks were pulled in, similarly crippled. Crating straps around their bodies had bitten deeply into their dorsal and pectoral fins as the fish grew, partially severing them and leaving gaping wounds.

The disabilities these encumbered sharks suffered would have severely handicapped them. The pectoral fins enable a shark to manoeuvre sharply in the water and the tissue damage these individuals had sustained must have been a great limitation. It is noteworthy that healthy sharks usually have large, oily livers, but in these specimens the livers were small, suggesting poor general condition.

The fate of these unfortunate creatures is symptomatic of the threat to sharks that is now posed by the advance of what purports to be civilisation – environmental pollution, excessive exploitation for sport and by commercial fisheries, habitat destruction, and simple nihilistic hunting down of what are popularly regarded as dangerous and undesirable killers could mean that the future of at least some shark species is already at stake. And yet sharks have survived and prospered in the world's oceans for well over 300 million years. They have out-lasted the dinosaurs, the sabre-toothed cat, and the Neanderthal cave men. Perhaps in the end they will also outlast Man himself, if the seemingly insatiable human appetite for conflict and destruction, fuelled by material greed and ideological bigotry, cannot be brought under control. Or can Man not only learn how to live in harmony with his fellow men, but also contrive to co-exist amicably with sharks, avoiding unnecessary conflict and recognising that planet Earth is the home of other species, as well as *Homo sapiens*, and that these species have an equal claim on the resources of the world.

Appendix: Check-list of Sharks Living and Extinct

The list includes the scientific names of all major genera, with common names in parentheses where applicable. Some poorly-known forms of doubtful status have been omitted. Extinct genera are indicated by †.

Class CHONDRICHTHYES
(cartilaginous fishes)

Subclass ELASMOBRANCHII
(sharks, skates and rays)

Superorder CLADOSELACHIMORPHA
(primitive extinct sharks of Palaeozoic age)

Family Cladoselachidae (Devonian sharks of north-eastern North America)
   †*Cladolepis*, †*Cladoselache*, †*Deirolepis*, †*Dicentrodus*, †*Ohiolepis*, †*Tamiobatis*

Family Coronodontidae (of Devonian age but slightly more advanced than the Cladoselachidae)
   †*Coronodus*, †*Diademodus*

Superorder SELACHIMORPHA
(modern sharks and their extinct predecessors)

Order CTENACANTHIFORMES
(possibly including the ancestors of living sharks)

Family Ctenacanthidae (common Carboniferous sharks)
   †*Bandringa*, †*Ctenacanthus*, †*Goodrichthys*, †*Phoebodus*

Order HYBODONTIFORMES
(known only from fossil material ranging in age from late Palaeozoic to Upper Cretaceous, but particularly abundant during the Mesozoic – the Age of Reptiles)

Family Trystychiidae (unique among sharks in possessing a gill cover)
   †*Trystychius*

Family Hybodontidae (the typical Mesozoic sharks)
   †*Acrodus*, †*Arctacanthus*, †*Asteracanthus*, †*Bdellodus*, †*Carinacanthus*, †*Coelosteus*, †*Dabascanthus*, †*Dicrenodus*, †*Doratodus*, †*Echinodus*, †*Eoorodus*, †*Holmsella*, †*Hybocladodus*, †*Hybodonchus*, †*Hybodus*, †*Lambdodus*, †*Lissodus*, †*Lonchidion*, †*Mesodmodus*, †*Monocladodus*, †*Moyacanthus*, †*Nemacanthus*, †*Onychoselache*, †*Palaeobates*, †*Petrodus*, †*Priohybodus*, †*Pristacanthus*, †*Prohybodus*, †*Scoliorhiza*, †*Sphenacanthus*, †*Styracodus*, †*Trichorhipis*, †*Wodnika*, †*Xystrodus*

Family Ptychodontidae (late Mesozoic forms with crushing teeth)
   †*Hemiptychodus*, †*Heteroptychodus*, †*Hylaeobatis*, †*Ptychodus*

Order XENACANTHIFORMES
(extinct freshwater sharks)

Family Xenacanthidae (formerly known as pleuracanths)
   †*Antarctilamna*, †*Mcmurdodus*, †*Strongyliscus*, †*Xenacanthus*

EXTINCT SHARK-LIKE FORMS OF UNCERTAIN AFFINITIES

Family Desmiodontidae
   †*Desmiodus*, †*Heteropetalus*

Family Eugeneodontidae
   †*Bobbodus*, †*Eugeneodus*, †*Gilliodus*

Family Caseodontidae
   †*Campodus*, †*Caseodus*, †*Chiastodus*, †*Erikodus*, †*Fadenia*, †*Romerodus*

Family Edestidae (Palaeozoic forms with specialised lower symphysial tooth whorls)
   †*Agassizodus*, †*Campyloprion*, †*Edestus*, †*Helicampodus*, †*Leiodus*, †*Lestrodus*, †*Metaxyacanthus*, †*Ornithoprion*, †*Parahelicampodus*, †*Parahelicoprion*, †*Physonemus*, †*Prospiraxis*, †*Sarcoprion*, †*Syntomodus*, †*Toxoprion*

Family Symmoriidae
   †*Cobelodus*, †*Denaea*, †*Stethacanthus*, †*Symmorium*

Family Orodontidae
   †*Orodus*

Family Helicoprionidae (effectively known only from involuted symphysial tooth whorls)
   †*Helicoprion*, †*Sinohelicoprion*

Family Squatinactidae
   †*Squatinactis*

Order CHLAMYDOSELACHIFORMES
(the frilled shark)

Family Chlamydoselachiidae
   Chlamydoselachus, †*Thrinax*

Order HETERODONTIFORMES
(the horn sharks)

Family Heterodontidae
   Heterodontus (the bullhead shark), †*Strongyliscus*, †*Synechodus*

Order HEXANCHIFORMES
(the six and seven-gill sharks)

Family Hexanchidae
   Heptranchias, *Hexanchus* (the six-gill), *Notorynchus*

Order LAMNIFORMES
(the most diverse and dynamic group of living sharks)

Family Palaeospinacidae
   †*Palaeospinax* (an extinct Mesozoic genus)

Family Orthacodontidae (extinct ancestral forms, known only from fossil teeth)

†*Eychlaodus,* †*Orthacodus*

Family Orectolobidae (nurse and carpet sharks)
†*Agaleus, Brachaelurus,* †*Cantioscyllium, Chiloscyllium* (lip sharks), *Cirrhoscyllium,* †*Corysodon, Eucrossorhinus, Ginglymostoma* (nurse sharks), *Hemiscyllium, Heteroscyllium, Nebrius, Neoparascyllium,* †*Orectoloboides, Orectolobus* (carpet sharks or wobbegongs), †*Palaeobrachaelurus* †*Palaeocarcharias, Parascyllium,* †*Phorcynis,* †*Squatirhina, Stegostoma, Sutorectus, Synchismus*

Family Rhincodontidae (whale sharks)
†*Palaeorhincodon, Rhincodon*

Family Odontaspidae
†*Anomotodon, Odontaspis* (sand sharks), †*Pseudoisurus, Scapanorhynchus* (elfin or goblin sharks) sharks)

Family Isuridae (mackerel sharks)
†*Anatodus, Carcharodon* (the great white), †*Carcharoides,* †*Isurolamna, Isurus* (mako sharks), *Lamna* (porbeagles), †*Leptostyrax,* †*Paraisurus,* †*Pseudocorax,* †*Squalicorax*

Family Cetorhinidae (basking sharks)
Cetorhinus

Family Alopiidae (thresher sharks)
Alopias

Family Pseudocarchariidae (the crocodile shark)
Pseudocarcharias

Family Megachasmidae (the megamouth shark)
Megachasma

Family Scyliorhinidae (cat sharks and dogfish)
Apristurus, Asymbolus, Atelomycterus, Aulohalaelurus, Cephaloscyllium (the swell sharks), *Cephalurus, Galeus, Halaelurus, Haploblepharus, Holohalaelurus, Juncrus,* †*Macrurogaleus,* †*Megascyliorhinus,* †*Mesiteia,* †*Palaeogaleus,* †*Palaeoscyllium, Parapristurus, Parmaturus, Pentanchus, Poroderma, Schroederichthys, Scyliorhinus,* †*Scylliodus,* †*Thyellina,* †*Trigonodus*

Family Pseudotriakidae
†*Archaeotriakis, Pseudotriakis* (the false cat shark)

Family Triakidae (the smooth dogfish or smooth hounds)
Ctenacis, Emissola, Eridacnis, Furgaleus, Gogolia, Gollum, Iago, Leptocharias, Mustelus, Neotriakis,

Proscyllium, Scylliogaleus, Triaenodon, Triakis

Family Carcharhinidae (requin or requiem sharks)
†*Aporomicrodus, Aprionodon, Carcharhinus* (grey sharks), *Chaenogaleus, Galeocerdo* (the tiger shark), *Galeorhinus* (topes), *Hemigaleops, Hemipristis,* †*Henningia, Hypoprion* (the dog shark), *Isogomphodon, Lamiopsis, Loxodon* (the cocktail shark), *Mystidens, Negaprion* (the lemon shark), *Notogaleus* (the Australian school shark), †*Paracorax, Paragaleus, Physodon, Prionace* (the great blue shark), †*Prionodus,* †*Protogaleus, Rhizoprionodon* (the sharpnosed shark), *Scoliodon, Thalassorhinus*

Family Sphyrnidae (hammerheads)
Sphyrna

Order SQUALIFORMES
(the smaller and less impressive of the two major living groups of sharks)

Family Squalidae (the spined sharks or spiny dogfish)
†*Aculeola, Centrophorus, Centroscyllium* (the black dogfish), *Centroscymnus,* †*Centrosqualus, Cerictius, Cirrhigaleus, Deania, Etmopterus* (the lantern shark), *Oxynotus* (angular rough sharks), †*Protosqualus, Scymnodon, Squalus* (the spiny dogfish)

Family Scymnorhinidae (the spineless dogfish and sleeper sharks)
Euprotomicroides, Euprotomicrus, †*Gyrace, Heteroscymnoides, Isistius,* †*Pseudodalatias, Scymnodalatias, Scymnorhinus* (the black shark), *Somniosus* (the Greenland or sleeper shark), *Squaliolus* (the dwarf shark)

Family Echinorhinidae
Echinorhinus (the bramble or spinous shark)
†*Paraechinorhinus,* †*Pseudoechinorhinus*

Order PRISTIOPHORIFORMES
(the saw sharks)

Family Pristiophoridae
†*Ikamauius, Pliotrema, Pristiophorus,* †*Propristiophorus,* †*Rhaibodus*

Order SQUATINIFORMES
(the angel or monk fishes)

Family Squatinidae
†*Parasquatina,* †*Phorcynis, Squatina*

Glossary

Amphistylic A type of jaw articulation in which the hyomandibular (*q.v.*) element is only moderately well developed as a prop between the brain case and the articular region of the jaws (see Fig. 4.2)

Ampulla A small sac-like structure which, in sharks, occurs in some numbers beneath the skin of the head region (ampullae of Lorenzini); they open to the surface by means of a pore and are sensitive to electrical fields (see Fig. 3.19). Also structures in the ear (Fig. 3.16).

Articulation Joint between two skeletal elements or structures.

Basals Skeletal elements forming the base of a fin.

Basicranium The posterior floor of the braincase.

Branchials The two paired skeletal components of which each gill arch is normally constructed: the uppermost is the epibranchial, with below it the ceratobranchial (see Fig. 3.3).

Centrum The body of a vertebra (see Fig. 3.4).

Ceratotrichia Ray-like structures that support the fin web (see Fig. 3.6).

Dermal bones Bones that form from skin tissue as sheets or plates instead of being pre-formed as cartilage in the manner of limb bones.

Dermal rays *see* Ceratotrichia.

Endolymphatic duct A tube extending upwards from the sacculus (*q.v.*) and utriculus (*q.v.*) of the inner ear (which contain endolymph) to terminate either at an opening on the top of the head or in a sac within the braincase (see Fig. 3.2).

Ethmopalatine ligament A ligament connecting the ethmoid (anterior) area of the braincase floor and the upper jaw elements (palatoquadrates *q.v.*). See Fig. 4.2.

Gill arch A paired structure in the throat region that supports the gill tissue (see Fig. 3.3). Sharks have from five to seven pairs of gills, with their supporting arches.

Gill lamellae Parallel structures forming the gill surface, richly supplied with capillaries for gaseous exchange with the water (oxygen is absorbed and carbon dioxide eliminated).

Haemal arch A series of paired structures beneath the spinal column in the tail region that protect blood vessels supplying the posterior part of the body.

Heterocercal tail A fish tail in which the spinal column is diverted upwards to form the upper lobe of a two-lobed structure (see Fig. 3.5).

Holostylic A form of jaw articulation in which the jaws are supported against the braincase principally by the hyomandibular (*q.v.*) element.

Hyoid arch The paired structures immediately behind the skull on either side of the throat comprising the hyomandibular (*q.v.*) above and the ceratohyal below; derived originally from a gill arch, but now functioning as jaw supports as well as forming the anterior part of the first gill opening (see Fig. 4.2).

Hyomandibular The upper element of the hyoid arch (*q.v.*). See Fig. 3.3.

Hypothalamus The floor of the brain's diencephalon (the unpaired posterior portion of the forebrain). The hypothalamus is a visceral nerve centre which in mammals, for example, controls sleep while in birds it controls temperature regulation; it also contains olfactory centres and exerts some influence on the pituitary (which secretes hormones that regulate the function of other vital hormone-producing glands governing growth, metabolism, and sexual function). See Fig. 3.14.

Lanceolate Of slender, elongate, pointed shape.

Maculae Sensitive areas of the inner ear's sacculus and utriculus (*qq.v.*) containing crystals (otoliths) within a sensory epithelium served by the auditory nerve. They register acceleration, the tilt of the head, vibrations of low frequency and, in some cases, may have a primitive auditory function (see Fig. 3.16).

Mesopterygium A subsidiary element of proportionately small size at the base of a shark's pectoral fins.

Metapterygium The principal element at the base of a shark's pectoral or pelvic fins to which most of the fin's supporting cartilages are articulated (see Fig. 3.6).

Neural arch An arch-like structure on top of a vertebra which protects the spinal cord (see Fig. 3.4).

Occipital condyle The protuberance at the back of the skull with which the first vertebra articulates (see Fig. 3.2).

Occiput The posterior surface of the skull.

Osteoblasts Cells around which bone is laid down by the deposition of calcium salts in a thick matrix containing fibre bundles.

Osteocytes The cells found in bone, derived from osteoblasts (*q.v.*) once their bone formation function has been completed.

Ovo-viviparous Reproduction in which fertilised eggs complete their development within the body of the mother but the young, although born fully formed, lack a placenta-like connection with the uterus and rely on a yolk sac (and sometimes on intra-uterine cannibalism) for nourishment.

Palatoquadrate The paired cartilaginous structure that forms the upper jaws of sharks; sometimes known as the pterygoquadrate (see Fig. 3.2).

Propterygium A subsidiary element of proportionately small size at the base of a shark's pectoral and pelvic fins.

Quadrate A skull element that, in bony fish, amphibians, reptiles and birds, forms the upper component of the jaw articulation.

Radials Stiffening structures (ceratotrichia *q.v.*) that support the web of a fin (see Fig. 3.6).

Renal corpuscle The hollow structure at the top of a kidney tubule containing a cluster of small in-going and out-going blood vessels from which waste products in the form of urine are filtered out for excretion via the tubule (see Fig. 3.12).

Rostrum The cartilages which support the nose of a shark (see Fig. 5.1).

Sacculus One (the lower) of two sac-like structures that form the inner ear; it incorporates sensitive areas (maculae *q.v.*) apparently receptive to low frequency mechanical vibrations and capable of a primitive auditory function (see Fig. 3.16).

Sinus venosus A thin-walled sac, at the back of the heart in sharks, where venous blood is collected before being passed forward through the heart for pumping to the gills where oxygen is taken up and waste products (notably carbon dioxide) are eliminated.

Symphysis, mandibular The anterior conjunction of the two halves of the lower jaw.

Trabecular dentine Dentine forming the body of a tooth in some cartilaginous fishes, usually capped by a crown of tubular dentine or orthodentine (enamel).

Utriculus One (the upper) of two sac-like structures that form the inner ear; it incorporates sensitive areas (maculae *q.v.*) which apparently record linear accelerations and the tilt of the head (see Fig. 3.16).

Viviparous Reproduction in which the young are retained within the mother's body until development is complete, nourished by a placental type of connection with the uterine wall.

Guide to Further Reading

Backus, R., Springer, S. & Arnold, E. (1956) 'A contribution to the natural history of the whitetip shark, *Pterolamiops longimanus* (Poey)' *Deep-Sea Res.* **3** pp. 178–188.

Baldridge, H.D. (1974) *Shark Attack* pp. 1–263. Berkeley Medallion Books, New York. (Paperback by Everest Books, London.)

Baughman, J.L. (1955) 'The oviparity of the whale shark *Rhineodon typus*, with records of this and other fishes in Texas waters' *Copeia* pp. 54–55.

Bigelow, H.B. & Schroeder, W.C. (1948–53) 'Fishes of the western North Atlantic. No. 1, Pt 1. Cyclostomes and sharks' *Mem. Sears Fdn Mar. Res.* pp. 29–546.

Bigelow, H.B. & Schroeder, W.C. (1957) 'A study of the sharks of the suborder Squaloidea' *Bull. Mus. Comp. Zool.* **117** pp. 1–150.

Budker, P. & Whitehead, P.J. (1971) *The Life of Sharks* (Translated into English by Whitehead, P.J.) pp. 1–222. Weidenfeld & Nicolson, London.

Clark, E. (1975) 'Into the lairs of "sleeping sharks"' *Natn. Geogr. Mag.* **147** pp. 570–584.

Clark, E. (1981) 'Sharks: magnificent and misunderstood' *Natn. Geogr. Mag.* **160** pp. 138–187.

Cohen, J.L. (1981) 'Vision in sharks' *Oceanus* **24** (4), pp. 17–22.

Coppleson, V.M. (1958) *Shark Attack* pp. 1–269. Angus & Robertson, London.

Cousteau, J.Y. & Cousteau, P. (1970) *The Shark: Splendid Savage of the Seas* pp. 1–277. Cassell, London.

Davies, D.H. (1964) *About Sharks and Shark Attack* pp. 1–237. Shuter & Shooter, Pietermaritzburg, Natal.

Devaney, C. (1975) *Killer Shark* pp. 1–64. Orbis, London.

Ellis, R. (1983) *The Book of Sharks* (Revised edition) pp. 1–256. Robert Hale, London.

Garrick, J.A.F. (1967) 'Revision of sharks of the genus *Isurus* with description of a new species (Galeoidea, Lamnidae)' *Proc. U.S. Natn. Mus.* **118** No. 3537, pp. 663–690.

Garrick, J.A.F. (1982) 'Sharks of the genus *Carcharhinus*' *NOAA Techn. Rep. NMFS Circular* No. 445, pp. 1–194.

Gilbert, P.W. (1962) 'The behaviour of sharks' *Sci. Am.* **207** No. 1, pp. 60–68.

Gilbert, P.W., ed. (1963) *Sharks and Survival* pp. 1–578. D.C. Heath, Boston, Massachusetts.

Gilbert, P.W. (1981) 'Patterns of shark reproduction' *Oceanus* **24** (4), pp. 30–39.

Gilbert, P.W., Mathewson, R.F. & Rall, D.P., eds (1967) *Sharks, Skates and Rays* pp. 1–624. Johns Hopkins Press, Baltimore, Maryland.

Gruber, S.H. (1981) 'Lemon sharks: supply side economists of the sea' *Oceanus* **24** (4), pp. 56–64.

Gruber, S.H. (1981) 'Shark repellents: perspectives for the future' *Oceanus* **24** (4), pp. 72–76.

Housby, T. (1976) *Shark Hunter* pp. 1–192. Priory Press, Hove.

Johnson, R.H. & Nelson, D.R. (1973) 'Agonistic display in the grey reef shark, *Carcharhinus menisorrah*, and its relationship to attacks on man' *Copeia* pp. 76–84.

Kenney, N.T. (1968) 'Sharks: wolves of the sea' *Natn. Geogr. Mag.* **133** pp. 222–257.

Klimley, A.P. (1981) 'Grouping behaviour of the scalloped hammerhead' *Oceanus* **24** (4) pp. 65–71.

Llano, G.A. (1957) 'Sharks v. men' *Sci. Am.* **196** No. 6, pp. 54–61.

Lineaweaver, T.H. & Backus, R.H. (1970) *The Natural History of Sharks* pp. 1–256. Deutsch, London.

Matthews, L.H. (1962) 'The shark that hibernates' *New Sci.* **13** 280, pp. 756–759. (Also in *Ann. Rep. Smithson. Inst. for 1962*, pp. 415–421.)

Matthews, L.H. & Parker, H.W. (1950) 'Notes on the anatomy and biology of the basking shark (*Cetorhinus maximus* (Gunner))' *Proc. Zool Soc. Lond.* **120** pp. 535–576.

McCosker, J.E. (1981) 'Great white shark' *Science, N.Y.* **81** 2, (6), pp. 42–51.

Moss, S.A. (1981) 'Shark feeding mechanisms' *Oceanus* **24** (4), pp. 23–29.

Moy-Thomas, J.A. (1971) *Palaeozoic Fishes* (Revised by Miles, R.S.) pp. 206–245. Chapman & Hall, London.

Nelson, D.R. (1981) 'Aggression in sharks: is the gray reef shark different?' *Oceanus* **24** (4), pp. 45–55.

Northcutt, R.G., ed. (1977) 'Recent advances in the biology of sharks' *Am. Zool.* **17** pp. 287–515.

Ryan, P.R. (1981) 'Electroreception in blue sharks' *Oceanus* **24** (4), pp. 42–44.

Smith, B.G. (1937) 'The anatomy of the frilled shark *Chlamydoselachus anguineus* Garman' *Bashford Dean Mem. Vol. Art.* 6, pp. 335–505.

Smith, B.G. (1942) 'The heterodont sharks: their natural history and the external development of *Heterodontus japonicus* based on notes and drawings by Bashford Dean' *Bashford Dean Mem. Vol.* Art. 7, pp. 647–770.

Springer, S. (1948) 'Oviphagous embryos of the sand shark, *Carcharias taurus*' *Copeia* pp. 153–157.

Springer, V.G. (1964) 'A revision of the carcharhinid shark genera *Scoliodon, Loxodon*, and

Rhizoprionodon' *Proc. U.S. Natl. Mus.* **115** No. 3493, pp. 559–632.

Standora, E.A. & Nelson, D.R. (1977) 'A telemetric study of the behavior of free-swimming Pacific angel sharks, *Squatina californica*' *Bull. South. Calif. Acad. Sci.* **76** pp. 193–201.

Strasburg, D.W. (1963) 'The diet and dentition of *Isistius brasiliensis* with remarks on tooth replacement in other sharks'

Copeia pp. 33–40.

Taylor, V. & Taylor, R., eds (1978) *Great Shark Stories* pp. 1–403. Bantam Books, New York.

Wood, G.L. (1982) *Guinness Book of Animal Facts and Feats* 3rd edition. pp. 124–137, 218, 230. Guinness Superlatives Ltd, Enfield, Middlesex.

Wright, B.A. (1948) 'Releasers of attack behaviour pattern in shark and barracuda' *J. Wildl. Manage.* **12** pp. 117–123.

Index

Numbers in *italic* refer to black and white illustrations.
Numbers in **bold** refer to colour plates.

Acrodus 163, 185
Agaleus 118, 186
Alopias (thresher sharks) 33, *104*, 115–16, 175, 186
Anachronistes 18
Ancestry of sharks 159–60
Angel sharks *see Squatina*
Aprionodon 112, 186
Apristurus 12, 128, 186
Archaeotriakis 124, *125*, 186
Asai, Iona 28
Atelomycterus 128, 186
Aulohalaelurus 128, 186
Australia, shark attacks 28, 30–32, 111

Banjo fish (*Rhinobatis*) 21
Bartle, Bob 112
Basking shark *see Cetorhinus*
Bdellodus 164, 185
Benchley, Peter 94, 173
Billies **39**
Biting capabilities 52–3, 55

Black-nosed shark *see Carcharhinus acronotus*
Black-tip shark *see Carcharhinus limbatus*
Black-tipped reef shark *see Carcharhinus melanopterus*
Blue shark *see Prionace*
Bobbodus 166, 185
Bone in shark skeleton 42–3
Bonnet shark *see Sphyrna*
Bource, Henry, **27**, 28, 89–90
Brachaelurus 117, 186
Brain *61*, 61–3
Bramble sharks *see Echinorhinus*
Brinkley, Jack 111
Brown shark *see Carcharhinus plumbeus*
Bull shark *see Carcharhinus leucas*
Bullhead shark *see Heterodontus*
Buoyancy 60

Campodus 166, 185
Cancer 180–82

Cape San Juan (troopship) 37
Carcharhinus (grey sharks) 31, *50*, 59, 62, 66, 70, 104–108, 178–9, 186
acronotus 105
amblyrhynchos **107**, 180–81
falciformis *12*, 13, 55, 105–108, 177
galapagensis 106
gangeticus 105
leucas 13, 32, 90, 105–106, 108, **178**, 180, 183
limbatus *13*, 105
longimanus *38*, 39, **104**, 105, *172*
melanopterus 105, **106**
menisorrah 106
obscurus 16, 29, 105, 183–4
perezii 108
plumbeus 105, 181
porosus 105, 180
Carcharodon 186
carcharias (great white) *9*,

10–11, 26, 28, 62, 65, 72,
85–86, *86*, **87**, 87–95, **95**,
95–6, 176
  megalodon 11, *95*, 95–6
Carcharoides 101, 186
Carinacanthus 163, 185
Carpet sharks 116–19
Caseodus 166, 185
Cat shark 128
Centrophorus 140, 144, 186
Centroscyllium 144, 186
Centroscymnus 140, 144, 186
Cephaloscyllium (swell sharks)
  127, 127–8, *128*, 186
Cephalurus 128, 186
Cetorhinus (basking shark) 10,
  130, 130–31, *131*, 132–4,
  179, 186
Chemical shark repellents
  39–40
Chiastodus 166, 185
Chiloscyllium 117, 186
Chimaeras *20*, 21–2, 164
Chlamydoselachus (frilled shark)
  44, *74*, 74–8, 185
Circulatory system 59
Cirrhigaleus 144, 186
Cirrhoscyllium 117, 186
Cladodus 158, 159
Cladolepis 159, 185
Cladoselache 47, *49*, 157–8, *158*,
  159–60, 185
Cobelodus 166, 185
Combat with captive sharks 23
Commercial shark fisheries
  176–80
Cookie-cutter shark *see Isistius*
Copplestone, Sir Victor 33
Cousteau, Jacques-Yves 39
Crocodile shark *see
  Pseudocarcharias*
Ctenacanthus 160, 185
Ctenacis 124, 186

Dalatias see Scymnorhinus
Darkie charlie *see Scymnorhinus*
Dean, Alf 90, 93, 173
Dean, Bashford 76–9, 157
Deania 12, 144, 186
Defence against shark attack
  39–41
Deirolepis 159, 185
Denaea 166, 185
Desmiodus 166, 185
Diademodus 159, 185
Dicrenodus 163, 185
Digestion *55*, 55–6, *56*
Dogfish 15, 121, 124, 126–7,
  142, 144
  common *see Scyliorhinus*
Doratodus 164, 185
Dusky shark *see Carcharhinus
  obscurus*

Ears 66–67, *67*
Echinodus 164, 185

Echinorhinus (bramble shark)
  149–50, 186
Edestus 164, 185
Eggs 58–9
Elfin sharks *see Scapanorhynchus*
Emissola 123, 186
Eorodus 185
Eridacnis 123, 186
Erikodus 166, 185
Etmopterus 186
  spinax (lantern shark) **143**,
    145
  virens (green dogfish) 15, *15*,
    144
Eucrossorhinus 117, 186
Eugeneodus 166, 185
Eugomphodon 120
Euprotomicroides 147, 186
Euprotomicrus 142, 146, 186
Eusphyra 103
Eychlaodus 129, 186
Eyes 63–4, *64*, 65–6
Exploitation, commercial 171–2

Fadenia 165–6, 185
Feeding frenzy 14–15
Fins 48, *49*, 50
Fishing for sharks 173–6
Folklore of sharks 22–25
Fox, Rodney 26, **26**, **27**, *27*, 28,
  88–91
Frilled shark *see Chlamydoselachus*
Furgaleus 123, 186

Galapagos shark *see Carcharhinus
  galapagensis*
Galeocerdo (tiger shark) 14, 28,
  29, 56, *104*, 109–10, **110**,
  111–12, 176–9, 186
Galeorhinus (tope) **111**, 112, 177,
  186
Galeus 72, 125–6, 186
  arae 13, *14*
  melastoma 59
  polli 59
Gilliodus 166, 185
Gills *45*, 45–6
Ginglymostoma (nurse sharks)
  23, 59, 117, **118**, 137,
  177–8, 186
Gnathodynamometer 52–3,
  53
Goblin shark *see
  Scapanorhynchus*
Gogolia 123, *124*, 186
Gollum 124, 186
Goodrichthys 160, *161*, 185
Great white shark *see
  Carcharodon carcharias*
Green dogfish *see Etmopterus
  virens*
Grey, Zane 92
Grey nurse shark *see
  Odontaspis*
Grey reef shark *see
  Carcharhinus falciformis*

Grey sharks *see Carcharhinus*

Halaelurus 12, 128, 186
Hammerhead shark *see
  Sphyrna*
Haploblepharus 128, 186
Hearing 66–7
Helicoprion 167–8, *168*, 185
Hemigaleus 105
Hemiscyllium 117, 186
Heptranchias (seven-gill) 45,
  69, 81, *83*, 83–4, 179, 185
Heterodontus (bullhead shark)
  43, 77, *78*, *79*, **79**, 79–81,
  185
Heteropetalus 165, 166, 185
Hexanchus (six-gill) 45, *81*,
  81–3, *83*
Holmsella 164, 185
Holohalaelurus **71**, 128, 186
Housby, Trevor 86, 176
Humantin *see Oxynotus*
Hybocladodus 163, 185
Hybodonchus 163, 185
Hybodus 49, 162–3, *163*, 164
Hypoprion (lesser blue) 112,
  186

Iago 123, *124*, 186
Ikamauius 156, 186
Indianopolis, US 37–8
Isistius (cookie-cutter shark)
  52, *142*, 146, 186
Isurus (makos) *49*, 62, 85, *86*,
  97–8, *98*, **99**, 99–100, **175**,
  186

Juncrus 128, 186

Kamo Hoa Lii 22
Kapaaheo 23
Kidneys 57

Lambdodus 164, 185
Lamna (porbeagles) 33, *47*, *51*,
  54, 62, 86, 97, *98*, 100–101,
  172, 179, 186
Lantern shark *see Etmopterus
  spinax*
Lateral line 67–8, *68*
Learning capacity 62
Lemon shark *see Negaprion*
Leptocharias 123, 186
Leptostyrax 101, 186
Lesser blue shark *see Hypoprion*
Lissodus, 163, 185
Liver oil 177–9
Lonchidion 163, 185
Lorenzini, ampullae of 71–2,
  72, 73, 103
Loxodon 112, 186

Mackerel sharks 97, *98*, 99
Macrurogaleus 129, 186
Mako *see Isurus*
Manta ray *20*

Marbled cat shark *see Galeus arae*
Mating 57–9
Maui 23
Medical treatment 30–32
Mediterranean, shark attacks 36
Megachasma (megamouth shark) 56, 137–8, *138*, 139, *146*, 186
Mesodmodus 164, 185
Mokoroa 23
Monk fish *see Squatina*
Moses sole *see Pardachirus*
Moyacanthus 164, 185
Mundus, Frank 92–3, 173
Mustelus 16, *45*, *72*, **122**, 123, 178, 181, 186

Nanaue 22–3
Nancy, US 25
Nasisqualus 144
Negaprion (lemon sharks) *14*, 15, 62, 64, 113–14, **114**, 177–9, 186
Nemacanthus 163, 185
Neoparascyllium 117, 186
Neotriakis 123, 186
Nictitating membrane 66
Notorynchus (seven-gill) 18, **46**, 69, 81, *83*, 84, 185
Nova Scotia (troopship) 37
Nurse sharks *see Ginglymostoma*

Odontaspis (sand sharks) *18*, 31, 59, *104*, 117, **119**, 120, 173, 186
Ohiolepis 159, 185
Onychoselache 164, 185
Orectolobus 117, **118**, 177, 186
Ornithoprion 164, 185
Orodus 167, 185
Orthacodus 129, 186
Oxynotus (humantin) *140*, 145

Palaeobates 164, 185
Palaeocarcharias 118–19, 186
Palaeorhincodon 137, 186
Palaeoscyllium 129, 186
Palaeospinax 129, 185
Paraisurus 101, 186
Parapristurus 128, 186
Parascyllium 117, 186
Pardachirus 40–41
Parmaturus 129, 186
Pentanchus 129, 186
Perception 70–73
Petrodus 164, 185
Phoebodus 160, 185
Phorcynis 155, 186
Pit organs 69, 69–70
Pliotrema 156, 186
Porbeagle *see Lamna*
Poroderma 128, 186

Port Royal Jack 24–5
Principessa Mafalda (Italian liner) 37
Priohybodus 164, 185
Prionace (great blue shark) 73, *104*, 105, 108–109, **110**, 186
Pristacanthus 164, 185
Pristiophorus (saw sharks) *155*, 155–6, 186
Proscyllium 123, 186
Pseudocarcharias (crocodile shark) 115, 186
Pseudocorax 18, 101, 186
Pseudodalatias 141–2, 186
Pseudotriakis 124, *125*, 186
Ptychodus 170, 185

Rays 20, 21, 73
Remora **71**
Reproduction 11–13, 56–58, *58*, 59
Respiration 60
Rhincodon (whale shark) 9, 10, 24, *50*, *131*, 134–5, **135** 136–7, 186
Rhizoprionodon 16, *112*, 113, 178, 186
Rodger, Brian **27**, 28, 89
Romerodus 166, 185
Round-nosed shark *see Aprionodon*

Sacrifice to sharks 23
Sand shark *see Odontaspis*
Sarcoprion 164, *165*, 185
Saw sharks *see Pristiophorus*
Scales 50, 50–51
Scapanorhynchus (elfin or goblin shark) 120–121, *121*, 186
Schroederichthys 128–9, 186
Scoliodon 105, 112, 186
Scoliorhiza 164, 185
Scyliorhinus 10, **11**, 67, *126*, **126**, 126–7, 181, 186
Scylliogaleus 123, 186
Scymnodon 140, 144, 186
Scymnorhinus (darkie charlie) *61*, *142*, 145, 177, 186
Seven-gill shark *see Notorhynchus*
Shagreen 177
Shanghai Bill 25
Shark, origin of name 25
'Shark papers' 25
Sharks, check-list of 185–6
Sharp-nosed sharp *see Rhizoprionodon*
Shovel-head *see Sphyrna*
Silky shark *see Carcharhinus falciformis*
Skate 20, 21, 73
Skeleton 42–3, *43*, 44–50
Skins 177
Skull *44*, 44–5, *85*, *141*
Sleeper shark *see Somniosus*

Smallest shark 10, *147*
Smalltail shark *see Carcharhinus porosus*
Smooth dogfish (smooth hound) 121
Social organisation 13
Somniosus (sleeper shark) *142*, 147–9, *149*, 178–9, 186
South Africa, shark attacks 32–3
Sphenacanthus 164, 185
Sphyrna (hammerheads) **54**, 59, 62, 66, 70, *102*, 102–104, *104*, 177–9, *184*, 186
Spiny dogfish *see Squalus acanthias*
Spiracle 45–6
Spiracular organ 68
Spiral valve 56
Squalene 180
Squaliolus 9, 10, 146–7, 186
Squalus acanthias (spiny dogfish) 15, *49*, 52, 70, *141*, 141–4, 176–7, 181, 186
Squatina (angel sharks or monk fish) 17, 151–2, *152*, 153–4, 186
Stegostoma 117, **119**, 177, 186
Stethacanthus 166, 166–7, 185
Styracodus 164
Sutorectus 117, 186
Swell shark *see Cephaloscyllium*
Symmorium *165*, 166, 185
Synchismus 117, 186
Synechodus 18, 185

Tagging sharks 16, 153–4
Tail 47, *47*, 98
Teeth *18*, 29, *51*, 51–52, *52*, 53, 55, *86*, *95*, *99*, *104*, *158*, *168*, *170*
Thresher *see Alopias*
Tiger shark *see Galeocerdo*
Tope *see Galeorhinus*
Tracking sharks 17
Triaenodon **122**, 123, **175**, 186
Triakis **122**, 123, 178, 186
Trichorhipis 164, 185
Trystychius 161, *162*, 185

USA, shark attacks 33–6, 90–91, 120

Valerian (British patrol boat) 37
Vertebrae 46–7, *47*, *141*, *152*

Whale shark *see Rhincodon*
White-tip reef shark *see Triaenodon*
White-tip shark, oceanic *see Carcharhinus longimanus*

Xenacanthus 160–61, *161*, 185

Zambezi shark *see Carcharhinus leucas*